THE RED CHAPELS OF BANTEAI SREI

Also by Sacheverell Sitwell

BRIDGE OF THE BROCADE SASH

GOLDEN WALL AND MIRADOR

THE RED CHAPELS
OF BANTEAI SREI

And Temples in Cambodia, India, Siam and Nepal

SACHEVERELL SITWELL

WEIDENFELD AND NICOLSON
20 NEW BOND STREET LONDON W1

To Reresby
who came with us
to India and Nepal

Printed in Great Britain by C. Tinling & Co. Ltd.,
Liverpool, London and Prescot

17/6228

CONTENTS

Book One

BANGKOK AND ANGKOR

Book Two

NEPAL

Book Three

A LITTLE OF INDIA

CONTENTS

Book Four

A VISIT TO CEYLON

LIST OF ILLUSTRATIONS

COLOUR PLATES

Illustrations numbers 1-3 and 6-9 are by Baron Studios, numbers 4, 5, 8, 10-20, 22-26, 31, 32, 35, 38 and 40 were taken by Georgia Sitwell and numbers 21 and 28-30 are by Reresby Sitwell. Number 25 was taken by Mr Pashupatis J. B. Rana and number 27 by Sir Christopher Summerhayes both of which are by courtesy of the Yetis, the Nepalese Students of Great Britain. Numbers 33, 34, 36 and 37 are by courtesy of the India Tourist Office. Number 39 is by courtesy of the Ceylon High Commissioner's Office. Colour plates I-III are by Baron Studios and number IV is by Georgia Sitwell.

Book One

BANGKOK AND ANGKOR

Chapter One

❖❖❖❖❖❖❖❖❖❖❖❖❖❖❖❖❖❖❖❖

BANGKOK

THE VERY NAME of Bangkok asserts a fascination upon nearly everyone. Why this should be so is still a little of a mystery though we hope to know the reason for it by tomorrow evening. For it is as imminent as that. Going to the hairdresser in the afternoon in London there is someone in the next chair who gives me messages to deliver to his father in the same hotel where we will be staying at this time tomorrow.

The Qantas aeroplane which has touched down at Rome and Cairo and Karachi, has flown over the Arabian desert in the night and crossed India in a huge leap from coast to coast, comes down for a last halt at Dum-Dum Airport, near Calcutta. It is only about three hours' further flying time to Bangkok, including the disappointment of just not seeing the golden spire of the Shwe Dagon at Rangoon for we pass almost directly over that city, but at special request are careful not to fly over the pagoda which springs from its terraced platform to about the height of St Paul's Cathedral. In fact we do not catch sight of Burma at all, cross another stretch of ocean, and arrive at Bangkok from London just exactly ten minutes late.

The only feature at the airport to make it different from any other air terminus is the number of monks in saffron robes crowding at the railings as though to watch a race meeting. After some delay we are through the customs and ready for the eighteen-mile drive into the city, past red or white frangipani trees in happy augury, and passing by shadow-like water-buffaloes, and a stork or two standing in the wet fields. It is explained to us that most of the trees beside the road are being cut down for a road-widening scheme, and canals are pointed out to us that are in the process of being filled in. The entrance into the town is unimposing, perhaps the more so because we are more tired than we realize, and in about three-quarters of an hour I am in the hall of the Oriental Hotel delivering the message with which I was entrusted scarcely twenty-four hours before. We dine in the roof-top restaurant overlooking the city and go, early and tired out, to bed.

It is a large old-fashioned room with a high ceiling, air-conditioning in full action over the door, and an electric fan of the sort that turns itself, irresolutely after an interval, from side to side. The windows and shutters are closed. There is no blanket on the bed. It is going to be very hot, that is certain. We have been told that our room looks on the river, and all night long we hear the chug-chug of motor-barges on the water. It is a delight to lie awake for a little in the early morning, knowing one is in Bangkok, but I can hardly wait to open the shutters and look out.

When the Chinese 'boy' who looks after us comes to take our order for breakfast, we ask for Java coffee (which is excellent) and fruit, and are brought a wedge of pineapple that must be cut out of the centre of a far larger specimen than any we are used to in England, and a slice of papaya with a piece of fresh lime lying on it. The pineapple and the papaya are delicious like vintage years of nectar, and during our three weeks in Bangkok, on and off, we only varied this by asking now and again for pomelo which tastes like the celestial offspring of melon and grape-fruit. To sprinkle any of these fruits with sugar would have been an insult to the whole vegetable kingdom, though a pomelo it has to be admitted takes rank a considerable way behind either a papaya or pineapple.

It was towards the end of February and the weather when looked out upon a sullen grey, but portending great humidity, not fog or rain. We were on the first floor of a building set back some way from the river, with a lawn leading down to that, and with flanking buildings to the water's edge at either side. The river, which is called the Chao Phya, of a dull brown colour at this moment, looked to be not quite as wide as the Thames at Chelsea Bridge. But it is much busier than the Thames. There is not a moment when a chain of barges, going one way or the other, does not pass in front of the window. Each barge tows five or six or seven others behind it, with little satellite boats alongside, or trailing at the back; and already one notices two things about them, that the families on board live at one end and under a roof or hood of corrugated iron that has been bent into shape, and that all the barges without exception are loaded too dangerously near the water-line. Often the gunwale is flush with the water, and there cannot be a dry corner down below. The far bank of the river is crowded with what look to be wooden warehouses and insignificant wooden huts. So the principal part of Bangkok must lie on our side of the river. At this moment, all evidence of humid heat apart, there is little sign of the Far Orient in the landscape; these might be the waters of the Scheldt and we could be at Antwerp, or Rotterdam, save for the low wooden huts opposite, and the suspicion that those are coco-nut palms above them.

There was not much to do that first morning except take a short walk into the town. The jet-stress from so long a flight requires a day at least before its strains begin to lessen. But the prime and essential memory of that morning in Bangkok is the moment of opening the bedroom door. This was not a question of opening a door and getting out of somewhere, but a matter of opening the door and going in; of leaving the vacuum of air-conditioning and luggage from London and stepping into something else. Already in that long dark passage one was in the stove-house heat. There was that little cubby-hole in the wall on the left where the Chinese 'boy' slept under a kind of lean-to mosquito-net with laundry hanging all round him—luckily our air-conditioning kept the mosquitoes out—and a court at the end with a tall palm-tree, and some bewildering turns, and then the stairs. These led to a bigger court with an attempt at a Japanese garden in the middle of it, and the hotel desk at the farther side. In the few moments of waiting there was time to look at the show-cases with Thai silks in them, and in a jeweller's window which had the 'princess' rings of semi-precious stones set in pagoda-shape like a Thai Dancer's head-dress.

If one went on further, there were rooms leading to a terrace and as one came nearer, the chug-chugging of the barges on the river. On the way there was a hall with a larger than life photograph of the young King, Orientally impassive of expression; a region, as indeed the whole ground floor of the hotel, and probably every other part of it except the air-conditioned rooms, patrolled and haunted by huge mosquitoes. But towards dark, not later than six or seven o'clock in this semi-tropical land, one could sit on this terrace, enjoying a cooling drink, and listening (not looking, owing to the sun-blinds) to the noises from the river. This, it was obvious, is the life-stream of Bangkok; and little as we have seen of it until now only looking on

it from between the side walls of the hotel, we are longing to know
more.

In the street in front of the hotel are taxi-drivers clamouring for
hire; and a few vehicles of cheaper sort, made in Japan, designed only
for a race of diminutive size, with a steering-wheel the shape of a pair
of cow's horns, an openwork body, and a roof like the canopy of a
perambulator. We were to find that the drivers of these latter never
knew the way anywhere, could not read a written address, and
would land one in the most unlikely places. A little experience of
them, however, is worth while for its Far Eastern flavour, a mech-
anized rickshaw being at least more pleasant, if it is more dangerous,
than its hand-drawn prototype. A horde of small children came
pouring out of school as we walked by; the little girls all alike as two
pins with their sleek hair and little slit eyes, and dressed in their blue
and white school uniform. It is a *lycée* run by French nuns.

The narrow, single file pavement led past shed-shops with Chinese
and Thai illustrated magazines in lurid colours. There were curio
shops, as well, selling temple bells; hideous statuettes that were half-
Boddhisattva, half Folies-Bergère; and open-work, Chinese lantern-
shaped contrivances of lucky fish in red and gold, that could be folded
up, or hung from the ceiling. At the street corner where the fat
Chinese proprietor sat, toad-like, at the cash-desk in his chemist's
shop, was the beginning of the trams. The pavement was being taken
up; and Chinese pedlars were trotting past with 'chop-chop' motion,
their step depending on the yoke they balanced on one shoulder. At
which point we climbed into a taxi and made for the flower market,
reaching it after a mistake or two by means of gesture language. It
was well worth the trouble. There were stalls of tuberoses, and pails
of lotus. But the market women had a way of folding back the lotus
petals that, one felt, must hurt or mortally injure the flower while
turning it into little more than the dull version of a tulip. It may keep
longer, but the lotus is prevented from opening.

This market was a first experience of their palm-leaf packaging.
Each stall had a neatly folded pile of palm leaves, looking like green
envelopes, and these they used instead of paper for tying up parcels.
A small fish done up in a palm leaf is somehow more appetizing than
a fish wrapped in old newspaper. The fish stalls were indeed almost
more interesting than the flower stalls; prodigious prawns and crabs,
fishes of the warm southern seas never before encountered, and dark

brown locust corpses, laid, neatly, side by side in rows. These last are very popular, though, I think, more as a condiment than a dish in themselves. Or one can see them pounded into a brown paste which they make into a sauce, or use as a dressing.

But the hour had come for luncheon and we embarked again for a famous Chinese restaurant, *The Golden Dragon*. This took us to a more modern and prosperous-looking part of the city. The address had been carefully written down for us at the hotel desk in beautiful Thai script with its many accents. We handed this to the driver, and were soon careering along the sides of canals, past the racecourse, by lawns heavy with hibiscus and walls overshadowed by the dark red frangipani. So the *Golden Dragon* must be in an outlying part of Bangkok, as the houses became fewer and poorer-looking again and we were almost out in the country? It was getting late, too, so that when we stopped and got out at a big building we quickly paid off the taxi without looking where we were going. It was not *The Golden Dragon* at all, but a notice in English over the front door announced that this was the Thai Amateur Weight Lifters' Association. The taxi had gone away by now, and we had to walk along in despondent mood, thinking of the late hour, walking for four or five blocks till another taxi came by and brought us back, past the hibiscus, frangipani gardens, to *The Golden Dragon*.

It had a décor of dragons at the door, all right, and this was opened for us by a pig-tailed Chinese girl in silk trousers. The place was nearly empty for the Chinese eat soon after midday, and air-conditioning had reduced the temperature to that of a floating iceberg in the Bering Sea. The shock of this after the humid heat outside was extreme, amounting almost to a direct promise of pneumonia. My wife, who had no coat with her, had to borrow a towel to put round her shoulders, and the sight of this was too much for the pig-tailed girl sitting at the door. She became quite hysterical. Each time she looked at us, she put her hand to her mouth and nearly fell off her chair. Chinese food is by now so much of a commonplace that it is almost superfluous to try to describe it. But *The Golden Dragon* must certainly be among the best of its kind. No one who has only eaten in Chinese restaurants in Europe or in America can know how good Chinese food may be. Now that the famous Chinese eating-houses in Peking are closed—the *Pei-I-Fang* celebrated for its lacquered duck, or the *Cheng-Lang-Lou*, open for nearly three centuries, its specialities, mutton grilled on an iron plate in winter, and crabs fed on sesame seeds in summer,[1]—and similar resorts in Shanghai and in Canton are no more, it is probable that the Chinese classical cuisine only keeps its tradition where the proper ingredients are available; in Hong Kong, in Taipeh on the island of Formosa, and in Bangkok.

At *The Golden Dragon*, for it is only fair to give some indication at least of its potentialities, there were some hundreds of dishes on the menu. Crab's claws in different forms were particularly good; and the 'hundred year old eggs', in reality buried for no longer than a year or two, were as satisfying as foie gras. Rice-birds, about the size of a field-mouse, and, at that, the smallest of the litter, came a dozen or so to a plate. The ortolans of the Landes are as the giant moa compared to them. They taste like soft brown paper macerated in vinegar, and there can be scarcely as much in a mouthful as a big bumble-bee. The poor little birds must be netted in their hundreds in the paddy fields. A meal at *The Golden Dragon* is anything but cheap, even if one is not tempted by birds'-nest soup from the isles, or by the varying grades of sharks' fin. At *Hoi Tien Lao*, another, perhaps even better restaurant in the Chinese quarter of Bangkok, the best kind of sharks' fin is ten pounds a portion.

But the grand objective at Bangkok is to get on to the river, and we were lucky enough to have this opportunity during the first days of our stay. We embarked at the jetty in front of the Oriental Hotel with a party composed largely of Danes and Norwegians working with the long established Swedish East Asiatic Company. It is true to say that Bangkok becomes transformed from the moment you are on its river. It reveals itself all at once as one of the water cities of the Orient, of the sort which reached to Europe a thousand years ago, but only on the lagoons of Venice. The water cities of the Netherlands are something different, cities that are as much canal as dry land on their town plan. Bruges, Ghent, the latter perhaps more river than canal; and in an ascending scale when we come to Holland—Delft, Leyden, Utrecht, Dordrecht, to end in the supreme canal town of Amsterdam with its canals in concentric rings, five-sided like the half of a decagon, Heeren-Gracht, Keizers-Gracht, Prinsen-Gracht, and Singel-Gracht, each with that terminal guttural that only a Dutch-man can pronounce—are all red brick towns of a northern civilization. People lived and died in the gabled, elm-shaded houses border-

---

[1] *Escape With Me*, by Osbert Sitwell, Macmillan & Co., 1939, pp. 234-242.

1   Aerial View of Wat Po Temple at Bangkok

2 The Supreme Pontiff
of Thailand

3 Silk Weaving

ing the canals, and not on and upon the waters as in the Far Orient. At Bangkok it is only necessary to push off shore and head a few yards into the stream to know this is a Far Eastern water town.

In a few moments coming round a bend in the river a huge pagoda appears straight in front of us, but it is difficult to know upon which bank it stands. An unfamiliar shape in any case, but a view of it that would have delighted Canaletto, painter of the palaces of the Grand Canal and of the steeples of white Portland stone along the Thames below St Paul's. Starting from a wide base, it towers up to a great height but is not in storeys like the pagodas of China and Japan. It is perhaps a mile away at this point, and hints that we may be nearing the dragon-roofs of the Royal Palace. The trains of barges are incessant, and the honking of their petrol engines is loud upon the water, but they are so closely covered in that it is impossible to tell their cargo. Also, there is much cross-river traffic in small, overloaded rowing-boats. Our hosts told us they had capsized one of these in midstream only a few days before, upsetting the occupants, a man and two women, and all their belongings into the water, but they had swum happily round, righting the boat again and retrieving their wet bedding without a sign of annoyance.

By now the pagoda that was straight in front of us has settled into position upon the left bank. It is the Wat Arun, 'Temple of the Dawn', and what looked at a distance like chimneys at its sides are four smaller pagodas of the same shape. Once it loses its dark outline against the sky Wat Arun is less impressive, and from being sombre turns to fun-fair gaiety for as we near the landing-stage it reveals itself as being coated with a mosaic of small fragments of porcelain. They could be the broken plates of the coco-nut shy; but, also, the pagoda is a little stumpy in shape at the start and then perhaps climbs too high. Nevertheless, one does not forget its outline against the sunset, or at early morning, and Wat Arun stays in the memory whenever one thinks of Bangkok. It was twinkling with lights when we saw it. There were strings of them linking the central with the smaller towers, as we disembarked to walk round Wat Arun among the youthful looking monks with their shaven heads and saffron robes worn toga-like with some little of a Roman air. Chinoiserie statues of sages and philosophers, or mere temple guardians and stone porters, make their first appearance here, but are as nothing to what we will see later on.

B

Crossing the river, our next call was at a dilapidated shed which housed the Royal barges. A wooden jetty led towards them, affording the most intimate views we had so far been given of life on the water. One could see right into the little wooden houses, which had mattresses to sleep on but no furniture beyond cooking utensils. Nearly every one of the sheds or huts was in the shadow of a coco-nut palm; and where flowers were the only luxury they had bougainvillaea on a wooden fence, beautiful yellow or tigered cannas, or often a flowering tree. What they must endure, though, from mosquitoes which are the prime nuisance of Bangkok! Yet we were told that malaria has been got rid of except in one small area of the town. The boat-house of the Royal barges is in a bad state with an ugly tin roof but the barges, themselves, fulfil all expectations. There are six or seven of them with dragon or seven-headed *naga* prows and serpent sterns. The Siamese Royal State barges have been described as the largest dug-outs in the world, exceeding in length the war-barges of any South Sea Island. Each is made of the trunk of a single (*dipterocarpus*) tree, and the longest are 150, or more, feet in length, the trunk 'being hollowed out with adzes, submerged in water until thoroughly soaked and then opened out over fire', the most splendid of them, which is the Royal Throne barge having a pavilion amidships for the King's throne.

The water processions which take place for the coronation, and in diminished splendour for certain religious festivals, include barges of the line, gold barges of the line, 'monkey and tiger' barges, garuda barges with trumpets and conches, barges with metal drums, the Royal pavilion barge conveying the King's state barge, the naga or Royal Throne barge, and Royal Reserve barge in the rear. The Royal Throne barge is rowed by seventy oarsmen 'in the crimson uniform of the ancient warriors of Siam', and has two steersmen and 'an official standing on a platform where he controls the stroke and keeps the time by tapping on the deck with the butt-end of a long silver spear'. The King is throned in his pavilion amidships which has a cloth-of-gold roof and side curtains under a gilded spire, and five tiered processional umbrellas are held fore and aft of his throne.

Interesting laws of taboo affect, or did affect, the water processions for we read that on board the Royal barges 'there are, or were until recently, bundles of coco-nuts intended to be thrown to the King or any members of the Royal family in the event of the barge founder-

ing, for it was forbidden on pain of death for any person to lay hands
on royalty to save them from drowning'. The first wife of King
Rama V (1868-1910) was drowned in full view of numerous by-
standers who dared not save her.[1] The draconian edicts in our footnote must have made the water processions into something of an
ordeal for all concerned. In the most elaborate of these not more than
thirty barges in all now take part; but in the past there were as many
as 150 to 200, including those of princes and nobles, all seated under
their umbrellas of state. It is interesting to note that Mr Quaritch
Wales from those book these details are quoted, notes a Burmese
influence in the design of the barges, and relates them to the golden
barges of King Thebaw and his predecessors on the moats and canals
of Mandalay. But river pageantry must have reached its greatest
heights here in Bangkok, and it is to be hoped that the craze for
speed and the idolatry bestowed all over the world on the internal
combustion engine will not obliterate all memory of these golden
dragons moving along the water.

Sunset is a beautiful hour on the river, and coming back from the
barges there was an intriguing view of golden dragon-roofs which
hinted at the Grand Palace and Emerald Buddha though we were
keeping these for the week following, and were determined not to
see them in detail during our first few days. But the distant view was
enticing enough for they do not come down to the water's edge but
stand some way back from it and are in a walled or forbidden city of
their own. And there are smaller and unimportant temples by the
river with the setting sun touching on their gilded eaves and glittering
across the water, and as we came by again Wat Arun stood up
against the darkening sky. However, this pagoda or chedi, to call it by
the proper name, has not the distinctive golden 'ox-horn' finials
which are in reality stylized naga-heads upon its gables. They are the
distinguishing feature in Siamese architecture, and their absence at
Wat Arun in at least the main building puts it a little apart from the

---

[1] Mr Quaritch Wales translates the following passage from the Book of Palace Law, a
manuscript dating from 1805, but of earlier origin: 'If a boat (Royal barge) founders, the
boatmen must swim away; if they remain near the boat they are to be executed. If the boat
founders and the Royal person falls into the water . . . let the boatmen throw the coco-nuts so
that he may grasp them if he can . . . If they lay hold of him to rescue him they are to be
executed . . . If the barge sinks and someone else sees the coco-nuts thrown and goes to save
the Royal person, the punishment is double and all his family is to be exterminated. If the
barge founders and someone throws the coco-nuts so that they float towards the shore (i.e.
away from the Royal person) his throat is to be cut and his home confiscated.'
Siamese State Ceremonies, by H. G. Quaritch Wales, London, Bernard Quaritch Ltd., 1931,
pp. 33, 111-115, 203.

other temples although after the Emerald Buddha it is the most memorable architectural feature of Bangkok.

It is a city where the days glide happily by in the humid heat, and where one is assured it is never cold. On the evening we arrived the lift boy who spoke a few words of English wanted me to tell him about snow. Had it been snowing when we left London? What did it feel like to touch? How deep was it? And so on. In the evenings there were the Chinese and the Thai restaurants to choose from, the latter offering a wide choice of their own; iced rice which was a new experience, various forms of curry, but, also, plakapong, an excellent salt-water fish, prawns, and much use made of coco-nut, particularly a whole coco-nut with a kind of trapdoor opening in its lid and the inside filled with the prepared pulp.

Morning and afternoon hours could be whiled away looking in the silk shops. This is a revived industry from the north of Thailand for which an American, Colonel James Thompson, is largely responsible. A taxi-driver who does not know one other word of English will call out 'Jimmy Thompson' almost before you have set foot inside his cab, and take you to his silk emporium. This is not mere commission-hunting for the 'Colonel' is rightly looked upon as a benefactor of the town. Thai silks of squared, almost tartan-like pattern are in dazzling, bewildering variety, in beautiful greens and blues, especially, and in crimsons and purples, in which latter colours some persons profess to see a Moslem influence, and in fact the Mohammedans of East Pakistan are not so many hundreds of miles away. But, also, Colonel Thompson has one of the oldest private houses in Bangkok, or, it is, in fact, four or five old Thai houses put together into one, and filled with antiques. It has rooms with superb teak pillars that elephants must have rolled and lifted with their trunks, and looks on to a canal which has a village of Thai silk weavers on the opposite bank.

In the interests of hygiene most of the canals or klongs of Bangkok have been filled in. It is part of the campaign to rid the town of mosquitoes, and has given all the opportunity and excuse for road-widening which is the craze with municipal bodies in nearly every town in the world. That this has largely destroyed the picturesqueness of Bangkok is obvious, and as in all such cases it may have been against the wishes of the inhabitants who usually prefer the environment they are used to, whatever its disadvantages. There are still some quarters of the town where the old disorder is undisturbed, as must

be the case where a population of more than one and a half millions
has begun to swarm, and the squalor of those may be enough to make
one change one's mind and come round to the side of municipal
improvement.

But the immediate fascination of the street scenes is in the groups of
children. Entirely naked babies are carried on their mother's back or
shoulder. Older children up to four or five years old are talking and
playing in groups; or it would be more sensible to call them bands
for it is probable that they meet all day and every day, and far into the
night. There is here an entire world of fantasy and study sufficient to
last a draughtsman or story-teller for a lifetime. Here is the Far Orient
in as immortal a potion as *The Thousand and One Nights*, all its action
in their little yellow persons with the scene unchanging and ending
at the next street, it being in their total and entire similarity to each
other that there are so many differences to look for. How much do
they know? What jokes and stories are they telling each other? What
riches of material in their slum-lore! But to Western eyes it is their
instant composition into Meissen or Chelsea figures that entrances,
derived, at that, from the doll shops of Kyoto. Here in Bangkok we
are never far from the land of bantam, though where that may be one
cannot precisely discover and it is even better not to look for it upon
the map, for it is their country of Cockaigne. Brueghel's painting of
'Children's Games', in the Vienna Gallery, in which more than eighty
different games are portrayed in action, is surpassed here at any hour
and along every street. It is inexhaustible, and perhaps the one kind of
folk-lore that is a living study.

But now a subtle change in the children and in the lettering over
the shops tells we are in Chinatown. The houses, too, are better built
and more substantial, and there are hotels for the Chinese who come
here from Hong Kong, Indonesia and Malaya. Sometimes there is a
shop sign in English, as, for instance, 'Birds' Nest Purveyors and
Suppliers' with all that implies and suggests, from the cliffs of the
Faifo Islands, off Tourane in Vietnam, name evocative of the 'fee-fi-
fo-fum' of *Jack and the Bean-stalk*, rocks of fantastic shape that should
have been transported into the classical gardens of China, and where
the best birds' nests are found, to the fleets of junks that sail as far
afield as Queensland and Arnhem and of the 'black fellows' in their
search for sea-slugs (bêche-de-mer), that other delicacy of the Chinese
kitchen.

Hereabouts in the Chinese quarter is that other restaurant, *Hoi Tien Lao* of the super-expensive sharks' fin, with Chinamen in new laundered white shirts lunching or dining upon four floors. There are, also, Chinese theatres and cinemas and Chinese music is in the air. An attraction all of its own pertains to the film posters whereon you may see the star, ten or twenty feet high, with the thin figure, sleek hair, slit eyes, and wearing the cheongsam of the Chinese canon. A living instance was the beautiful air hostess from Saigon who welcomed us aboard the Vietnamese jet at Angkor, on our flight back to Bangkok some days later. This interpretation of the 'moth-eyebrows' of the Chinese poets was borne out on those posters, but no one knew if they were the work of local artists, or if there is some central agency that supplies the film posters for Chinese audiences all over Indo-China and Malaya. It may be their origin is in Hong Kong. They give, at least, a new allurement to films that have had their day in Europe and the West.

Perhaps the noisiest place in Bangkok with 'tinned' music at full blast is the café just outside the Boxing Stadium. This, in spite of the slighter physique of the contestants, is a good deal more serious and less amusing than the Sumô wrestling in Japan. A direct kick below the eye, even from a foot only wearing a sock, or a riposte aimed at the area over the appendix, may have semi-permanent or long term effects. The music of a pipe and a pair of drums, and the preliminary prayer dance, are unrewarding. One of a pair of wrestlers staggered from the ring in unfeigned agony, and we wondered if he would ever fight again.

Thai Classical Dancing is as graceful and harmless as the boxing is dangerous, though, unfortunately, the performances of the great corps de ballet of the Fine Arts Department were just ended at the time of our visit. Instead we saw a small number of performers at an old school of fencing, and were handed fans of gilded palm leaves as we took our seats. The Khon (masked pantomime), a scene from *The Mahābhārata*, was long and tedious; the character dances were too 'peasanty'; but in the Lakon (operatic ballet) the glittering spired head-dresses of the classical Thai ballet came on, and there was the beautiful and sinuous back-bending of the fingers, and even the elbows. The girls are charming and graceful to look at. The ratio of feminine good looks in Bangkok is high indeed; and the dancers apart, who look their best in the costume that many centuries of dancing tradition have evolved for them, there is hardly a shop or an office in Bangkok where there is not a good-looking young woman at the desk or counter. They form an endearing memory of Thailand. It would seem that the social conscience which bedevils other large populations has not yet raised its head; or it may be that a benevolent, but enervating climate has joined with the gentleness of the Buddhist faith in giving contentment. How long this settled condition can go on is another matter for Thailand has dangerous neighbours.

We were long enough in Bangkok to get to know by sight some of the vagrant characters of the main streets; a tall thin man in a turban with a long staff in his hand, an Indian ascetic of lost vocation, ceaselessly wandering, but we never saw him begging. And an old white-haired woman, at times sitting on a step, or walking along muttering as she went, who, I saw, had European features and blue eyes. On inquiry, having seen her often, we were told she had been stranded here with a circus company many years ago. A friend had tried to speak to her, and found she talked a few words of English and Russian in her addled fury. I think she must have been Russian, and would like to know more of her history. There may come a day when the memories stored in a human brain can be photographed, and then from such a source as this would come soliloquies more revealing than the trauma of Mrs. Bloom in Joyce's *Ulysses*. The same friend, who has lived long in Bangkok, told us that Tibetan pedlars still come here by devious routes from Burma, visiting on their way the holy places of Buddhism. Their journey can be only less arduous than that of a mediaeval pilgrim to Jerusalem after the failure of the Third Crusade.

The exigencies of a semi-tropical clime that flatters, but never quite fulfills its promise, are made manifest in a visit to the snake pit of the Pasteur Institute. The climate has suppressed many of the pains of husbandry till it is indeed hardly necessary in glades of pineapples and under groves of mango and coco-nut to do more than wait until the fruit falls off the trees, yet it has allowed venomous snakes to multiply. A table of figures hung on the wall gives the fatal casualties which run into many hundreds for every year. It was nasty in the great heat leaning over the pit to watch a snake waken out of its sloth, make a flickering dart at a live white mouse which was paralysed in a few seconds, and wriggle off with it into the water.

The circular pit was divided in two like a double bullring, and attendants went down into both halves of it, one after the other, catching the snakes with a forked stick, lifting them up, and pressing the venom from the sacs or glands at the backs of their heads into a little receptacle. It seemed only natural that the products of this should be made use of for, among other maladies, venereal disease and madness.

We went straight from the snake pit to see the pavilion and garden belonging to Princess Chumpot. This has tropical flowers and flowering trees and a lacquer pavilion supported upon teak columns. Not the least charming feature is the courteous old Siamese gentleman and former diplomat, in old Thai court dress of white 'plus-fours' and blue frock-coat, who leads one up the ladder. The pavilion was once the library of a temple. It is of diminutive size, and confers a new probability upon the so-called 'libraries' at Angkor. The interior is a double shell and the walls are lacquered in black and gold, the interest being that the figures include late seventeenth-century French and Dutchmen, both nations being clearly identified by their clothes. The Dutch have their baggy breeches, and the French their long surcoats and plumed hats. It may have been painted soon after the Embassy sent to Siam by Louis XIV in 1685, of which l'Abbé de Choisy left a sparkling account. It seems that there is no other library, or, for that matter, old house left in Bangkok, which in any case has only been the capital since the establishment of the present dynasty in 1782. Ayudhya, the old capital, had been entirely destroyed by the Burmese a few years earlier. Little, if anything in Bangkok is older than the last decade of the eighteenth century, which only makes more remarkable the picturesqueness of the Emerald Buddha and the Grand Palace. Of this the lacquer pavilion is as a little foretaste; but, before the experience, and leading up to it, must come the early morning excursion upon the river-boats.

Chapter Two

✦ ✦

TEMPLE OF THE EMERALD BUDDHA

THE JOURNEY TO THE FLOATING markets begins at half-past six in the morning. It starts from the landing-stage in front of the hotel, and continues along the river to Wat Arun, the 'Temple of the Dawn', then crosses over to the boat-house of the Royal barges where we have a glimpse of their dragon prows, and soon after that takes a right turn down one of the side canals. These are no longer the klongs of the city but country water-ways, though just at this beginning there is a wide expanse of water. The sun has not yet climbed above the trees. All the buildings are low sheds with palms behind them. The river is a muddy yellow, then suddenly as we turn into the quieter waters there is a flashing of gold from the eaves of a small temple. It comes from the naga finials and from its fronton which is an intricate carving with much gold in it, a carving that in the West would be work of a ship or coach builder's yard. The carved and gilded barge-boards of the temples in Siam are a little and special art to themselves; and our eyes follow along the green tiles of the roof line to the 'ox-horns' on the gables that give to these temple roofs an incongruous look of the dragon finials of a Norwegian 'Stave' church, though we know they are really naga-heads. There are many scores or even hundreds of such temples, and each one of them is a delight to look upon, this no less than all the others, with the bright blue shed in front of it, and next to that an open shed piled high with red petrol drums.

There are barges with bent hoods of corrugated iron, and soon where the canal is still wide we come to a great raft of teak logs that has floated down from some forest in the interior, a raft with a little hut at one end of it where a whole family lives. Over their heads just at this moment a flower rocket has burst high in the palms—not palm-trees—for these are the sort with fronds that spring straight out

25

of the ground without stems, in fact the palms of Edwardian drawing-rooms and palm courts at home here in their native habitat, and the bursting, falling, crimson rocket must be a rogue bougain-villaea that has escaped into the trees. From about this point the water trip becomes an experience always to be remembered. Before the canal narrows we pass other smaller boats with awnings over them. The only annoyance is the loud noise of our motor engine; with a passing aggravation at the sun-hats worn by everyone in sight, straw hats the shape of circular, double waste-paper baskets or lamp shades, one inside the other for coolness, with a round flat crown, for the tourists off a cruise were wearing these last evening all over the town.

We float by large warehouses under big, tall trees, and soon after have left civilization, as we know that. The klong, which must be the branch of a river, is overhung by a forest of strange trees and palms of exotic kind and of a luxuriance that only douanier Rousseau has painted; and then only in the one or two of his pictures drawn from his experiences as a soldier under Marshal Bazaine in Mexico. There is no more inspired painter of the tropics, not even Gauguin; and anyway this is Indo-China and it is different. We pass a hut with gorgeous scarlet or yellow cannas growing beside it, and with hanging baskets below the eaves with orchids trailing from them. It is an entire solitude in the tropical morning. In some places a tree pushes itself in front of the others, and right into the water, as though to make more room for its huge leaves. Brilliant and nameless flowers hang from other of the trees. Occasionally a wide spreading tree, almost the size of a small oak, is a mango tree, and one wonders in passing what else there can be to do but wait for the fruit to ripen and let itself be loosened from the leaves. More flower rockets are bursting in the top boughs under the canopy of sky.

We overtake an old man paddling his way to market in a blue shirt and sun-hat. He has nothing to sell in his boat, and is probably going there just for the excitement of it. Now even his sun-hat fits into the picture, and is part of the long, lacquered morning. After him there is entire silence, unless the flowering trees on both banks can work upon a sixth and lost sense in some language we do not apprehend. And we come to where a much smaller raft of teak logs has pulled up beside a provision store which has the lower part of its roof made of corrugated tin like nearly all the farm barns at home in

I   Canal Scene at Bangkok

England. At the side of it, just where the teak logs lie along the shore, is a tall bush that I mistake for a poinsettia, not in flower, but it has avocado-shaped fruits high on its leaves and is a papaya. Many of the isolated huts are in fact country farms, and these hamlets spread out along the klongs have their village stores and even here and there a chemist's shop. Here are three or four of the huts, together under a lively skyline of palm fronds. Their porches come out into the water on poles and the naked infants are playing there. One imagines how completely dark it must be here at night between the amphibious farmsteads, and with what nocturnal sounds unknown to our ears. Just the one splash could be a snake gliding into the water, and there must be flowers that only open in the night.

The ribbed palm fronds are throwing tigerish-striped shadows. Beside many of the huts there is a wooden post with a structure that looks like a miniature house upon it, and always of more elaborate design than the hut itself. It is some kind of a household shrine. The sun is now high enough to look down to the forest floor, and we have a long straight stretch of water in front of us which is so perfect in balance of slanting stem and tossing palm crown, though still now for there is no wind, that it could be a panoramic wallpaper if from the brush of a greater genius than ever set hand to such a scheme. The crowns of the palms are as bunches of feathers, but arranged for the scene, and as appropriate as the trees in Fragonard's paintings. The forest glades are like marvellous scenery that extends and dissolves into more scenes as though to music, and yet it is the lacquered Indo-China all the time. Something in the spatulate spread of the palm boughs, even in the interval between their fronds, is of this land of dragon-roofs and frangipanis. Why it should not be of the South Sea Islands one does not know, but this is a journey along a canal or klong that could lead in no great exaggeration from Phnom Penh or Saigon to Tongking, Hanoi, Haiphong, and with the changing sound in the names, to Southern China. Perhaps we are becoming a little drugged with the scene.

But suddenly the canal widens. We have reached the water market. There is a great concourse of small boats ahead under the palms, and the palms have become wider spreading, more domesticated. Each is standing straight in plumed arrogance, as regular as a feather duster set on end. And where the black bulblet grows at the base of the leaf of a lily, there are the golden coco-nuts, or the lopped stems where they have been. It is a water market in a glade of palms, with the *klong* leading off below it for as far as one can see, and at this moment like the pleasure pond in a public park for it is entirely covered with little canoes or boats. There is a canoe full of melons and another of pineapples, and the objectionable sun-hats altogether rid of their former association fit into the picture. What is entrancing is that the water-way now narrows into a green tunnel and stretches still farther ahead with little boats all along its length.

We are alongside a palm-tree that leans right over the water, trying to get past a boat with a little boy in the prow with his back to us, wearing one of the hats that is much too big for him. Another of the hats with its immaculate waste-paper basket finish lies on one of the seats, and an old woman in a boat beside it wearing yet another is lifting and moving something from one boat to the other. The Chinese-looking hats have become an integral part of the scene. We are at the centre of the market, and the wooden verandas are crowded with every sort of merchandise. That the verandas have tin roofs is of no moment. There are hoop nets hung from a rafter, and a number of pot plants which must be for sale, and at a glance everything there should be in a village post-office store in the tropics, except the facilities to post a letter. Pineapples the size of fire buckets have a corner to themselves. Probably they do not bother to put mangoes and papayas on sale because everyone has them growing in his or her back garden.

The next shed is nothing but baskets of all shapes and sizes. One would like to buy several of these if it were not for the difficulty of getting them home. Even the cheapest kind of tinware looks interesting in this setting. One canoe has round baskets full of prawns crawling over each other with uncertain movement of claw and jointed shell, like creatures from another element just landed. And there is a tethered houseboat which is a crockery store, with brightly enamelled cups and plates of the kind to catch the eye of bargees on any canal in the world. Lean and famished-looking dogs, limping and covered with sores, are the bane of the scene, for the Buddhist religion does not inculcate kindness to animals, while, at the same time, it forbids the taking of life so that a diseased creature is left lingering on and cannot be put out of its misery. The dogs seem to lead a life apart from human beings as though they do not like humanity but cannot get away from it. I do not remember seeing a child playing with a dog anywhere in the water market. But children are idolized, especially by their grandparents, and we passed a small boy eating with his grandmother at a table which had, surprisingly, bottles of '7 Up' and 'Yorkshire Stingo' upon it.

All this time we have been passing through the market and now, sadly, are coming out of it at the far end. The dream-like aspects of the first part of the journey, which became fulfilled or realized in this market on the water, are as quick in returning to normal save that the ordinary, itself, becomes transcended as one is regretting going back to a town of trains and motors, and in that very moment catches the glitter again of a small temple, standing back from the water with a white stupa mound beside it to give mystery. This temple seems, too, to be a school for novices. All males in Thailand are supposed to spend a year of their lives as monks, and they are certainly very young bonzes in their saffron robes who come down to the water's edge to watch us go by. How beautiful were the over-arching coco-nut and the bushes of scarlet hibiscus at the railing as we caught the last gold of the temple finials, and turned back again into the river!

But it is the larger temples of Bangkok that now beckon. Even the Marble Temple begun by the reigning family in 1900, built like some of the government offices in traditional style, is to be preferred to its equivalents in other Oriental lands. It is quiet and elegant in its precious woods and marble, and in its cloister were a group of bonzes with no less a figure than the Buddhist patriarch in person enjoying a late vegetarian breakfast, their last meal in the day. This is no unjust comment on the architecture. The older temples are both more fanciful and more serious. Perhaps it is best to begin with Wat Rajprohit, enclosed within its high white wall on a morning of blazing heat, when the grey humidity of the days of our first arrival had given place to a clear sky. It was necessary almost to run from the car into the dark shadow of its porch. The splendid old wooden double doors were open wide, but the two bodies of building within were locked, and it took long searching to find the bonze with the key.

It is in an open space beyond this temple that the Swinging Festival takes place. This is, or was, one of the most curious of the Siamese State Ceremonies, and while the key was being looked for we walked to see the swing. Persons with long memories of Bangkok give con-flicting accounts of the ceremony, but it is of ancient Hindu origin and conducted by the Court Brahmans, themselves of Indian descent many centuries ago though intermarried with Siamese women and showing no sign now of Indian blood, and in themselves a curious anomaly in that they are performing Hindu ritual in a Buddhist land. The swing consists of a pair of huge teak pillars like ships' masts, eighty feet high, painted red, sloping inwards a little, and crowned with a carved cornice. It looks like a gallows at first sight, but something gayer about it conveys its festive purpose, and would lead one, even in ignorance, to inquire what it is there for.

The ceremony is a pantomime of the yearly arrival on earth of the Hindu god Shiva, a cheerful god of impish character, and the acrobats and the swinging are in order to amuse him. The King appoints a nobleman or high official as temporary king to impersonate the god, and he goes in procession to the ceremony in a tall pointed hat and wearing robes that are only subtly different from the State robes of the King. The procession includes 'a number of acrobats and persons dressed as sprites from celestial spheres'.[1] There are three sets of swingers, four to a team, and it is only typical of Indo-China that their peculiar head-dresses are in symbol that they are nagas. The object of the swinging is to catch with the teeth a purse hanging from a bamboo pole, and as with the trapeze artists of our circuses they make many feints at it in order to amuse the crowd. At each success gongs are beaten and conches blown. The ceremony is repeated two days later in the evening when the naga-swingers perform a circular dance around the swing, and throw water over each other from buffalo horns. It is no doubt a solar ceremony of ancient Indian origin. As noted by Frazer in *The Golden Bough*, 'in the Rigveda the sun is called, by a natural metaphor, "the golden swing in the sky" . . . and about the middle of March the Hindus observe a swinging festival in honour of the god Krishna, whose image is placed in the seat or cradle of a swing and then, just when the dawn is breaking, rocked gently to and fro several times. The same ceremony is repeated at noon and sunset.' A further piece of evidence which seems to prove this Indian origin and meaning is the presence in the Brahman temples of Bangkok, 'of pairs of posts about four feet high, from which on certain occasions are suspended small swings on which the Brahmans rock to and fro the image of the gods. But the original

[1] The best account of the Swinging Festival, which is also described in Frazer's *Golden Bough*, is to be found in *Siamese State Ceremonies*, by H. G. Quaritch Wales, London, 1931, pp. 238-255.

connection with the sun has been forgotten, and they place in the swing whichever god they wish to placate at the time.'[1]

The Swinging Festival has been compared a little cruelly to our Lord Mayor's Show, and pondering on that and thinking of those cold November days, we walked back to the temple where there was still a little time to wait in the long cool corridors and look out upon the carved and gilded fantasy of the two prayer halls. For just a moment one might wonder if the Thais of the end of the eighteenth century had been in telepathic communication with the Norsemen of a thousand years ago for the golden finials on the gables, call them 'ox-horns', but they are really (cobra) naga-heads, bear a fortuitous resemblance to the dragons or sea monsters of the Norwegian 'stave' churches. The angle of the projecting dragons' heads on the gables of those wooden churches on the fjords is almost exactly the same. It is no more than the coincidental resemblance due to identity of material in all wooden building, but nevertheless it is quite striking. This is all the more so where, as in the two prayer halls of this temple, the wooden superstructure of roofs and gables is above plain white walls. Then, the 'ox-horns' make this immediate impression which is not that which one would anticipate from a Buddhist temple. In other of the Bangkok temples the curious Norse look of the gables is lost in the whirl and glitter of exciting incident which alas! is more true of the exterior than the interior of Thai buildings.

Wat Indra and Wat Traimit are other temples we visited. In one of these, even persons who have lived many years in Bangkok get confused about their names, the interior was more interesting. It is reached by boat up one of the klongs, and being older than the other temples may date from before Bangkok became the capital. It has the oldest paintings and door panels inlaid with mother of pearl. A Siamese friend who was with us bowed her head to the floor being a devout Buddhist, and it was little different from going into a church in Italy or Spain except for the taking off of shoes at the doorway, the bowls of frangipani petals and the dark red and white frangipani bushes that scented the air as we came out again.

But the grand picturesque in its utmost expression is to be studied in Bangkok as in few other cities in the world, if always with the reservation that it is pantomime scenery with a touch of genius to it. The accumulation of incident may be haphazard but its results are

[1] H. G. Quaritch Wales, *op. cit.*

quite thrilling. Wat Po, the Temple of the Reclining Buddha, is a prime instance; all the more so because the statue, 160 feet long, lying on its side and like a stranded golden whale, is one of the less interesting things in the whole temple. It is as though a dead whale has been towed into a boat-shed. Another of the high white walls surrounds Wat Po, and the enclosure is so near to the Emerald Buddha and the Grand Palace that the gilded eaves and 'ox-horn' finials showing over their respective walls combine into giving an impression of one great Kremlin. In fact the approach to Wat Po is down a lane between two long white walls, and the living quarters of the bonzes are behind the long wall to the right. There are long walks between whitewashed buildings, and many fine plants in pots and tubs outside the doors. The monastery or 'bonzery' gives a feeling of contentment and well-being, and the monks in orange or saffron robes look youthful against the white walls.

Crossing the lane is a considerable excitement. This first moment in one of the two great temples of Bangkok is different from the experience of any Hindu temple in India in there being nothing either fanatic or horrid about it. That is because it is Buddhist and therefore gentle. Under Buddhist influence the grotesque is no more than picturesque. There is no Ganesh, the elephant god whose statue is always smeared with ghee (clarified butter), generally dyed red. Instead, it is as a glorious dream-like performance of the Oriental scenes from 'Sinbad the Sailor' with backgrounds by the scene-painters of the great days of pantomime, which indeed is exactly its date for Wat Po, difficult as it is to believe this, was only begun in about 1860. It is just how the scene-painters for Drury Lane, for Sadler's Wells, for Astley's Equestrian Drama would have visualized a temple or palace scene in Peking, being more than a little uncertain of their facts. In the result it was the China of the tea-chest, the engraved bill-heading, the lacquer cabinet, all deriving from their main source, Les Indes Occidentales et Orientales of the seventeenth-century Dutch engraver, Romeyn de Hooghe, but resembling very closely the temple of Wat Po in Bangkok.

It is that scenery not just painted, but built and brought to life. It has indeed so much incident that one does not know where to look first. There is a long cloister or arcade of gilt Buddhist images, all alike, so one need not walk down the length of them. But all around, walking farther inside, are stone statues of sages, or, in fact, panto-

4   Water Market at Bangkok

5   Emerald Buddha Temple at Bangkok

6 & 7 Gilded Figures at the
       Emerald Buddha
       Temple, Bangkok

8   Temple Guardian

mime Chinamen, clipped trees as if from the scissors of a professional poodle-trimmer, and chedis (pagodas) like thin tapering spires, three or four or five of them in a row, which are cremation monuments. These are made of a sort of vitreous paste of broken bits of china. Not far away is a half life-size bronze horse that, some little crudities in head and neck apart, could be the enlarged replica of a silver statuette off many a dinner table in sporting circles or in an army mess. Wat Po is like a junk shop in a vision. You never know what you may be finding next. Everything is near together without context to its neighbour. It is this fairy-tale-like fantasy and lightness, and the improbability of incident, that Mrs Leonowens suggests so well in her narrative, however much it has been travestied by rougher hands. Indeed it is nearly impossible to describe the scene except with her touch of mingled ignorance and innocence. At this moment we may have no fewer than four of the cremation monuments in our direct line of vision like much enlarged pagodas of Delft china, or china tulip-holders, and next to it a building with an extraordinary complexity of gables, double or tandem, jackanapes or galligaskin we will call them, after the double or freak primroses, one inside the other, of the Jacobean age, each with the golden 'ox-horn' at the tilt of the gable, and only the more fascinating if we know their secret and can turn them in our minds to golden cobras. The aesthetic success of all this incident which 'comes off' so brilliantly goes to prove that the Thais must possess some quality akin to 'green fingers' in their building. Everything grows so naturally next to everything else however diverse in character. It must be a trait of their individuality as a nation, and from its presence among them so short a while ago there may be some hope that they keep it.

Before looking at the Grand Palace and the Emerald Buddha there is room in a single paragraph to speculate upon what other architecture there may be in Thailand. In a kingdom which reaches six hundred miles to the south down the thinning isthmus of the Malay Peninsula, and five hundred miles to the north to Chiengmai, which city is only half as far as that again from China. Ayudhya, fifty miles from Bangkok, and the old capital of the Kingdom, has ruins that are the version in stone of what many tastes would consider to be the gimcrack buildings of the newer city. But it is arguable that this kind of thing is better in plaster than in stone, and that its quality

C

is its impermanence. We were not able to visit Ayudhya, nor yet Lopburi with its memories of the Greek adventurer Constantine Phaulkon and the ruins of his palace. Chiengmai, a living city and the northern capital, must be more interesting. The shops in Bangkok have cotton stuffs from Chiengmai which are only less distinctive than the Thai silks. But the interest of Chiengmai is its old temples, six or seven of them, and in another style from those of Bangkok, for Chiengmai was an independent kingdom which did not become a part of Thailand until 1764. It would be natural to expect more Burmese influence, that country being so near, but there is no means of finding out about such things except for oneself. It may be some criterion of how difficult the temples of Bangkok are to describe in words that no one who had been to Chiengmai was able to give me any verbal description of what he had seen there. It is a pity on the whole that I was not able to go there in person.

Wat Phra Keo, the Temple of the Emerald Buddha, is to be seen on all accounts after, and not before Wat Po. For the temple of the Emerald Buddha compared with that latter is the pantomime with the final harlequinade as well. There is perhaps no more glittering collection of buildings in the world. Probably it is at its most intriguing if entered through the Grand Palace where the lamp-posts, or, rather, lamp-clusters are on the lines of those outside all casinos from Deauville to Monte Carlo and there are clipped trees of wildest fantasy trained to grow in an espalier of blobs like full stops. They appear to be signalling in some Morse or other code from their casino-like balustrade. There is a model of a funerary pagoda which is like a small temple in itself, a throne room in Thai style which has beautiful gold-work, and in another hall are portraits of the Kings of the reigning dynasty in their robes of ceremony. There are gateways which led, or still lead to forbidden parts of the Grand Palace, doors which perhaps Mrs Leonowens was allowed through, and in general some slight apprehension that the sacred White Elephant may be at hand.

We had in fact caught a glimpse of the new White Elephant in his cage while passing the zoological garden. He had shortly before been awarded estates and honorific titles and was soon to be promoted to higher rank; and the reader will forgive the digression in remarking that the ideal White Elephant is not white at all, but an albino, and should possess, 'if perfect, pink and yellow eyes, a light reddish brown skin, white at the edge of the ears, and at the top of the trunk, white toe-nails, and red hair'. Mrs Leonowens in her *The English Governess at the Siamese Court*, describes the death of the White Elephant in 1862, and how the King read aloud to her the official description of it: 'His eyes were light blue, surrounded by a salmon colour; his hair, fine, soft, and white; his complexion pinkish white; his tusks like long pearls; his ears like silver shields; his trunk like a comet's tail; his legs like the feet of the skies; his tread like the sound of thunder; his looks full of meditation; his expression full of tenderness; his voice the voice of a mighty warrior; and his bearing that of an illustrious monarch.' And it should be said in conclusion that his companions in captivity were, by tradition, a white monkey to represent Hanuman, the monkey hero, and a white crow for the sacred bird Garuda; that it was formerly the custom to provide him with a large number of human wet-nurses, and that he was greatly esteemed as a rain-maker.[1]

After which overture we change our minds and now think it better to enter the Temple of the Emerald Buddha, as we did on our second occasion, not from the Grand Palace but through the gateway in its high wall for that gives opportunity to stand back from it and admire the marvellous panorama of its tilted roofs and gilded finials, and to enjoy the sensation that we are about to set foot inside this magical and enchanted Kremlin. For that is how it appears from whatever direction you look at it outside its walls; and a Kremlin, at that, scarcely more than a hundred and fifty years old, and of a gentle, not cruel enchantment thanks to the Buddhist faith that built it. Once inside its gateway the glitter is nearly overpowering. But one is pushed by the crowd of worshippers and sightseers up some steps and towards the main buildings. Or one can turn round, look back, and admire the statues of the temple guardians. But it is better still to go on a little farther to where one can see a whole row of them standing on duty, both hands upon their staffs of office.

To many persons these figures are the chief curiosity of the Emerald Buddha Shrine. They are pantomime ogres twenty-five feet tall, at least, for the tops of their gold hats are as high as the roofs. Each stands with his gold boots in red or green socks on a solid white pedestal. They are porters or door-keepers on watch, night and day,

[1] H. G. Quaritch Wales, *op. cit.*, devotes a whole chapter to the White Elephant and quotes from Megasthenes who wrote of these sacred animals in 300 B.C.

and we must comprehend that in their time they were really frightening. They have blue or red or green faces and grimacing expressions, and are wearing lacquered armour in many colours. Their hands folded on their door-keepers' staffs are to match the colour of their socks and faces. And it should be added that for ornament they have a pair of flares or wings to each knee, and peaked shoulders; that their gilt ears are enormous and in the attempt to make them suitably threatening they have come out as bats' ears. Now they no longer terrify, but are endearing and grotesque, and are the plaster giants of pantomime. One does not know whether to like them most on standing duty each side of a door, and as high as the roof; or seen sideways, six or eight of them in line, as though dressing their ranks. One is always coming back to them at the Emerald Buddha, and trying to count them, and losing count, and having to begin all over again.

The next sensation is the material and texture of the chedis as one comes up nearer to them, and hears the music of the temple bells. Many of the pagodas are made of broken china, and it is as though one's grandmother's favourite tea-service has been broken by the servants into unusually small pieces and then shipped out to Bangkok. It is just exactly the china of which a cup or saucer may still be left in the china-cupboard in an old house. And the effect of a whole chedi made of broken bits is as bright and gay as can be imagined what with the chiming of the temple bells. The pink roses of the china can be identified singly, one at a time; and then the whole airy structure blends together and is no more unlikely than that mosaics should be made of cubes of coloured glass.

The buildings are so near together you have almost to squeeze in order to get between them, and as haphazard of purpose as the kiosques at an exhibition. A scale model of the temples of Angkor, itself on a terrace, stands near a gilt shrine at the foot of which are seven-tiered umbrellas of state in sign of high rank, and the monument is complete with four statues of elephants to guard its marble base. Where nothing else is going on, and wherever there is room for them, are little open pavilions for worshippers to rest in from the heat, and bring their picnics if they want to. And we find ourselves walking round the outside of a golden stupa that is as round as a gasometer. Just beyond this we get the view of the temple guardians, standing in line, and come back from that to the platform in front of

II Part of Wat Po Temple at Bangkok

the main temple, emerging on to it from under a porch that is shaped like the spired head-dress of a dancer.

On this raised platform stand the gilded figures that are the most beautiful works of art within the precincts of the shrine. There are eight or ten of them; angels or bird dancers for some have birds' thighs and a bird's rump and tail feathers, but the head and body are those of a bayadère. All are female, about Thai life-size, and the most seductive of them for their physical attraction is undeniable, has her hand on her hip just where her tail fits on, and a pair of human legs. She stands in her corner, with youthful pretty face and spired head-dress, and a strange ornament rises at the back of her over the low balustrade. It is like a fantasy evolved from a green artichoke. The 'choke' is there for a base, and the flower rises above that, but tapering and elongated, and climbing high against a tilted roof.

This, till our attention is held by another of the statues with an animal's legs, and a lion's tail curling upwards higher than her head-dress, or the gold rod she holds in one hand, with her other hand upon her waist. Who made these figures? How old are they? And what is their meaning? Were they here in the time of Mrs Leon-owens? Probably the inspiration for them may have come from among the troops of Amazons. The Kings of Indo-China, whether Khmer, or Cambodian, or Siamese, have always had companies of Amazons in their retinue; and the angels or bird dancers of the Emerald Buddha if this is their ancestry are more attractive of feature than the apsaras of Angkor.

The temple has the gold figures in front of it, and at its sides. It is a large high hall with a colonnade of presumably teak pillars all round it, but gilded and spangled, and with a much convoluted skyline. There is the feeling of a holy place as you take off your shoes and go inside, and the sense that it is a Royal Chapel. It is always full of worshippers, and of course the effect is enhanced if there is chanting. The interior of the chapel is late nineteenth century, but not incon-gruous to the giant temple guardians we know to be at their posts not far away. It is interesting to know that various sacred vessels of nephrite in this temple were made by the Russian jeweller Fabergé to the order of King Rama VI; and did the crowd of worshippers permit of nearer approach we would see the statuettes with names and titles of the twenty-one White Elephants that have belonged to the present Chakri reigning dynasty of Siam. All this is in keeping with the scene; with the women praying on their knees, and with the mystery of the golden altar where is the sacred image, carved, it would seem, from a solid block of jasper resembling emerald. Like the images in many Catholic countries it has a large wardrobe and its garments are changed according to the season of the year.

But one does not want to stay long inside the Emerald Buddha. It is so gay and cheerful outside. The temple bells are lazily lolling, and now and again chiming, all in their different tones in lovely evocation of the heat. We come out and down some steps, and past a blue and gold building with tall pillars, hundreds of bells hanging from its complicated cornice, and a blue and gold pyramid of naga-heads, indeed an ordered, an arrogant nest of serpents for its roof. Is it another, or the same temple we have just been in? The enchantment of this magical Kremlin is at work, and in a moment or two we will be mistaking the temple guardians for living giants. Once again, and for this last time, they dress their ranks, but never turn their heads. The golden figures on the terrace perform the figures of their harlequinade. And we come away from this magical pantomime at the Emerald Buddha into the hotter, duller world outside.

Chapter Three

✦━✦━✦━✦━✦━✦━✦━✦━✦━✦━✦━✦━✦

THE FIVE TOWERS

THE ROAD LED STRAIGHT ON to the five towers, the corn-cob towers. They were the shape of corn-cobs stood up on end with the tallest in the middle. And they were like wild bees' nests formed in the angle between some wall and ceiling of an empty building, old honey-cells and honey-stalagmites taken down and set up with the front pair of them hiding the pair behind it, so that there are not five but only three towers rising and growing bigger as we come towards them. And so they stay for a moment or two until each one of the hinder pair shows the fretted cone of its summit a little lower and to the right of its companion as the road comes out in front of the whole huge structure, and across a wide stretch of moat we have high in front of us the five corn-cob towers of Angkor Wat.

Looked down upon only a few minutes earlier from the aeroplane when after an hour or two of the paddy fields and then the blue-green jungle below we had come over something straight and ordered just underneath us, if it was only the work of a child drawing lines in the mud and playing at making a building. The plan of it was one rectangle within another with a line of water between and a cluster of towers in the middle, such as a child might make playing on the sands at bringing order into a foot or two of what had been uncovered by the tide and would be submerged again and swept away in only a few hours. A human being at work if only playing in order to amuse himself; or it could be the work of a multitude of six-legged beings, ants or bees. As to the scale of it this was difficult to guess at while we circled round and made a turn cutting off one of its corners, came straight on down one of the long arms of its canals, and flew off abruptly as if we had been shown enough of it and had something better and more interesting to do.

Then back to it some half-hour later along this road with the five towers growing bigger and taller every moment, but now at last risen to their greatest height until we walk nearer to them along the causeway. And so in fact to the water's edge of what was clearly ornamental water. They were waters of ceremonial or ritual on a scale far surpassing the basins and long canal of Versailles. But was it a temple, a tomb, or a palace? For to eyes free of knowledge or prejudice it could be either, or any two of them, or all three. Whichever, it was the work of some human being of tremendous, and forgotten importance who when he disappeared for ever from the human scene left this giant structure of stone behind him in the lotused waters.

This is what we think in the first moment of seeing the five towers rising before our eyes; that some being of Pharaonic importance whose very name has been forgotten lived here, that he reigned here, or came here to be buried. In which moment we are driving down the half-mile or so of embankment which is but a half of this one arm of the canal in front of Angkor Wat, and coming to an open quadrangle of white-painted, one-storeyed sheds where we are to stay. It is towards a far end of this one of the moats with the five lotus-bud towers rising a little way to the left of us, for now they are more the shape of an opening lotus bud than of a corn-cob. And the bus comes to a stop in front of the Auberge des Temples with its mosquito-netted beds and shower-baths and its relics of former Western 'culture' in the shape of bottles of Vichy and even one or two French wines.

Having arrived at Angkor at last after half a lifetime of anticipation it is impossible to rest, and at half past two in the afternoon, at the hottest hour of the day, we start off on what is called '*le petit circuit*', determining though to break it in the middle in order to have an evening walk over the causeway into Angkor Wat. It is therefore but a preliminary look at some of the ruins, and we do little more than drive into Angkor Thom, the ancient city, for Angkor Wat lies outside that. We follow the whole mile-long length of the moat, see another of its arms opening a mile long to the right of us, and are soon passing ruined buildings to either side. And soon we come to the moat of the city and are on one of the causeways crossing it, bordered with stone giants and demons holding the serpent body of the naga in their hands like a stone cable they are laying, or the stone rope of a never ending tug of war. There is only time to see they are giants on one side of the road, demons on the other, to be known by their benign or ferocious expression, and we are going under a triple gate-tower below stone faces of Buddha looking in all four directions under their tiaras of stone flowers; the highest turret in the middle with a Buddha on both fronts of it, and a Buddha's face in profile on the smaller turrets to either side. Buddha-faced towers and gateways are the familiar hallmark of Angkor; what one was not prepared for were triple-headed stone elephants, just their heads and trunks coming out of the wall, tuskless elephants feeding on lotuses and about to lift the stalks and lotus buds into their mouths.

Next, we pass an enormous stone-faced mound of a temple which is the Baphuon, or all that is left of it for it is in extreme ruin and delapidation, and soon after that some low ruins like open porches in a wider space to either side, and we are at the Elephant terrace and the Terrace of the Leper King. We are in the grand plaza or great square of the old city in utter silence with the heat seeming to drip down on us from the trees. The left-hand wall, which is 400 yards long, is sculptured down all its length with bas-reliefs of elephants in procession, one following another; and the heat and the hallucinatory silence that must affect everyone who comes here begins to distort and extend the limits of its own reality.

The elephants, which are animals of a circus or quasi-theatrical connotation to any Western mind, together with the dancing figures of apsaras which one knew to be present in their hundreds in the sculptures of Angkor but curiously had not encountered up to this moment, together with the obsessive naga-motif evident in the serpent-balustrades, all of these things heightened the ritual panto-mime. The very names, the Elephant Terrace, the Terrace of the Leper King, were the acts given on a circus programme, or signs put up to delude and deceive one in the haunted forest. How old were the trees growing out of the stone terraces? Were they centuries old, and the progeny of still older trees; or had they grown up in the night? Or come up through traps in the stone floor of the stage?

And we climbed up a narrow and steep stair on to the terrace of the Leper King, a stair in the thickness of the stone wall past tier on tier of stone princesses, seated figures of goddesses or devatas, sitting cross-legged, watching the play, row above row, and now there was no pantomime or pageant for them, with their eyes on ourselves except that, when we were within a few inches of them, one could see that their eyes mostly were withdrawn and looking down into themselves. Up above, where the weeds grow and one can see how the trees have rooted themselves in the stonework, is the seated statue that local tradition calls the Leper King, one of the only sculptures in the round at Angkor, but in fact not king, nor leper, for he has no marks of either, though the lichen has left blemishes on the statue's naked arms and legs; or it could be that the stone itself is diseased. There is nothing else in any way remarkable about the statue, and one can only wonder why this sculpture in particular has had a legend attached to it. Probably only because of its prominent position sitting there overlooking the great square.

Opposite, across the open space are the dozen small towers, structures of little interest, but flattered by another local tradition into being the Twelve Towers of the Cord Dancers, according to which legend leather ropes were strung from one tower to the other and acrobats advanced along them holding fans of peacock feathers in either hand in place of balancing-poles. Here we have a case of a story invented, one could almost say, in order to give employment to the hundreds of dancers, the vast corps of heavenly ballerinas from all the bas-reliefs. It is a much more obvious theme for popular tradition to grow up about, this retinue of all the huge theatrical and pantomime company from the temples of Angkor.

The heat during this time had been of a kind and degree never experienced before. The humidity, too, was something excessive and to give excitement there was a mutter of thunder in the distance which was to continue every day we were at Angkor. We came back by another way, passing more ruins, and ordered iced drinks, only to be warned by a khaki-clad, Indian Army figure in shorts and bush shirt who was shepherding a group of middle-aged ladies from Chicago: 'You'll forgive me interrupting, won't you! But you're drinking the water. I'd say you've quite likely bought it already. You'll forgive me, won't you! But it is more than likely that you've had it!'—and we were ready for the evening walk across the causeway into Angkor Wat.

Chapter Four

‡‡‡‡‡‡‡‡‡‡‡‡‡‡‡‡‡‡‡‡‡‡‡‡‡‡‡

ANGKOR WAT

JUST THE APPROACH TO Angkor Wat is on a grander scale than anything in the living world. The piazza of St Peter's at Rome, down the
triple passages between Doric pillars of either arm of Bernini's
colonnades, is as nothing in comparison to it. At Angkor Wat there
is, first, the half-mile walk from the end of this half of the arm of the
canal or moat that lies in front of the temple. Then, arrived directly in
front of the middle of it, there is a step or two up on to the causeway,
and you are crossing some 220 yards of water with a naga-rail or
balustrade, broken in many places, on both sides. About half-way
along this, two ceremonial stairways go down into the water to
either hand.

This causeway leads to a flame-crested, five-storeyed gateway in
the middle of the 600 feet long outer enclosure of the temple which is
continued in the form of galleries in both directions, and along all
four sides. Once through this gateway you are on another raised causeway nearly 400 yards long, still guarded by naga-balustrades, and
leading to the landing or platform at the foot of the inner shrine. You
have already walked a mile and 100 yards by the time you reach that.

Half-way down this second stretch of causeway, where nearly
everyone would be inclined to rest for a moment and look at what
lies in front of him, there are two 'libraries', so-called, standing out in
the parkland of this inner enclosure with square ornamental tanks or
water lawns in front of them, buildings which it has been said long
ago 'would anywhere else be considered of importance, but here may
be passed over', as is indeed the case for it is quite impossible to look
at anything else but the fantastic five-towered structure rising before
our eyes. Until, that is to say, we have come nearer still and our gaze
is distracted by the finials of the naga-balustrades running about in
both directions on the stone landing, now that we have reached it;

43

running towards us as we come a step forward, that is to say, and again to the sides or flanks of the stone platform; stone serpent-bodies that lift their seven hooded-cobra heads and give the effect of peacocks darting to and fro, dancing with spread tails at the foot of the temple.

The serpent or polyp-heads, for they carry that suggestion, too, are followed immediately by another animal, or, rather, reptilian sensation which comes at the moment of setting foot inside the porch of the main building. It is the bat-smell or bat-presence which is all pervasive in every temple at Angkor. At the first sensing of it one looks up uneasily into the stone vaulting and hears sure enough the rustling and scraping of bat-wings. This ammoniac stench has not the sickly sweetness of the smell of death but it is dead, dead, and yet shrilly and scratchily and pinchingly alive. There is nothing of reptilian sloth and torpor about a bat. They turn every dark corner they inhabit from a tomb into a ghetto. The stone floors of Angkor Wat are slippery from their droppings, and one is disinclined to touch the stone walls with a hand. There seems to be a thin film or deposit upon most of the stone surface. What can be the total bat population of the ruins, for they have formed their cities and centres of urban population in the ruined temples? No comparable area of jungle or forest can have anything approaching this number of bats in it. They have swarmed here and proliferated.

Their unseen presence urges one to pass quickly under any covered part of the building, and some stretches of gallery and colonnade are doubly darkened at thought of their membrane wings. At which point the steep steps begin. And if we climb them, which is the most likely thing for us to do, we will miss the long gallery of bas-reliefs which runs round all four sides of the main mass of building. Continuing, then, up the steps to the second storey, looking on to grass-grown courts with more 'libraries' in their fore-corners, we climb yet another steep flight of steps and look down to find there are four deep basins obviously intended for water, though one does not know the method for keeping them filled. From here the stone mass climbs again with the four towers at its corners and the central and taller tower in the middle rising to 180 feet from the ground, and now from near to, more like a fir-cone, with the stone-tiled roofs of the 'libraries' and the long galleries with the pagoda-cresting of stone flames below us. A headlong vertiginous staircase leads from here upward to the central sanctuary or main tower which is in fact an anticlimax for it is no more than a small, dark cell.

All the enormous stone mass has no hall of even modest proportions within it. There are but endless galleries and stairs, and except that at least there is a roof overhead Angkor Wat is as useless a structure as Carnac or Stonehenge. It could accommodate great crowds but to no other purpose than their crowding; galleries and stairs only leading to more galleries and further stairways, but no inner chamber of any size or for any purpose. The 'libraries' which are most intricately worked upon stone bases of the utmost elaboration are so wasteful of their own space that they occupy only a small portion of the plinth on which they stand. They could qualify almost as 'sham buildings' and look as though intended to stand in water up to their doorsteps. There could be the green tank water lapping all round them. Their fretted lines must be in order to throw reflections. What other purpose had their steep bases but to be seen through water? Had they in fact any use at all? The doorways are so low that even the slightly built Cambodians would have to stoop in order to enter them, and they must have been almost completely dark within. Looking down again at the 'libraries' in the courts below we may think they had no more use than the thatched hut on the little island in a pond for ornamental ducks. Yet each of the 'libraries' has had as much time and labour expended upon it as any of the chantry chapels of Perpendicular Gothic, or such a 'gem' of the Italian Renaissance as the marble encrusted church of the Madonna dei Miracoli on its canal bank at Venice.

At Angkor Wat we are standing on a mountain of worked stone nearly at its cone or summit, and it can only be described as a more lively sensation by far than that of looking down from the Great Pyramid of Egypt. That is an ant-heap, and this a honey-hive. For the Great Pyramid has nothing but its labour to show, stone upon stone, as it could be the grains of earth or sand of the ant-hill; but this has the mathematical intricacy and the precise repetition of a honeycomb, the richness of the honey-cell and only the thronging crowds are fled. The bulk or mass of it looked down upon from nearly its highest point, the canals and causeways apart, is of the scale of the largest of mediaeval cathedrals. Moreover it is contemporary to those within a century or so for it is supposed to have been completed soon after 1150.

Yet, curiously, Angkor Wat does not seem mediaeval. The regularity of its plan, the fact that it is all of one date and has not grown gradually as did the mediaeval cathedrals by slow accretion over the whole span of the Middle Ages, together with the formal straightness of its ornamental waters, bring it forward in time and relate it more to a palace than a temple. But after much disputation the historians and archaeologists have pronounced it neither temple, nor palace, but a burial-place, and the King whose ashes were brought here and probably put below this central tower emerges from the mysterious past of Angkor as Suryavarman II, the suffix 'varman' which was given to all the Khmer Kings of Angkor being of Indian origin and derived from an Indian title or honorific meaning 'up-holder' or 'protector'. The names of other of their kings, Indravar-man, Rajendravarman, Jayavarman all have Indian echoes or con-notations, the last in particular for the 'Jaya' part of the name implies from Java and that he was vassal or tributary to the utterly mysterious 'King of the Mountain'. This great conqueror and potentate, now altogether forgotten in history, was a Hindu prince from Southern India who setting out in the eighth century 'to conquer the world' like a second Alexander subdued Java, Sumatra and the Malay Peninsula. Because of the Indian laws of taboo his name could not be pronounced, and is not known to this day, but his comtemporaries called him Sailendra or 'King of the Mountain'. It is to him or his successors that the great temple and stone mountain of Borobudur in Java—as great a marvel as Angkor Wat—would appear to be due, and it was he who sent his relative Jayavarman I to rule over Cambodia. The second Jayavarman is said to have gone to Java to pay homage to the Sailendra King and it was he who made Angkor his capital, and later established his independence from the 'King of the Mountain'.

Suryavarman II, on whose stone mountain we are standing, inherited from the earlier Kings in title, if not in blood, and like the 'King of the Mountain' was Devaraja or 'God-King' in his own life-time, a cult of self-glorification in which the symbol or palladium was a sacred lingam or phallic emblem. This object which only much Hindu palaver and mystification can elevate above a very primitive culture level, was 'imbued with the essence of divine Kingship and installed in a temple-mountain'[1]—Borobudur or Angkor Wat—and

---

[1] *Towards Angkor*, by H. G. Quaritch Wales, Harrap & Co., 1937; and *The Art and Architecture of India*, by Benjamin Rowland, Penguin Books, 1959.

the perpetuation of the dynasty and the security of the race were dependent on its safe keeping. There is nothing at Angkor Wat to suggest that it was ever the King's residence. He must have lived in a compound of wooden buildings, long vanished, but resembling the gilded kremlins of Bangkok and Phnom Penh. Angkor Wat was the shrine of the 'God-King' in his immortal aspects, living and dead; and it is this which gives to it that extra concentration of a single person-ality that obliterates all comparison with the Versailles of Louis XIV, and quite puts out of mind such personal and Roman grandeurs as Diocletian's palace at Spalato, or the Leptis Magna of Septimius Severus.

Climbing down from the base of the great tower of Angkor Wat, and it is nothing if not a precipitous and even perilous descent, we make acquaintance with the first of the huge company of heavenly dancers or apsaras, scarcely noticed before in the excitement of the ascent. The various troupes of them are subtly differenced. Singly, at times, on the corner of a wall between the stone bamboo stems of the false windows—in themselves typical of nearly every temple at Angkor—there is an apsara with a whole pilaster to herself, carved in bas-relief under a flame-like canopy; an apsara, not dancing, but standing still, bare-breasted, with triple and even quintuple-spired head-dress, doubtless of the same gilt material as those worn by the Cambodian Royal ballet of today, but in their multiple form they look like 'corn dollies' of straw and moulded paper. A solo apsara of this type is likely to be wearing long ear-rings and many necklaces, and a skirt that only begins at her waist and has a stiffened sash flaring out from that which takes the form almost of a train, or wings, but starting from the waist not the shoulders, and trailing down to the heavy anklets on her feet. Others are in companies of fours, or fives, or sixes, sometimes with a single dancer to fill in the empty space at the side of one of the sham-bamboo windows.

The more active of the dancers are nearly always in company as though for greater freedom of gesture, in rows like a chorus, and often with skirts swung aside to show their sturdy legs. They are wearing several forms of head-dress, in one of which their hair appears to be frizzed up like a wig framing the face, and with the long ends of it plaited and touching on both cheeks. So much for their hair; but the head-dress is not the spired pagoda type, it is of fronds which wave about and must make a rustling noise, to add to which one of the row of maidens holds some sort of a rattle with a long handle over her head, much resembling one of the instruments in a Cuban dance band. At certain points the dancing maidens have linked arms; and always and everywhere they have the same eyebrows joined in one line, flat faces and thick lips. Nowhere is there the slightest sensual suggestion about them. That they have their breasts bare is of no import for this was the universal custom in Indonesia, continuing so in Bali until the tourists came with their cameras between the two World Wars. Or, as it has been put by one writer, Khmer art 'is extremely sensual and completely sexless'. The apsaras 'are extremely voluptuous, curved and adorned with an obvious appreciation of human beauty, but with no desire', and he gives it as his opinion that 'the Khmer were an opium-soaked community'.[1] This conviction which grows upon one with every walk over the causeway into Angkor Wat becomes a certainty when we see the obsessive and megalomaniac Bayon.

By now the dancing apsaras, the sham-bamboo stems of the false windows taking the place of the arcading in a Gothic cloister, the naga-rails rearing their huge hoods, and the flame-crested gables rising above the long galleries which have their every individual tile cut in the shape of a lotus petal,[2] are all combining to form that same impression. It is so strong that no subsequent visit in the early morning, at evening, or by moonlight will ever alter it, and it is that there is nothing at Angkor Wat to enter or go inside. It is all long galleries and steep stone stairs. Nowhere else are there such long roofs, but no rooms within. The Khmers had not the technical knowledge to cover any wider space, so that Angkor Wat is as big in mass as the biggest mediaeval cathedral but with no interior, only stairs and cloisters. All this on a rectangular stone platform with sides 1,000 yards long, lying in a moat which is nearly two and a half miles round, and with the impress of one single human personality upon a scale like nothing else on earth.

Yet Angkor Wat is Indian and not Indian. It is Hindu, not Buddhist, and in fact there is no trace of Buddhism in any of the bas-reliefs. That it has now been taken over by a few saffron-clad bonzes from a wooden monastery within the temple precincts does not alter this. Angkor Wat is of the same Hindu culture as the island of Bali, a

[1] *Bali and Angkor*, by Geoffrey Gorer, Michael Joseph Ltd., 1936.
[2] Benjamin Rowland, *op. cit.*

9   Landing Stage at Angkor Wat

10   The Bayon at Angkor

11   Terrace at the Bayon

12   A Gateway at Angkor Thom

further or overseas India of a thousand years ago, and at the other end of the trajectory are the hull shaped gopurams or gate-towers of the Indian temples. Having seen Angkor Wat it is only necessary to be shown a photograph of Madurai, or of any of a dozen other temples in Southern India, in order to be convinced of this. That the central tower of Angkor Wat, once crowned by a golden lotus, has been found to have a well 120 feet deep with golden objects lying at the bottom of it, directly below the shrine which housed the Devaraja or sacred lingam, and that this well was a symbol for the world pivot or pestle employed by the gods and giants in their churning of the Sea of Milk; all shows Indian derivation. Its builders knew the sacred places of India, and the authority of one extraordinary person or potentate had put order into the confusion and planned his own tomb-temple not with Indian haphazard, but with the regularity of our Augustan age.

There is indeed no sensation comparable to that of treading the causeway and walking into Angkor Wat. It is an Indian temple and an Escorial; and it has the bas-reliefs of Nineveh or of Persepolis with the waters of Versailles. And after the first flame-crested gateway, as one walks for nearly a quarter of a mile down the second causeway still guarded by the naga-rails, there is time to think and to fancy oneself 400 years ago crossing the causeway into the ancient Aztec city of Tenochtitlan. This, because there is no sight in the world stranger or more exotic than the five towers and long cloisters rising with the grid-iron precision of the plan of the Escorial before our eyes. It is the regularity of planning together with the tropical or even equatorial detail and motif that are the wonder of Angkor Wat.

For now we are in the long gallery or cloister of bas-reliefs that runs round all four sides of the temple. But the aggregate length of these scenes from the Hindu epics of *The Rāmāyana* and *The Mahāb-hārata* is some 2,000 feet, implying that it is a walk of not far short of half a mile to inspect them all, and when it is said that a 'fair average' of the number of figures of men and animals represented would amount to between eighteen and twenty thousand the feeling of mental suffocation induced is index to the actual experience. There are, alone, many hundreds of elephants involved. It is probably true that statistics when made use of in order to add interest to architecture always fail of their purpose, and the galleries of bas-reliefs at Angkor Wat are no exception. The scenes were planned in order to be seen while walking round them counter-clockwise or 'withershins', that

D

is to say, with one's left side towards the bas-reliefs, and at about a quarter of the way along they become forced and mechanical. They have turned into something as monotonous and soul-killing as the mere copying out and reiteration of a sacred text, and interest dies out altogether round the three further sides of the cloister. Yet it is not untrue to say that these bas-reliefs of Angkor Wat are in descent from those in the Egyptian temples and from the sculptured walls of Persepolis, just as much as the winged, man-headed bulls of the Assyrians have their belated and probably last progeny in the temple guardians of the Emerald Buddha at Bangkok.

If the impression of walking along the causeway into Angkor Wat is itself ineffaceable from the memory there is as well the sensation of coming upon it again from the back when returning from more distant temples far out in the jungle. Another of the huge water-tanks lies out in this direction, with a great stone stair leading down into it where some of the many hundreds of elephants of Angkor must have had their bathing-place. It is as big as the reservoir of some modern city of a million or more inhabitants, and has a small island and a tree growing on it left there in the middle of the water by some caprice or oversight of the surveyor or borough engineer, it being impossible at Angkor not to equate in one's mind the ruins of a stupendous past to the necessities and requirements of London, Chicago, or New York. The road now runs beside perhaps half a mile of water, and into the jungle again, and after a distance equiva-lent to the length of Fifth Avenue as it runs beside Central Park, or the outer circle of Regent's Park, there are the five towers in front but a little to the right of us, and unmistakable as Radio City or the Seagram Building, those wonders of the modern world.

A few moments later we come out at one corner of the rectangle where two arms of the canal meet, banishing by their scale any com-parison we may still have in our minds to the formal waters of Versailles, and the road runs parallel to one of the longer flanks of Angkor Wat with the moat between, beside one of the interminable cloisters of stone tapestries. At the half-way mark along this we pass the water-gate with the huge corn-cob tower exactly in place behind it, and go down the other half of its immense length to where we turn the corner and have the front of the great temple before us across another stretch of water. Seen thus, it has the monotony of some overwhelming personality upon it, a potentate or 'God-King whose old age must have been oppressive and never ending, and if one's senses are to be believed, its share of the bad luck always attendant upon a building exaggeratedly finished and completed. Is this not true of both Versailles and the Escorial, structures perfected in good time to see the ill-omened deaths of their possessors? It is not to be denied that Angkor Wat is pervaded by some aura of this sort.

A hundred years have now passed since the French naturalist Henri Mouhot hacked his way through the jungle to the edge of the moat and saw the five towers of Angkor Wat rising before him. He was the first European to reach the ruins.[1] Since that day two generations of French archaeologists have worked upon Angkor with the result that it is now no more difficult to visualize the city nearly a thousand years ago in its prime than it is to take in Angkor Wat with the forest trees and lianas that had grown here since the city was abandoned by its inhabitants in 1432 splitting the stones apart. Both states of the Khmer city are a strain upon credibility, and it is easy to comprehend Mouhot's remark that to look upon Angkor Wat after the jungles he had traversed was 'to be transported from barbarism to civilization, from darkness to profound light'. But this light to which he refers is no clarification; it only heightens and obscures the mystery by revealing it in all its detail.

If our cities were deserted, what would be left of them? What would there be of London—let us imagine the Mall from Admiralty Arch to Buckingham Palace, miraculously preserved with the litter and the decorations from a Royal wedding—or even Paris, except that avenue of splendour from the Place du Carrousel to the Arc de Triomphe! The shops and trees and lights would be gone, and where are the fine buildings? Probably this is irrational. For the greatest geniuses of the human race are not to be judged by their individual environment, or what would one expect of the homes of Shakespeare or Beethoven! Or, where earthly potentates are under discussion, what would one deduce from the Osborne House or the Balmoral of Queen Victoria! But the arts are where the arts have flourished, and where this is so Angkor Wat long lost in the Cambodian jungle has to be considered although it is all exterior walls and no interior, and even if it only slept there unknown to the world for four centuries.

[1] But the presence of gigantic ruins 'built by the Romans, or by Alexander the Great' had been reported in the middle of the sixteenth century by two missionaries, Fathers Ridadenyra and Gabriel de Sant' Antonio; and later in the century Father Chevreuil mentions a temple 'called Onco, once as famous among the Gentiles as St Peter's of Rome'.

For that is no time at all. It is only four times the slumber of the princess in the fairy story. And it is no farther back into the past than many of our existing schools and colleges.

But the sleep of Angkor Wat is a deeper and drugged slumber, and while we were walking round it for a last time there was that mutter of far-off thunder. The great cloister of bas-reliefs was deserted. Only when we had turned the first corner and had three more sides of it to walk along, each a furlong in length, did a couple of Cambodian children come up who spoke a few words of French, and were trying to learn more. In which manner it was a slow progress as we went along pointing to one object after another in the carvings, an elephant, a dragon-beaked boat, or a chariot, and telling them its name. Their little slit eyes and small wrists and feet were very clearly of the same race as those portrayed in the bas-reliefs.

Tiring of this after a while, and walking ahead so that there was the length of one whole gallery between us, it seemed a good idea to stop and rest a moment at the last corner. Here, just at this point, a loud and menacing croaking came from nowhere. And again, seemingly from outside and below the outer wall. It could have been the croak of a raven, and an ill-tempered one at that, but there was no hopping or flapping of wings. Or could it be a vulture, or some other bird of prey? But, whatever, there was no sign of it and nothing to be seen. After a few moments the two children came along. It croaked once more, and they pointed to a creature like a lizard, nearly invisible, high up and flat against the wall. So that was one of the ghosts of Angkor; and on our return we saw and heard the same creature, and found there was at least one of them in most houses in Bangkok. The thunder muttered; and disturbed at our footsteps bats flew out of the gate-tower with us as we came for the last time down the steps and out of Angkor Wat. In another land they would have been swallows skimming the earth with forked flight just before it rained. And as it thundered again, not far off this time, 'the burden of Babylon' came to mind with the determination to look it up in Isaiah, 13. 'Wild beasts of the desert shall lie there; and their houses shall be full of doleful creatures; and owls shall dwell there, and satyrs (perhaps monkeys?) shall dance there. And the wild beasts of the islands shall cry in their desolate houses, and dragons in their pleasant palaces.' Precisely that is to be seen and heard in this most withdrawn and portentous of all human buildings half a mile away into itself across a lotused moat.

Chapter Five

❖❖❖❖❖❖❖❖❖❖❖❖❖❖❖❖❖❖❖❖❖❖❖❖❖❖❖❖

THE BAYON

AFTER ANGKOR WAT ONE might go away expecting nothing more. But the wonders of Angkor are only at their beginning. The Bayon, which comes next, is no less unique and extraordinary. It leaves as strange an impression as that of finding here in the Cambodian jungle a companion to Gaudí's 'Templo de la Sagrada Familia' at Barcelona. At first sight it is a capriciously fantastic, much weather-worn imitation of a dolomite, doubtless a copy of some holy mountain in China. A few such mountains in the far interior of China have been illustrated in recent books; and also there are the water-worn stones off lake beds that are the chief ornament of Chinese classical gardens. Could it be a Stonehenge-like concatenation and gathering of these? But it is not as simple as that.

This extraordinary mock-mountain, of which we are now turning the third or fourth corner, for the road goes right round it, looks at this moment like the Khmer imitation of a holy mountain. That there are real mountains of this character in China only gives it a different and Khmer flavour. But now we see that what we took for rocky pinnacles of the dolomite are towers or turrets carved with the four faces of Buddha. There are fifty of the towers, and every one of them has a huge mask on each of its four sides, the masks varying between five and eight feet high. All are exactly alike, so that having begun to climb on to the stone platform wherever you turn you see nothing but the stone heads.

There are innumerable steps and intricately worked and recessed stone plinths, and in order to explore the Bayon you have to climb or jump from each to each. This gives something of the sensation of walking on the rocks at low tide. At about which point the Bayon is still the mock-dolomite but is becoming many other things as well. The Catalan-phantasiast, Gaudí aspect of it is growing more and more

apparent. In one of the main streets of Barcelona there is the apartment house built by Gaudí in the shape of the mountain of Mont-
serrat with wave-like balconies to suggest its dolomite striations.
Opposite, across the street, is the house that Gaudí built to simulate a
breaking wave. The walls surge or splash wildly upwards, and the
roof with its cresting of green tiles represents the foam and spray;
which said, it is no longer like the Bayon. But Gaudí would certainly
have fallen under the spell of this dolomite temple with its fifty
towers of masks; while it is Picasso, another Catalan, who proposed
to buy a stretch of Mediterranean shore and erect apartment buildings
along it in the shape of gigantic women's heads.

At this very moment of thinking of Gaudí we may have as many as
six or seven of the huge faces looking at us, as well as three or four of
them that we see in profile. After all they are only a few of the 200
and more Boddhisattva faces of the Bayon. It is the Boddhisattva
Lokesvara, 'Lord of the World', that they portray; but it is thought
that into their features has been worked the likeness or the idealized
portrait of Jayavarman VII who began to reign in 1180 and died at
about ninety years old in 1220. He may have been 'the King of the
Angels' to whom the local villagers ascribed the building of Angkor
when questioned about it by Henri Mouhot, the first European to set
eyes upon the ruins. Or, just as well, this could have applied to his
predecessor, the builder of Angkor Wat if, by 'angels', they implied
the countless dozens or even hundreds of apsaras, dancers 'said to have
no fathers or mothers, but to be born on the spray of the ocean',[1]
'nymphs given to dancing, flying, and throwing flowers'.[2]

Other answers given to Henri Mouhot by the villagers: 'It is the
work of giants', 'We owe these buildings to the Leper King', 'They
built themselves', are no more helpful, except for the last reply which
is something one thinks of for oneself after only a few moments at the
Bayon. For it does really look as though human hands were not
responsible for it. Or, at least, if human handiwork, that it has been
left to crumble for centuries at the bottom of the sea. Photographs of
raised or dredged up wrecks covered with weeds and barnacles recall
the Bayon, for the hulls have the same, worn away calcareous outline,
like that produced by water working on limestone, a rubbing and
fretting away, only it is not that but an accretion, an adding and not a

[1] *Angkor*, by Malcolm MacDonald, Jonathan Cape, 1908.
[2] *Escape With Me*, by Osbert Sitwell, Macmillan & Co., 1939.

III   The Great Stairway at Angkor Wat

diminution, and now that we put our heads into one of the small, cell-like turret-chambers of the Bayon, we may think we have the answer. For the bat-stench of all Angkor comes out of that dark door-way and the stone step is slippery and green with bat-droppings. For a moment or two the Bayon may seem to have risen in this way by slow deposit at the pace, and like the forming of a coral atoll.

A curious phenomenon about the Bayon is the continual alteration of its own scale. Seen another time from the road it looks like a tray-garden, not a Japanese bonseki, but something shown on the child-ren's stall at the local Women's Institute. There it stands on its stone tray all ready to be lifted up and taken away. But in the next moment the Bayon becomes inexplicable and huge. Not beautiful. It would be true to say that the Bayon is never beautiful. But neither is the Pyramid of Kheops. Nor can that have been intended of the Bayon. But, rather, the intention was to frighten, a supposition which is born out in the city plan of Angkor Thom. For the Bayon stood at its centre and symbolized the temple-mountain, or Mount Meru of Hindu mythology, which was the abode of the gods—a mountain that had five peaks like, again, the five towers of Angkor Wat—while the outer walls of Angkor Thom stood for the cakrevāla or mountainous rims or edges of the world, and the moat of the city for the outer ocean. This gives the clue, too, to the double rows of stone giants and demons holding the serpentine body of the naga on their laps to each side of the main gate of the town. They are twenty feet tall, even squatting on their heels; and the thirteenth-century Chinese pilgrim Chou Ta-kuan, so frequently quoted by all later writers on Angkor, says of them: 'On either side of the bridges are fifty-four stone demons, like stone generals, gigantic and terrible.'[1] That is exactly how they appear, even now. They have the look of execu-tioners and killers. But the real import of them is that they are holding the coils of the naga and assisting in the churning of the Sea of Milk.

The richness and intensity of symbolism in Indian and near-Indian building perhaps comes to its climax at Angkor. Buddhism and Hinduism in their varying forms are so intermingled and involved at the Bayon and at Angkor Thom, in general, that even the foremost authorities are unwilling to commit themselves to a straight statement as to which is which. It could be said that Angkor Wat is a Hindu

[1] Chou Ta-kuan went to Angkor with an embassy from China in 1296-1298. His account of it, found in the Imperial Archives in Peking, was first published in a French translation by M. Pelliot in 1902.

temple with no trace of Buddhism, although Buddhist monks now pray there, unconcernedly; while the Bayon is steeped and altogether founded on Hindu mythology but has its fifty-odd towers all crowned, as we have seen, with the idealized faces of a king masquerading as a Boddhisattva. That the lingam or male emblem of the Hindus is also present in the Bayon is but another curiosity of their dual worship. Probably they had reached a state where like the later Romans they prayed impartially to the different gods, but certainly the depths and degree to which religious symbolism entered into their architectural planning has no parallel in Europe. None of our mediaeval cathedrals was so closely calculated to fulfil the quirks and curves of religious legend. In order to attain to anything approaching this degree of complexity we would have to imagine an architecture following strictly on the 'conceits' and imagery of the metaphysical poets. By shifting the centuries to fit such improbabilities we would have buildings on the scale of our largest churches, which is to say no bigger than the Bayon or Angkor Wat, following, detail by detail, poems by Vaughan or Crashaw. Only in the Wieskirche and other Rococo churches in Bavaria is there this closeness of instruction so that religious symbolism gives meaning even to the painted colours of the scagliola. But their small scale, no larger than that of a theatre, and howsoever profound theatrical intention, put no weight on the scale beside the ponderous and mortal seriousness of the Bayon. The eighteenth-century Benedictine iconographers who, 'as was their custom, had the decoration executed to a programme which is carried through the church like a sermon'[1] in larger foundations such as Ottobeuren or Zwiefalten would have been defeated by this deeper symbolism which dictates the entire construction and has a whole city and the capital of an empire conforming to a sacred legend.

The outer walls of the Bayon are even more crowded with bas-reliefs than the long cloisters of Angkor Wat, scenes from daily life and from the *Rāmāyana*, elephant-haunted as ever, but with fewer of the dancing apsaras, and in a rounder, fuller technique of carving or incising that must more nearly resemble the bas-reliefs of the great temple of Borobudur, in Java. Despite their greater factual interest than those of Angkor Wat they do not invite inspection in the same way, or, as those do, challenge one to an endurance contest in

---

[1] *From Baroque to Rococo*, by Nicolas Powell, Faber & Faber Ltd., 1959, p. 113.

walking their entire length. Instead, one is drawn, irresistibly, on and upward into the dolomite.

There are extraneous considerations that enter into this. Or it may well be that they are not unrelated to the reality. Certain little clues or keys to this are to be sought almost everywhere. There is the cliff-face in Arizona carved with the profiles of George Washington, and others, bastard descendant of Michelangelo's plan to carve a giant statue out of the marble quarries at Carrara. There are the grotesque sculptures at Bomarzo, and the 'bruto seicento' doorway in the shape of a grotesque face in the Via Gregoriana at Rome, none of these being far removed in spirit from the distorting mirrors of the fun fair. Or, for that matter, from the cabezudos (big heads) of religious pro-cessions in Spain where the Gigantones de Tarasca, as the whole collection at Toledo is called, including a comic giantess called Anna Bolena, is stored in the cathedral tower. The gigantes y gigantones of Spain, of Toledo, of Burgos, of Zaragoza, do undeniably come to mind when encountering the giant faces of the Bayon. The repeti-tion, the reiteration of the same face is what gives it seriousness. Had they been of different, and not identical Bodhisattvas, their impact would lose in force. Of the two hundred masks some would be less severe of mien; or would be expressive of another, and not the same mystery. Each of the huge faces has been carved *in situ*, and one wonders if the same sculptor carved them all; and in parenthesis whether he ever did any other work afterwards. One sculptor could be employed for ten years upon them if all the towers were ready and waiting for him to set to work. But the Bayon must have been longer than that in building, and we may think it probable that he spent his life on them.

But all conjecture is useless, and thinking in the next moment of the rows of 'stone demons, like stone generals, gigantic and terrible', fifty-four to a side, 'holding the serpent in their hands', we see the absurdity of ascribing all those to the same carver. Or, for that matter, every elephant of the Elephant Terrace which is sculptured along all its length and is a quarter of a mile long. But at least it is probable that their tasks were specialized; that one sculptor in parti-cular carved the heads of the stone demons, and a subordinate or apprentice the demon's arms and hands which are in every instance identically the same and rendered from a like number of blocks of stone. As for the snake-body of the naga, it is no more interesting than the stone pipe of an aqueduct until it rears up its seven hooded-cobra heads that in this humid and intense heat seem to dance like a peacock with spread tail, yet with something of the swaying movement of a polyp or cuttle-fish in its dark pool and, withal, somewhat of a phallic connotation. What curious division of labour, and bizarre pre-eminence, to be sculptor in special of huge seven, or nine, or eleven hooded-cobra heads, and always in pairs, one to a side, to guard an entrance or a landing-stage. Thinking of them once more, there is the suggestion as of coral seas and atolls in the stone nagas of Angkor, as though they had emerged from, and would glide back again into the snaky waters. It is because of the branching heads of the nagas, that, it would seem, might snap and break like stems of coral.

Clambering about now among 'the more than twenty towers of stone and a hundred stone chambers' of Chou Ta-kuan, who in this instance is inaccurate in his numbering, we may like to fall in with the theory of the local population, as reported to Henri Mouhot, that these things 'built themselves'. And indeed there are moments at the Bayon when one could nearly believe it. But, also, the Bayon recalls many other things seen and experienced and at one point in particular I found myself remembering days and nights long ago in the First World War, in 1917-1918, when my brother and I amused ourselves by climbing about Dr Phéné's house in Chelsea. This 'eccentric', who built the half-timbered 'Six Bells' in King's Road and the barber's shop next door with the flight of swallows on its ceiling (now destroyed), 'went peculiar' on his wife's death, so went the story, leaving some of the rooms untouched as they were on the day she died, and building all manner of strange things in the garden. One could climb in at the back and go all over the house which was empty of furniture, but had elaborately carved ceilings and fire-places. There were stone figures of swans on the garden steps, and other ornaments, but the greatest eccentricity was the garden, entirely overgrown with trees in blitzed London-ruin parody on the temples of Angkor, and with a tumbled down, collapsed structure in the middle said to be a copy of the Indian 'snake mound' of Illinois. Below it a horse was supposed to be buried; and there were stories I heard at first hand of a studio at the back, looking on to the garden, being haunted by a horse, perhaps the genuine and original nightmare of Fuseli's once celebrated painting. Dr Phéné's house, which was probably built in the 1880's, was pulled down soon after 1925, and few people remember it now. But most persons will have had experience of some similar 'eccentric's' dwelling, and it is undeniable that the Bayon enters into this category though conducted with every energy of one of the most complete despots in human history. Angkor Wat of Suryavarman II and the Bayon of Jayavarman VII, 'god-Kings' whose very recent emergence at the hands of archaeologists out of oblivion leaves them unreal, shadowy, and of no historical substance, prove their builders to have had powers of construction greater than those of any Roman Caesar or Egyptian Pharaoh. That these forces were exercised with so giant a hand by these two forgotten Khmer Kings makes small play of a Philip II, a Louis XIV, a Catherine of Russia, and for a fantasy of egoism on the scale of Angkor or of the Bayon it could be that we must return to the *Domus Aurea* of Nero.

The more unreal, therefore, the stone turrets with the four faces at their different levels that are like different degrees of consciousness. For it is certain that they have, and that it was intended that it should be so, a hypnotic effect. The proliferation of masks of the 'god-King's' features was meant to beam forth his omnipotence in all directions to every quarter they were facing, and to the far limits of his kingdom. The stone Buddha with an ornament like a lotus leaf as a shield behind it found in the ruined central tower of the Bayon was also the King's idealized portrait, though probably the laws of taboo forbade it to bear any physical resemblance to him, and in position in the central tower of the Bayon it could with little exaggeration be described as in control of the radio station. It has been said that the 'stone chambers' or chapels of the Bayon all bore dedications from different provinces of the Kingdom, and had Brahmanic or Buddhist statues in them that were locally worshipped in those places,[1] thus gathering in or receiving as well as giving forth his divine Kingship. During the lifetime of the King it was the nerve centre and transmitting station of his Kingdom. Jayavarman had twice in his lifetime been a Buddhist priest or monk and the Bayon was his magic power centre, not a temple or palace, but a conjuror or magician's tent, made permanent in stone, and endowed with hypnotic forces.

Reiteration of the same brooding face with half-closed eyes, identical high head-dress of jewels, long dangling ear-rings with immense ear-lobes, and all the pearls of Coromandel for necklace,

[1] Benjamin Rowland, *op. cit.*

exactly echoed in every direction you look, and not so much carved in the stones of the towers as growing out of them, certainly produces an effect of hypnosis. Whether this is greater *in absentia* now their message is gone from them so that they are out of order, or while they were new and transmitting his magical authority, day and night, is a matter of your own receptivity. When brand new, the Bayon would have affected ourselves like a fun fair combined with a visit to the phrenologist while under influence from some heady drug. In no other way could the vision be explained were one to believe one's eyes. Preliminary experience, too, led up to this and strengthened the illusion. To what other purpose are the stone genie on each side of the causeway over the moat of the city? In the words of our Chinese pilgrim of eight centuries ago: 'they hold in their hands as a parapet a serpent with nine heads, and look as though they were trying to prevent his escape.' It has been further suggested that in his time the moat was full of crocodiles as a protection against live enemies, which would render still more impressive the arrival at the main gate of the city with mesmeric faces carved on it, an archway high enough for elephants with howdahs on their backs to ride through, and triple-headed stone elephants coming out of the wall with their trunks feeding upon the stalks and buds of lotuses. After such preliminaries who indeed would not be in the mood to be hypnotized by the same brooding countenance repeated over and over again upon the fifty stone towers of the Bayon?

But the truth of such impressions is even stranger than it seems. For among all the ruins of Angkor there is not a single human dwelling. It is not that it is uninhabited, but uninhabitable. Yet of the crowded life of the capital there are the bas-reliefs for witness, and in particular those on the lower walls of the Bayon below where we are standing. Also, there are the descriptions by Chou Ta-kuan. He is writing of a city of perhaps 1,000,000 inhabitants though some authorities would double this figure. But both Hindu and Buddhists burn their dead so there is no cemetery or burial ground.[1] Were this not so, it would be one vast charnel house of bones. Of all the uncounted millions who may have inhabited Angkor over the four or five centuries when it was a great city, no human remains are left.

---

[1] Chou Ta-kuan has this to say. 'They do not use coffins for the dead, but a kind of mat, which they cover with a cloth. They leave the body in some far off and uninhabited place outside the city, and go away. They let dogs and vultures devour it.' They may have changed over from cremating their dead, one way or the other, when the Hindu religion was replaced by Buddhism, but the inhabitants of Angkor never had cemeteries or burial grounds.

This gives to so gigantic a series of ruins an even more shadowy substance in some respects than that of the ancient Mayan cities in Central America where the archaeologists engaged in excavation hope to find a burial more than anything else. It is the burial-chambers that have the best preserved wall-paintings and where the finest artifacts are found. But there is no hope of this sort in the ruins of Angkor.

It was a stone city of ritual and ceremony, but no dormitory. The wooden and reed huts of the poorer population stretched out for miles into the rice fields, and can have been little different except in multitude from the present-day villages passed on the way to the more distant temples. What are gone are the wooden buildings that stood, for instance, on the stone walls of the Elephant Terrace, above that quarter of a mile of bas-reliefs of elephants in procession; 'the great hall of mirrors' of Chou Ta-kuan, which may have been a wooden building with an interior ornamented with small pieces of looking-glass resembling the audience or throne halls in the modern palaces of Phnom Penh and Bangkok. The palaces of Suryavarman and Jayavarman must have been of this character, and with certainly much gilding. Where Chou Ta-kuan talks of 'gold': 'a golden bridge and eight golden Buddhas . . . a tower of gold marking the centre of the Kingdom' (at the Bayon, this) . . . 'a square tower of gold, and a golden lion and golden Buddha' . . . he surely infers, not gold, but gilding. This is not Cuzco of the Incas, but the gilt spires of another and earlier Bangkok or Phnom Penh.

It was within such walled, but wooden Kremlins that the King lived with his women, and thence he issued forth in solemn procession. 'Horsemen always come first, then follow the standards, the pennants and the music, and after them, between three and five hundred girls of the palace, in flowered dresses and with flowers in their hair, holding huge wax candles which are alight even in daytime. More girls of the palace now bear the royal vessels of gold and silver, and many ornaments of different kinds, and of which the use is unknown to me. Behind marches another company of girls of the palace, carrying shields and lances; Amazons, who are the body-guard of the King. After them, carriages drawn by goats, and carriages drawn by horses, all ornamented with gold.' Then, ministers and princes mounted on elephants under red parasols and, at last, on the back of a huge elephant—its tusks sheathed in gold—

the King, with the sacred sword in his hand, and a shield of twenty white umbrellas around him. The Chinaman was witness of all this, and comments on the dark skins of the ordinary people, contrasting that with the paleness of the palace women 'who never see the sun, and are white as white jade'. He mentions the public festivals of Angkor, the rockets and fire-crackers fastened to scaffolding and high masts and to the tops of four or five wooden stupas put up for the purpose, and let off at the New Year ceremony. 'The rockets soar up into the heavens, and the crackers as loud as cannons shake the whole city with their bangings. This goes on for a fortnight . . . But every month there is a festival of some kind; Throwing the Ball; or a Grand Parade when the whole population passes in procession in front of the palace; or the Washing of the Buddhas; or Sailing Vessels on Dry Land; or The Burning of the Rice (which women like very much, and come to it by goat-carriage or on elephants), or Dancing to Music; or Fights between Wild-Boars and Elephants.' And he concludes, innocently: 'Other of the festivals escape my memory.'

The streets were crowded: 'but they do not have shops, but a kind of mat, each occupying a particular piece of ground, and they have to pay rent for these to a mandarin . . . The women, who never hesitate to show their breasts, tint the soles of their feet and the palms of their hands . . . Both men and women scent themselves with sandalwood and with musk and other essences.' And the Chinaman mentions 'the Buddhist priests who go barefoot, with shaven heads, and wear a yellow skirt and a yellow robe that leaves the shoulders naked,' just, in fact, as nowadays, and nowhere more aptly, though incongruously, than at the aerodromes. And he tells of the Brahmins 'who dress like everyone else, except for a piece of red or white stuff wound about their heads,' no doubt in sign of their Indian origin and as vestigial turbans. Some few of these priests or monks would be seen at night on the temple steps cooking at a fire, and they might unroll a blanket or mattress, or, more probably, they just lay down to sleep on the stone terraces wrapped in their saffron togas as do the white-clad Indians on the streets of Calcutta or Bombay. It is a shock to see how simple are the sleeping arrangements in Buddhist temples in Japan. No more than a rolled up mattress in the corner of a tiny room may be the abbot's bedroom. It is unlikely that the Khmers were more luxurious in this respect than the modern Japanese. There surely did not exist such a thing as a recognized bedroom. It was only a question of which corner you were going to lie down and sleep in. The *bonzes* probably took their turn of duty in the temples, and then went back to their monasteries which were wooden buildings like those in the temple enclosure of Wat Po, the Sleeping Buddha, in Bangkok, where there are prayer halls and sleeping-quarters and refectories. The monasteries and palaces were impermanent buildings. They were wooden, while the temples were built of stone.

The Bayon would not burn; nor would Angkor Wat. Neither one or other could be set on fire. And it would be the wooden, not the stone buildings which would be pillaged. There may have been golden images, but there were no tombs to be robbed. After lying empty for five centuries (since the Wars of the Roses in England) it would be unreasonable to expect any of the wooden structures to be standing. The ant-hills, ten or twelve feet high, passed on the way to outlying temples are, alone, reason and excuse for this destruction. It is curious that in their tapering forms the ant-hills seem almost to imitate the thin golden spires above the Buddhist fanes. But the real enemies of the stone buildings have been the forest trees. They have seeded themselves, and wrenched and torn and split the stones apart. This carnage of the cold stone has its extraordinary parallel in the ruins of that other tropical civilization in Guatemala and Yucatán. If one has seen both it is impossible not to compare the Further Indian with the Central American, and to contrast the one with the other in one's mind. To anyone who has climbed over the ruins of Angkor, and of Uxmal and Chichén-Itzá, there is the supreme mystery of how such vast schemes of building were undertaken in the enervating heat, and under temperatures and conditions which have reduced the present population in both places to supineness and lethargy. This tenacity of purpose is something that surpasses all comprehension. To imagine that it would ever again be possible for the existing inhabitants on either side of our world is not in question.

But these schemes were not only undertaken; they were carried on and finished. They are not giant torsos, but completed buildings. They are not public utilities like the Roman aqueducts and circuses. In no instance at Angkor is the reason for their conception the accommodation of large crowds. The great pyramids of the Mayans were for ceremonies and rituals in open air. The priests and their sacrificial victims could be plainly seen on the platforms at the top of those pyramids. If, like the Khmers, the Mayans had not the skill and capacity to roof over large areas and like them could only construct little cells and long covered passages, at least their intention was to accommodate the whole population of their cities and in that sense was for the public. But at Angkor Wat the long galleries or cloisters of bas-reliefs seem to lose themselves in magic formulas and interminable narrations.[1] Attention quickly tires of them, as it must do faster still at Ramesvaram in Southern India where the sculptured corridors, 'the glory of the temple', are twice as long and extend to 4,000 feet of bas-reliefs, a dullness painfully evident from any photograph. Ramesvaram is a late example (seventeenth century), but it is to their Indian forbears that the temples of Angkor are constantly returning, but from a distance and as though they were losing touch, or had no close knowledge of their antecedents.

It is an India transformed and constructed with hallucinatory conviction in the tropical heat. But a personal vision, and not in answer to the demands of the population. The message out of the ruins of Angkor is personal in both instances, at Angkor Wat and at the Bayon. When Chou Ta-kuan saw them, Angkor Wat had been completed for about a hundred and fifty and the Bayon for nearly eighty years. The buildings of the Khmers may have been more imposing than any in China. But if they struck the Chinaman with astonishment it is evident in his account that, his native xenophobia apart, he looked on the Khmers as half-barbarian and it is true that they lacked the painting, the philosophy, the literary tradition of classical China. Also, they were deficient in the minor arts, in ceramics, and in everything that would appeal to a practised dilettante or a gourmet, categories which were well established with long precedent in China. He had not been to India; or he would have seen that it was an attempt at being Indian, the land their dual religions came from, and a conscious copying of Hindu models with a Khmer accent.

But the most curious feature of the Bayon, of the bridge leading to it over the moat with the 'stone demons, like stone generals, gigantic and terrible' holding the naga-rail in their hands; of the darting, swaying, hooded cobras that are their finials; of the triple-headed gateways with the four faces; and the triple-headed elephants of the

[1] 'It must be remembered that the bas-reliefs at Angkor were specially chosen, more as ornaments magically appropriate to the palace of a god than as didactic scenes destined for the edification of man. Their arrangement was certainly determined by a magic principle of orientation, which we do not know, rather than by a desire to instruct the visitors to the sanctuary.' Benjamin Rowland, *op. cit.*, p. 224.

13 & 14 Faces of Buddha
from the Bayon
at Angkor

15　Angkor Wat

16 Doorway at Angkor Wat

17 Pediment carving at Banteai Srei

18 Doorway carving at Banteai Srei

side walls that are feeding upon lotuses—all on the way to the Bayon —the greatest curiosity about these is their unreality. Their spirit demands that they should have been made in papier mâché, and instead they are carved in stone. They are puppet or pantomime properties made permanent. What should have been put up for a night has lasted for the greater part of a thousand years. Short of systematic demolition it has undergone more perils and dangers than could have befallen it in temperate lands. Nature has not this savage hand in Greece or Rome. There are ruins at Angkor which could have been brought to the surface from the bottom of the seas, with the pressure of deep waters on them and all the turmoil of a millennium of Atlantic storms, with the coils of the huge kraken round them and the giant growths of the profound abyss. All the more haunting, at Angkor Wat, the companies of dancing apsaras lost in the deep woods.

But the Bayon is not of this character. It is more hallucinatory, more obsessive still. A dolomite, fretted and worn into turrets, and all marked from the same mould. The human, yet inhuman countenance faces in every direction from under its tiara of jewels or flowers. It looks into itself in contemplation, and as though in reservation of its inward powers. Bodiless, but with somewhat of the Mongoloid staring downward at its own navel. It is possessed of those traits of character of the Mongoloid that it knows what is going on, but makes no comment. It does not see clearly for its eyes are half shut; but it feels and knows. It is too far gone into itself to speak. But it is not unconscious. This message, or diagnosis, is repeated every way you look, and always, and everywhere the same. To the extent that the Bayon has almost ceased to be the work of human hands. There are moments when you may find yourself confronted by any number of the gigantic faces, and enfiladed by more of them if you turn around. It has the multiplication of an endless number of mirrors reflecting into each other. But the faces are no smaller. They are all of the same size. If the Bayon was built in order to effect some degree of auto-hypnosis it has not lost its powers.

E

Chapter Six

THE RED CHAPELS OF BANTEAI SREI

IT IS A DRIVE of rather under twenty miles from Angkor to the chapels of Banteai Srei along a road that is impossible during the rainy season. Their very existence was only reported or *signalé* in the phrase of the French guide book, in 1914; and ten years after that, before the archaeologists had begun to work on them, some of the sculptures were stolen and removed by 'amateurs' from Europe and are now in museums and private collections in France and the United States. The public conscience has only lately stirred itself over such matters, but this is not the place to discuss the ethics of the origin of many museum treasures, or how many of them should be returned of right to the countries whence they came. What is probable is that the disturbance of the stones at Banteai Srei may have still further complicated the restoring work of the experts but, whether this be so or not, so beautifully has it been accomplished that Banteai Srei emerges from what we shall find to be its exceptionally shadowy and shifting past as one of the jewels of architecture, not only of the Far Orient, but of the world at large.

In a little while after leaving the canals of Angkor Wat we are passing villages that can have changed but little in a thousand years for the possession of a box of matches, an electric torch, or even a bicycle, has not really altered the mode of life. The children still play naked at the roadside and the thatched huts still stand on stilts above the ground. 'They cook rice in an earthenware pot, and make the sauce on an earthen stove. They bury three stones for a hearth, and help themselves to the food by using a coco-nut as a ladle . . . They help themselves to the sauce with leaves of which they make small cups, that, although full of liquid, never let it run out. For spoons, they use smaller leaves that can be thrown away when finished.' But this account by Chou Ta-kuan of the villages as they were just before

the year 1300 while the Khmer civilization was at its height should be
qualified by saying that the cooking is now done mostly in a big iron
cauldron, and always, unless it is the rainy season, in the open air
outside their huts.

In the space under the huts there are nearly always a cock and hens,
the male bird so brilliant in plumage that it must be near in descent to
the red jungle fowl that is its ancestor. The huts are a few feet apart,
and the flashing colours of the cockerels are conspicuous and glorious.
What would seem to be golden duck wings with crimson hackles and
green-blue metallic wing-bars catch the eye and would delight the
English 'fancy'. Under one or two of the huts an entirely naked child
may be lolling in a hammock. And the account by the Chinaman of
so long ago only needs further qualification in saying that the 'sauce'
is the ubiquitous dried fish paste, the smell of which pervades all of
Thailand and parts of India, and is near relative to the Bommeloe
fish or Bombay ducks, relics of the seastrand, that we eat with
curry.

We are passing ruins all the time, and a wooded hill appears which
is Pnom Bakheng according to the map, with what seem to be more
ruins on its flanks, being in itself an object of interest in this flat plain
for it is the only hill for miles around. There are coco-nut palms near
the huts, but soon there are fewer villages, the track becomes rougher
and rougher and we are out in the wilds. The birds were a disappointment; there are brackish lagoons with one or two storks; but we see
no parrots, and sadder still, no hornbills, which is a loss to any
admirer of the coloured plates in *A Monograph of the Bucerotidae, or
Family of the Hornbills*,[1] one of the most splendidly lavish of Victorian
bird books. A lesser reason in coming to Cambodia in order to see
Angkor had been the hope of encountering a hornbill in its natural
surroundings. But it was not to be, and for a view of parrots we had
to wait till India; curiosity being only assuaged during our journey
and not satisfied at sight of what I take to have been the Homrai, a
perfectly enormous hornbill from Borneo and Sumatra, in the
Zoological Gardens at Colombo. It perched there in the dark at the
back of its cage, as solemn as any owl on a telegraph pole at mid-
afternoon, in sober vest of black and white, quite four feet high from
the summit of its extraordinary double casque of horn, curving backwards and placed with double edge or rim on top of its excessive

[1] D. G. Elliot, with fifty-seven coloured plates by Keulemans, 1882.

beak, to the ends of its tail-feathers of white and black.[1]

That there are hornbills in the woods is certain, and now the land-scape takes on more and more the character of a celestial park. The trees are taller, a little sparse of leaf, and with immensely elongated, or they could be termed, webbed trunks, or, rather, buttress-trunks running down from the mother trunk and then sprawling laterally along the ground. One cannot disassociate them in mind from the triple-headed elephants of the town gates at their meal of lotuses. They are rain-trees, the bane and ruin of the temples, and the lesser roots at the tree foot are like a writhing mass of snakes. So continual and oppressive is their wrestling with the stones that from the one or two of the temples that have been left undisturbed by the restorers in order to show the process of destruction, one remembers the extra-ordinary trees more even than the temples lying in ruin. But it is not so at Banteai Srei. The aerial roots or lower ramifications of the tree-trunks are less convoluted, and they are not strangling the stones. Their snaky coils are not so evident. The forest is gayer and lighter here. There is not the sensation we will get later at Ta Prohm and Prah Khan that visiting them is a sub-aqueous, sea-bottom adventure.

We have a longing to get down out of the jeep and listen. Monkeys unseen till now, live up in the trees, and herds of wild elephant are not far away. This sacred or celestial parkland is nearly unique in experi-ence and surely among the beautiful things of the world. The only approach to what is, up till this moment, its ecstatic silence is the park surrounding the ruins of Polannaruwa, in Ceylon. But, there, a huge red lotus grows 'in profusion' in the artificial lake or tank—though, alas, not in the month we went there—descendant of those grown a thousand years ago for use in the palaces and temples of the ancient city; white frangipani, superlative in height and of ideal shape, and a marvellous yellow-flowering tree, its name not known to me, grow near together close to the rock-cut statue of Buddha, lying in Nirvana; and in fact the sacred park of Polonnaruwa is Buddhist and only Buddhist in inspiration and in feeling. There, too, whole monkey-families were leaping like satyrs on the rocks. With

---

[1] Incommodious in flight, one might opine of the Homrai in Victorian language, but Wallace has this to say of it in his *Malay Archipelago*, (1869). 'Its voice is very rough and grating, and not to be surpassed probably by any sound that an animal is capable of making. Its flight is heavy, and performed by repeated flappings of its huge wings. It proceeds in a straight line and sails only when about to alight upon some tree. The strokes are made with great force, and the noise of its wings can be heard for more than a mile.'

its mile and a half of ruins it is a sacred park that has more the character of a huge and deserted garden.

But Banteai Srei, to which we are coming, is more lost and remote. Forgotten, till between the two World Wars, though the length of its oblivion is not determined, is even still in argument, and when we get to it, this temple seems not slumbering like the other ruins, but to be wide awake. Immediately you climb down out of the jeep, and the engine stops, you hear the noises of the forest. But only for a moment or two and then comes the rapturous silence. The road stops at a low wall or a bank where there are exceptionally tall trees, and beyond that you find yourself in a narrow aisle between the stumps of pillars. At first it is a disappointment as though the beauty of Banteai Srei can only be how deep it is in the forest, and no more than that. Then, walking away from where the temple must lie there are low stone doorways leading into roofless calls, and the lintels of these doors are more intricately carved in a manner richer and withal a little different from anything at Angkor Wat or at the Bayon.

Turning in our steps, now, to walk back again over a stone pavement that has been worn away into mere stepping-stones, we come to a low wall and arc in front of the outer gatehouse of Banteai Srei. The side walls have door openings of almost classical Italian pattern as to their mouldings, and are pierced as well by windows barred with the sham bamboo-stem motif that was one of the inventions of Khmer building. The colour of the stone is a light red with darker shadows from its many fretted cornices, and through the portal there are more of the red chapels.

But the gatehouse itself is in a new and strange style. It is in the technique of sandalwood carving with even an Indian scent to it, that is how I would describe it, with an extraordinary aura of India over it all. But this is either of an India that has long disappeared, or of one that only had existence in the craftsman's imagination. An Indonesian evocation of India for the breath of Sumatra, even of Java is on it too; a not distant affinity because of the connection of its Kings with the mysterious Sailendra, the Hindu 'King of the Mountain and Lord of the Isles' of whose empire Sumatra was part; while there is certainly some racial tie between Banteai Srei and the barns and long houses of the Batak and other Sumatran tribes who have developed a wild fantasy in their roof-shapes and gable-ends, 'and have store-chambers and tribal meeting-places in which the architectural fantasy runs riot

to produce buildings more eccentric than any European Rococo'.[1]
Banteai Srei is Indonesian, but its craftsmen had the classical India
before their minds.

The gateway is a porch supported on four plain stone columns,
unless indeed these are a restoration for the French archaeologists
have done their work here with such delicacy that it is next to
impossible to detect their handiwork. One of the stone columns is
cracked right through which should prove it genuine; but as against
this the columns are left plain and without ornament, and this is most
unlike the craftsmen who were at work on Banteai Srei. It is the roof
of the porch that simulates carving in sandal or other scented wood,
being formed out of stone beams that have the ornament worked
along their grain. This illusion is carried further in the stone returns at
the edges that curve upwards in 'S' shape, but precisely like the knot
in a sawn log, or the limb of a tree that has been sawn longitudinally,
along its length, and shows the fault or knot. This idiom has been
allowed to flower out of its idiosyncracy into a fantasy of its own; and
the entire lintel is repeated a second time and on a larger scale
immediately behind it, like its own taller shadow, giving to it a
marvellous, and I would say in parenthesis, a doubly-scented
richness.

But it is time to step inside while there is still that rapturous pause
of silence; or it is that we are in no mood to listen for the moment.
For just the sensation of coming into Banteai Srei is something
beyond ordinary experience. One has come into a walled enclosure
made alive by what seems an incredible number of architectural
units, all of the reddish-pink coloured stone, little stone buildings, in
fact small chapels, in every direction and round every corner, and all
seemingly in nearly unbelievable perfection of preservation. Through-
out, and everywhere, it is the sandalwood technique applied to the
pinkish stone. One can almost breathe the sandalwood in that first
moment.

There are three shrines, side by side to each other, standing on a
richly corniced stone platform about three feet tall, that exactly
follows and repeats the contours of each of the chapels. Sitting on
this platform at the heads of flights of steps, and scarcely higher than
those, are pairs of statues that might be mistaken for monkeys come
down from the trees. They are guarding the open doors of the

[1] Geoffrey Gorer, *op. cit.*, p. 25.

sanctuaries, and if come upon in three-quarter darkness one would take them for monkeys from their attitudes and the way they are sitting. What more natural than that monkeys should inhabit these chapels which for that matter are as though the monks or nuns only left them yesterday! Having perhaps invited the monkeys to look after the chapels during their absence which began, incredibly, more than five hundred years ago, chapels and woods having entered meanwhile into another dimension or measurement of time!

The statues squat there like monkeys sitting on one knee, and will be off in a moment on all fours, not quite human enough to walk upright unless led by the hand like a child, but lumbering along on their hind legs as though walking on their hands, curling and uncurling their tails, and thus over the low walls and up into the trees! And indeed a pair of statues is of Hanuman, the monkey general, dressed up in a loin-cloth and what one may presume to be a general's head-dress, and like all the others, with one hand placed upon his knee. The rest of them are more human still; and one pair of them wearing short pleated knee-pants have wild cat masks or parrot heads. They are all birds and creatures of the woods, metamorphosed into half-human beings for the time the priests are away, which must by now be for longer than was expected.

In addition to the three shrines there are two temple 'libraries', five buildings in all of the pink sandstone, none of them bigger in scale than a grandiose kennel or a monkey-house, all of them of a size for animals to inhabit, and enclosed by the wall with the fantastic outer and inner gatehouses. The inner portal, now we turn to look, projects forward from the two recessed bodies of building flanking it, the outer of the pair being placed slightly to the back, behind the nearer. These little bodies or rooms of stone are of the utmost elaboration of carving, each with its five-barred, bamboo-stem window simulated in the red stone; and each body raised on a base or plinth which is worked into at least some half-dozen mouldings. A pair of the bamboo-stem windows, therefore, one slightly behind the other, is on each side of the door, and a couple of lion statues resembling Chinese kylins sit there on guard before it.

The stone waggon-roof of the portal has end gables like flickering flames of fire in their outline, while the gateway has for its scale an immensely high and tower-like tympanum which encloses a pediment carved with a whole scene or episode from the Hindu fiction—

forest or jungle of The *Mahābhārata*. Above this it climbs to its peak in some three or four tiers of stone flames. The flame-edging may not be intended to portray fire. It may be meant rather for some curling fern-fronted motif. But the effect is of flame, and it is for flame we take it.

The whole of this gatehouse could be an extra large cabinet of sandalwood, the size of a small room, and executed as a *tour de force*, but no more so than any other of the chapels, gatehouses, or 'libraries', the bamboo motif for the false windows somehow adding to the illusion that the pinkish-red stone is some kind of precious, scented wood. Turn every way you will, and there is another of the little buildings with sculptured figures standing in niches at its door, and double or even triple frontons of the red sandstone, one behind the other, framing the sculptured pediment with triple edges of carving in sandalwood technique, and tossing the flame or the spray of their outer and topmost fringing against the forest trees.

If we move now to look at one of the 'libraries', and the buildings at Banteai Srei are so near together that we have to squeeze in order to get between them, we find ourselves unable to take our eyes from the pediment carving. It has a multitude of little figures, the subject being the giant Ravana shaking Mount Kailasa. This is carved upon the squares of reddish-pink sandstone in entirely, once more, the sandalwood technique, and with an extraordinary flat clarity of detail that even resembles the glass-cutting on Orrefors or Steuben glass. Hanuman, with monkey head, and Ganesh, the elephant god, are to be recognized; and the little manikin figures in their vivacity of detail belie their antiquity and could be prize reliefs in plasticine.

Another pediment from one of the 'libraries' portrays no less lively and playful a scene, and once again the little figures have had their red sandstone background carved into half-conventionalized trees as though the sculptor while at work, was thinking that Banteai Srei was deep in the woods. The triple fronton, pretending to be of precious wood, and not of stone, frames and towers above this, and the naga motif never far away in any Khmer building returns in the topmost and largest, or outer of the frames or tympana. This spreads at its bottom corners into the multiple hooded-cobra heads, looking here more like polyps or stems of coral, while down below to either side are more upraised and swaying naga-hoods for finials to the roof crests of the flanking walls on either side. The effect is of ferns and trees and little human or semi-human figures under a triple cresting of tongues of flame, and with darting, swaying naga-hoods at the principal corners, all in the red sandstone that purports to be of scented timber and never to have known the quarry.

The two 'libraries' are small buildings indeed, and whatever else they may have been, the use suggested for them seems improbable. It is more likely they were sacred storehouses like those at Ieyasu's Shrine at Nikko, in Japan. But the mere comparison, having been to Nikko, returns us in thought to this deeper and more serious work of art from which the more bizarre elements of Japan are lacking, carried out in this red sandstone reminiscent of that from which Lichfield Cathedral and the churches of Nuremberg were built, but with an elaboration of ornament that was never attained by the Gothic craftsmen even during the Flamboyant and Perpendicular periods. In degree of execution there may be nothing to surpass Banteai Srei anywhere in the world. That it has some affinity to the Rococo of Southern Italy, even to the Churrigueresque of Spain and Mexico, is a thought which passes by and vanishes, or we would find ourselves comparing the red chapels and libraries of the deep forest to the Wieskirche in the sub-Alpine meadows of Bavaria, to golden façades and balconies in Lecce and Noto, fretted pilasters and fluttering cornices of white stucco at Granada,[1] or the gilded altars of Mexico.

At Banteai Srei it is sufficient but to shut one's eyes and open them again in order to see that the true affinity is Indian. The red sandstone, never the pleasantest of mediums, has been worked into an evocation of India. But at a distance, and from hearsay. The true comparison must be to such temples as Halebid, in Southern India,[2] the date of which it is useful to state at this point is the middle of the twelfth century. The poetic inspiration in these red chapels has a divine origin or afflatus to which mere skill and technique cannot aspire, and it can be that the copy undertaken in this fever of creativity is finer than the original.

Not that these chapels and 'libraries' can be qualified as being of the highest order of beauty, or that they are entirely satisfying as works of art. For they are not. They are stone structures, but hardly buildings at all, for their interiors are but little cells. There are elements of Toy Town in this collection of tiny buildings that are not

[1] In the Sacristia of the Cartuja.
[2] 'Surpassing all others in the prodigality of its sculptural embellishment . . . a Churrigueresque riot of carving that defeats description,' Benjamin Rowland, op. cit., p. 104.

much bigger than dolls' houses; then, as one listens for it, there come the sounds of the Cambodian woods; a high pitched, staccato piping repeated like a signal from no particular direction as we are sitting not far from the monkey statues on a stone ledge in the shade.

And having rested for a while, we come round a corner face to face with the tower or gopuram over one of the chapels. We look up at the hooded pediment over its door, and at the tympanum repeated over and over again, five times in all, diminishing in size and with different carved figures on each storey. Looking round, we see another of the gopurams rising on our right and one of the 'libraries' on the left, conveying all the crowded effect of some narrow street, but not of Toledo, nor Siena, of no one of our mediaeval cities. It is an Indian gate-tower or gopuram in an Indonesian setting. It is only necessary to be shown an illustration of Madurai, or of any of a dozen other temples in Southern India, to be certain of this. The great temple of Madurai with its four giant gopurams 150 feet high, and its seven lesser ones, eleven of them in all, more crowded with statues than the benches at the Easter bullfight, in fact four towering and crowded seat stands, for that is the effect of them above the temple courts and the bathing-tank or 'Pool of the Golden Lilies'— all such, and many others, are as these towers of Banteai Srei in decadence, being late in date for they were only built early in the seventeenth century, and belong to a culture from which all of Angkor, itself, was in decline from earlier Hindu temples according to the purists.

We look at the carved ornament round the niches in which the guardian spirits stand for the lettucy, even kale-like foliation of its leaves recalls something else, and that is the two pairs of monolithic marble pilasters in the Basilica at Leptis Magna. These are carved with vine tendrils and clusters of grapes, while the undercutting of the marble shows Actaeon and his stag, centaurs and satyrs, and various anthropomorphic figures. They are among the wonders of the ancient world but they do not surpass the marvellous vegetative richness of the carved detail at Banteai Srei. The pilasters at Leptis are indicative of what must have been the finest technical resources of the classical world gathered from all the Mediterranean littoral at the command of a Roman Emperor, Septimius Severus, who wished to adorn his African birth-place. This was during the decline of classical architecture six centuries after the Age of Pericles. But, also, the pilasters of the Basilica could be Italian work undertaken in the first excitement of rediscovering the ancient world. Berenson compares the architecture of Leptis to buildings in paintings by Mantegna, and speaks of 'pillars sculptured as richly as the panels on the façade at Orvieto, but deeper cut and even more ivory-like in quality'.[1] But they suggest even more strongly a building still marked by the Gothic, such as the Certosa di Pavia. And stemming from that comparison we could perhaps best explain the chapels at Banteai Srei to someone who has never seen them, in saying that they could be a collection of hermitages built to the orders of Sforzas or Viscontis in the Valtellina, maybe, or in the hills near Bergamo.

But look up to the cresting of the chapels and they are Indonesian in their outline which suggests the gilded spire-like head-dress of a Siamese or Cambodian dancer. Or is it that the head-dresses, themselves, mimic the golden spires of Bangkok and Phnom Penh? At the back of the compound there are further buildings where the inmates had their living-quarters, and traces of a moat. We saw some of the ruined cells before entering the temple but they leave little impression. Yet it is as though the chapels and 'libraries' had been lived in by hermits. It is difficult not to regard Banteai Srei as a Camaldoli or a Vallombrosa, and see it inhabited by Hindu monks or Brahmins rather than by sadhus and devotees of Shiva and Vishnu. Yet two of the shrines of Banteai Srei are dedicated to just these gods and the lingam had its place here. The architecture is indubitably of a late Renaissance phase as that term is understood in Europe, and the only explanation is that the arts everywhere in the world are subject to the same rules and that this Indonesian rebirth or Renaissance of classical India is no exception. It follows just the same course of primitive and poetic awakening, mature exuberance, and quicker or more prolonged decay. The chapels of Banteai Srei are the climacteric, the peak or summit of this rise and fall.

But now comes the mystery as to the date of the red chapels of Banteai Srei. The chronology of the ruins of Angkor has ever been of shifting character with the temples shunted backwards and forwards from century to century inside an orbit of some three hundred years and more. And each time the dates are announced as final they are liable to be changed again. That this is less likely of occurrence now the French archaeologists are no longer in control and restoration is

---

[1] *A Vicarious Trip to the Barbary Coast*, by Mary Berenson, London, 1938, p. 21.

proceeding more leisurely, if at all, has not prevented the date of Banteai Srei from being in dispute even in the last few years. Thus, the guide to Angkor by Henri Parmentier, in its third edition, revised and edited by his widow, and printed at Phnom Penh as lately as 1960, states that its date 'qui présenta longtemps un curieux problème', has been lately decided by the discovery of new inscriptions according to which it was built by Jayavarman V (1068-1101) and begun in 967. But Benjamin Rowland in the Penguin *Art and Architecture of India*, second edition reprinted with corrections, 1959, says Banteai Srei was founded by the teachers and relatives of King Srindravarman in 1304—a difference of three hundred and thirty seven years—adding in a footnote that the temple 'is built on an earlier foundation of 969 which used to be accepted as the date of the complex as it now stands'. 'The carving', he continues in the text of his book, 'is of a crispness and extravagant richness that are typical of this final "Rococo" phase of Khmer art.' Between these two authorities Malcolm Macdonald in his *Angkor*, 1958, once more puts the clock back where Banteai Srei is concerned in saying it was completed and dedicated in 968, and that: 'Owing to a misreading of certain inscriptions, it was at one time considered a product of the fourteenth century, and so judged to be the last of the great buildings in the classical Khmer style. A later correction established that it was in fact the first of these—the tentative introduction, not the refined finish.'

There is here a direct contradiction in that one authority says the misread inscription puts Banteai Srei back from the fourteenth century to the tenth century, while the other blames the misreading for an attribution to the tenth century which should really have read the fourteenth. This argument as to two dates which are nearly four hundred years apart shows how wrong it may be to ascribe a date entirely on stylistic grounds. One would like to think the earlier to be correct because then it would be a closer evocation of classical India. It would be wonderful if one could believe the chapels in this sylvan remoteness to be more than a thousand years old. But a last walk in the precincts taking in the general effect of the chapels must, I think, convince one that the early fourteenth century is correct. It is the classical Indian in an Indonesian accent, in the latter phase of the Indian when it approximated to flamboyant Gothic or the Rococo, in which connection the dating of the temple at Halebid as mid-twelfth century is valuable for that would allow of a century and a half for the influence to seep through from Southern India to Indo-China.

A morning or an afternoon at Banteai Srei is an experience that compares with that of seeing so many shrines in Italy or Spain. It rouses just the same expectations, and for a moment at a time one may be deluded into thinking it concerns the same sort of personages who ordered the work to be done and perhaps had themselves entombed in the end at Orvieto, or the Certosa di Pavia, in late Gothic Burgos, or the Plateresque churches of Salamanca. But then comes the difference, and it overwhelms one in a rush. The similarities in conception and execution at different sides of the world are farther apart than the mere sum of their distance. Indeed, they are only alike in antithesis to each other, and it is only because they are so dissimilar that they are in some respects the same. To the extent perhaps that all human beings are born with a head and two legs and arms, and within those limits and from those beginnings there is all the difference in the world between them.

That difference comes in a rush if you look up into the trees and listen, and then down again to get that impression of sandalwood from the red sandstone chapels. Then, indeed, you are in Indo-China and as fast as you breathe the air into your lungs. But the surprise is that they are solid buildings of stone and not mere wood and tinsel. It was the rumour of great stone buildings on the Roman scale lost in the forest that drew on explorers and naturalists and that form the contradiction to the flimsy present. They have this similarity to the Mayan temples at the other side of the world, but in the same belt of climate, that in our Western understanding of the word they are elaborately planned and executed stone shelters, but hardly buildings. How many persons could the red chapels of Banteai Srei accommodate; or the Bayon under and among its giant heads of stone; or even the long stone galleries of Angkor Wat? Were we able to continue our journey into Indonesia to end at the temple of Borobudur in Java, we would find it to be a nine-storeyed stone pyramid or casing to enclose a natural mound or hillock. Marvellously beautiful as may be the bas-reliefs along its terraces, and subtle as may be the ritual symbolism of its planning, Borobudur can hardly be called other than a monument and not a building. This stricture must apply to Angkor Wat; still more to the Bayon, and no less than that to Banteai Srei.

The temperature of excitement rises at the fantastic gates of the city, at its wide moats which magnify the sense of expectation, at the rows of stone giants holding the naga on their laps, the dance of the hooded-cobra heads at the end of those stone rails, and indeed the whole corps or company of stone dancers. But it is a yet stronger sensation to get away from all that, to put those stone pantomime props at a distance, and come upon these chapels in their exquisite state of preservation some miles distant in the woods. If you listen for it, there are none of our sounds in the trees. No cooing of doves at the tree foot, treading on violets or anemones, and a month later, when it is a wood of bluebells, looking up into the boughs. Instead, it is a shaking, for the sake of shaking of the branches, as if it were a party of acrobats or trapeze 'artists' in the trees. They begin their shrill calls to each other but, maddeningly, are gone before we catch sight of them. We hear their shrill comedian chattering, their monkey-pretence that they are speaking, and they go swinging from bough to bough where we will never see them. But the monkey statues are here still. And so are the red chapels of Banteai Srei, yet they are gone, too, in the instant we leave them; though the vision of them is so entire in detail that we may find ourselves wondering if we really saw them.

Chapter Seven

✦✦✦✦✦✦✦✦✦✦✦✦✦✦✦✦✦✦✦✦✦✦

STORM IN THE DEAD STONES

THE QUANTITY OF RUINED sites in and around Angkor forms an ensemble of ruins not less imposing than those on both banks of the Nile at Luxor. That these are some thirty centuries or three thousand years earlier in date makes the temples of Egypt more interesting historically but it does not confer greater aesthetic value upon them. Despite their disappointing interiors—there being nothing at Angkor that can for instance offer any comparison at all with the great hypo-style hall in the Temple of Amun which was considered one of the wonders of the world among the ancients—the temples of Angkor, nevertheless, though none of them older than ten centuries, are beautiful where that other is not, and it could be said that what they lose in age they gain in mystery.

It would take many weeks to visit all the Khmer ruins, there being some thirty or forty groups of them within a radius of as many miles around Angkor. Others, too, within the present frontiers of Thailand, for while we were in Bangkok an acquaintance was just returned from seeing ruins in the northern part of the Kingdom covering a larger area than that of Angkor Thom (the city proper), but where 'the sculptures were not so fine'.[1] These are sites that, now, in all pro-bability will never be reached by the excavator's spade. Mayan ruins in Central America, remote as they are, lie nearer to American university sponsors, and hold more promise to modernistic trends in architecture and in sculpture. The restoration of Khmer ruins is likely to have reached to its completed state, and the shrinking world which seems to diminish in direct ratio to the acceleration of air travel over its surface will probably neglect further exploration in this part of the world even while the augmenting crowds of tourists pour into it, and are gone the next day, or by the day following.

[1] Probably at Lamphun, near Chiengmai.

It is only proposed in these pages to give some impression of the more immediately imposing of the ruins, and to write of them from the point of view of someone lucky enough in his life to have seen many of the works of art of the world, and therefore to discuss them in that context and from those comparisons. That they are ruins is melancholy enough, and we have to people them by an act of imagination while considering also that the gilt and tinsel and the impermanent wooden buildings have long disappeared. It could be compared to seeing the raised hull of a liner, without deck-houses, interior fittings, or passengers. These few sentences taken haphazard from Chou Ta-kuan's description of the living Angkor will illustrate my meaning. 'On the city gates there are five stone heads of Buddha, their faces turned to the west, the middle one being adorned with gold.' (This must be the central tower of the Porte de la Victoire or great gate of Angkor Thom.) 'A golden bridge and eight golden Buddhas lie west of the walls; and the centre of the realm is marked by a tower of gold,' (the central tower of the Bayon). 'The palace is to the north of the golden tower and the golden bridge. The tiles of the King's apartment are of lead; those of other people are of yellow earthenware. The piers of the bridge are immense, and there are painted and sculptured Buddhas on it.' Even these few sentences by the only eyewitness whose account is preserved to us bring back some of the colour to the dead city.

Another sentence by the Chinaman could be said to give the clue to the life secret of Angkor. It is where he writes: 'The council hall has golden window frames below which elephants are sculptured,' for this is the Terrace of the Elephants which until one has read his few words is a structure without point or meaning. Once we know that the endless quarter-mile long procession of elephants was the basement of a great council hall, 'salle de conseil, d'audiences, ou même des fêtes', and that Chou Ta-kuan describes it as 'ornamented with mirrors', many more stone walls and mounds in the woods of Angkor renew their life again, and we begin to people the Towers of the Cord dancers with acrobats. Their use for that purpose being no more than a legend and a piece of folk-lore but at least the hundreds of apsaras of the bas-reliefs had their reality within the walls of the Royal palace.

If we begin to think of street scenes it is as well to remember that the impression of only an hour spent in Bangkok would be the

19   Monkey Statues at Banteai Srei

20   Panel of Sculpture at Banteai Srei

mulitude of naked babies. It would be a pity to dilate upon this point after we have left there but the living chinoiserie of their slit eyes, their black hair and yellow skins transfers easily, and as of nature, to Angkor. For the temple of Angkor may be Buddhist-Indian or Hindu in intention but the inhabitants had little Indian about them, except that they wore garments of cotton of which 'the most esteemed kinds', so says Chou Ta-kuan, 'come from the western seas' which means Indian flowered cottons. And deserting the naked babies for a moment we read further in the Chinaman, 'only the King may wear a thickly flowered material . . . He usually wears a golden diadem, but when without it he rolls some garlands of scented jasmin flowers round his chignon . . . He wears nearly three pounds weight of large pearls in his necklace' (like an Indian Rajah). 'On his wrists, ankles and fingers, he has bracelets and rings of gold set with cats' eyes' (to show that he can see in the dark). 'He goes bare-foot, and the soles of his feet and the palms of his hands are dyed with a red pigment . . . Among the people only the women are allowed to tint the soles of their feet and the palms of their hands. The high mandarins may wear a material with a few flowers upon it. The palace attendants wear cotton ornamented with a double row of flowers, but in the poorer classes only the women are permitted to do so.' And Chou Ta-kuan goes on to tell of a Chinaman, newly arrived, who wore cotton of this kind, but was allowed to go free, as he did not know the local custom. All of which reads like Indonesian effect, but Indian aspiration.

The naked babies, to return to them, form the 'instant' chinoiserie of Thailand and Cambodia (and of Angkor, therefore), in just the sense in which we speak of 'instant' coffee. Inferring that it makes coffee, then and there, on the spot, and in a second. These are the lands of chinoiserie; and the figures off lacquer cabinets, and on Meissen teacups, are more reminiscent of Indo-China than they are of China or Japan. This is by accident; but both the 'stone generals, gigantic and terrible' of the causeways, with their pantomime, Gog and Magog affinity, and the straight canals and 'water lawns' of Angkor which look as though Le Nôtre had lent a hand in planning them, give a semi-demi European air, or as much of that as if it were a chinoiserie in reverse and their own Indo-Chinese attempt at being European. But, really, by trial and error they were trying to be Indian; and it was this attempt at being something they were not

F

naturally and of themselves that is part of the secret of these mysterious buildings.

No small portion of this mystery is how they attained to such energies in this enervating heat. But this, too, is the riddle of the 'Indian' cities in Central America. The Khmers may have got here before the coming of malaria and other tropical diseases. Certainly the impression given by the swarms of children in Bangkok is not one of idleness or apathy. Still less can it have been so among those playing at the foot of the temples of Angkor. It was in fact an invasion from Thailand that was the ruin of Angkor, after which the Khmers moved their capital in order to be farther away from the Thais and established it at Phnom Penh. There it has remained ever since; and one authority even suggests that the golden sword of the King mentioned by Chou Ta-kuan, 'when the King goes out he holds a golden sword in his hand', is the Phra Khan, the sacred sword of Cambodia, 'perhaps the same one that is still preserved with such care by the Court Brahmins of Phnom Penh'.[1] But, also, the arrival of another, the Himayana form of Buddhism, in place of the Mahayana Buddhism, sapped the energies of the Khmers, and turned them finally from the Hindu worship of Siva which had been the fountain of their creative powers.

To a stranger's eye there are only slight physical differences between the Thais and Khmers. The Thais were a people who had been driven by Mongol pressure from Southern China into Indo-China not later than the thirteenth century, and who were lacking in the religious and cultural inspiration from India that enabled the Khmers to build the temples of Angkor. If it be true, as another writer remarks, that 'Vietnam' (capital, Saigon) 'is Little China and Cambodia' (capital, Phnom Penh) 'is Little India', the racial differences may be said to become, in contradiction, both clearer and more confused. Nevertheless, this is a helpful summing up of the situation for it tells us once again that the influence upon the Khmers came from ancient India. It was in fact a part of that greater or overseas India which spread its influence as far as Java, and even beyond it, to the isle of Bali. The 'earthly paradise' of the Java seas is Hindu in inspiration whether its gamelan music is classical Indian in origin or classical Chinese. But the 'instant' chinoiserie must be there, too, as it

---

[1] *Towards Angkor*, by H. G. Quaritch Wales, Harrap & Co., 1937, p. 232. The quotation in the following paragraph is from an article by J. Duval Smith.

is in Java and all over Indo-China, to include present day Thailand and Cambodia, no less than Laos and Vietnam.

The living Angkor would have been the most wonderful spectacle of all Further India or Indo-China, even as its ruins are to this day unparalleled, for 'here Oriental architecture and decoration reached its culminating point'.[1] Such statement must go without qualification unless it be for the Imperial Palaces in Peking—for certainly there is nothing in the Middle East, or in India, or Japan, to compare with Angkor. The only strictures on it are that it is in ruin, and that the ruins are late in date, in fact about contemporary to the oldest buildings in Peking. That 'the Khmers left the world no systems of administration, education or ethics like those of China' is the reason why so much more is known about China, their painting and their poetry being left to be added to this enumeration of the Chinese achievement. It is not difficult to people the unruined buildings of Peking for there is plenty of evidence as to their inhabitants, but Angkor is left to the imagination and the ruins of her temples are conclusive to a highly coloured interpretation of the scenes along her streets.

We must account it the prime wonder of Angkor that it was lost for 400 years, though this is hardly the term to apply to something discovered which it was never known had disappeared. There was no reason to look for this city that is scarcely mentioned in history. But the vanishing of Angkor is no more sensational than the disappearance from history of Sailendra, the King of the Mountain, the mysterious Hindu conqueror and founder of Further India, of whom all that is known can be put into a few sentences. Yet in his reign, or in that of his descendants, so vague is the chronology, the temple of Borobudur was built which Benjamin Rowland writes in his *Art and Architecture of India*, 'holds locked within its hidden galleries the final development of Buddhist art in Asia', and Borobudur was lost for even longer, forgotten for a thousand years from the ninth until the nineteenth century. But the bas-reliefs of this Javanese temple, and the three circular terraces at the top of its stone-cased hill with concentric rows of Buddhas, seventy and more of them, each sitting under, or rather, inside his openwork stone stupa the shape of a perforated hand-bell, cannot, surely, add up to any one of the profounder architectural sensations of Angkor.

It is what we would call the pantomime aspects of this 'culminating

---

[1] *The Ancient Khmer Empire*, by L. Palmer Briggs, Philadelphia, 1951.

point in Oriental architecture and decoration' that make the ruins of Angkor almost too good to be true. Who would think for instance that in these ruins lost in the woods—in a land where every child at school would guess there must be elephants—on a wall over half a mile long there should be 400 yards carved with elephants! Or, again, that in this land where snakes would be any schoolboy's guess, the very serpents should be made into ornamental motifs many hundreds of feet long! How many elephants all told in the bas-reliefs of Angkor: and how many hundreds of yards of stone naga bodies? Or that the hooded-cobra heads should be multiplied, seven, nine, even eleven times over, till they rear themselves up and dance like peacocks with spread tails! After this, the tug of war of stone giants and demons holding the naga-rail upon their laps seems but a natural development and the obvious next step to take; and the pantomime becomes entirely realized, theatrically, in the many hundreds of stone dancers in the corps de ballet.

But even the stone giants and demons of the main gate of Angkor Thom are surpassed by the naga-balustrade of another huge temple, Prah Khan, where the giant figures along the causeway are twelve feet tall. Moreover, in this instance they are seated not in a slanting position looking in your direction as you come towards them, albeit with half-closed or downcast eyes, but facing directly to the causeway. It is no longer a tug of war, but the carrying of a burden. Their head-dresses are different; less conventional and more hieratic, and in their solemnity it is as though they wore high head-dresses of flowers. Where the serpent body ends at last and is about to lift its many heads, a quite enormous giant is sitting. He cannot be less than eighteen to twenty feet high. The serpent body begins its lift upon his lap. His right hand holds its neck where the multiple hoods should branch forth from the stem, but they are broken just at that point. There is nothing left of them. And now we see distinctly even in the injured state of the statue that he had more than one pair of arms.

His head, towering over those of the other giants, and which looked as we were coming nearer to it as though it had an exaggeratedly high head-dress, is in fact a tiara of diminishing heads with his own features. Four of them, one to look in every direction, with a head-dress formed of four smaller heads, and above that what seem to be but two heads, ten in all. To the cranium of the topmost of them it must be all of twenty feet, or more, and the stone general of the demons looks even taller because of this tapering head-dress of his own physiognamy. His enormous shoulders supporting so many heads, one on top of the other, are in the giant canon of Giovanni di Bologna's crouching statue of the Apennines at Pratolino. Not four, but three arms, looking closer, for this gigantic demon who could have as many arms as he asked for. That extra arm and hand holding the many headed serpent, with one knee out, and one tier of his heads facing them, must have been as though he sat there in double profile holding a spray of stone water in his hand, grasping the nozzle of it which was the serpent's neck. We are to imagine that it must have been the biggest of all the polyp-nagas of Angkor, eleven-hooded at the least, and may have risen as high, or higher, than the topmost head of the stone demon's head-dress.

This causeway of Prah Khan with its avenues of demons, its triple gate-towers with three entrances, and the forest trees that have taken root in the stones, but their buttress-trunks appear as though poured down into the ruins instead of growing up from them—all this is for a transformation scene in pantomime—for a performance by scene-painters and machinists of genius of *Jack the Giant-killer*, or *Jack and the Bean-stalk*, and one can almost hear the noises of the stage machinery. If one listens for but a moment there are strange sounds indeed, coming from the trees. The demons of Prah Khan demand Bengal flares to light them and the perpetual, expectant hush and hiss of fireworks in the night air. Not only at night, but all around, above the great reservoirs and artificial ponds, the elephant tanks and lotus pools.

One is taken to temples beyond number at Angkor, of which it is impossible to remember the names. Often, for a ruin which would be remarkable anywhere else but here, it is not worth while getting out of the car, or climbing down out of the bus. One may find oneself without warning at the head of Sras Srang, a huge reservoir, larger than the Grand Pièce d'Eau des Suisses at Versailles. You get down to look at it, and find a stone landing-stage with steps, statues of lions to guard the stairs, and a naga-rail running to the edge of the water. There are no such steps for embarkation even in Venice, though the repertory of invention at Angkor may be growing monotonous, and one laments such opportunities for a great sculptor. This stone platform going down into the tank must have been for festal occasions, and had some sort of temporary pavilion erected upon it. At Sras Srang we must keep the barges and the water processions of Bangkok and Mandalay in mind. Their ancestry surely goes back to the canals and lakes of Angkor. Or some temple of which one is never told the name may present rather the form of a Roman basilica, and is an earlier building than most. Only 100 yards away through the trees, a similar group of buildings reveals itself to be of brick with stone lintels to the doors, and hence the suggestion of early Roman churches, but never anywhere a trace of human dwelling. Angkor is in this respect as Henri Mouhot saw it, where he finds it 'remarkable that none of these monuments were intended for habitations; all were temples of Buddhism.' They are monasteries but without cloisters, refectories or dormitories.

On the afternoon of which I am thinking we drove for miles with buildings out in the woods on either hand. There are ruins for some fifteen miles out of Angkor in this direction, their tower-like structures following closely upon Indian models for it was before the Khmers had begun to build their pyramid temples, or had thought of bas-reliefs, or planned the pantomime adornment to Angkor Wat and Angkor Thom. Such temples may be of the ninth or tenth centuries, three hundred years earlier than Angkor Wat or the Bayon. There is no fantasy about them; they are plain buildings for ascetics to pray in.

The absence of any sign of human habitation beyond their religious or meditative needs, but with such evidence as there is spread over so large an area, is something to wonder at in this humid siege of heat. For the moment we are among the plainer buildings in the knowledge that there were other and more interesting ones not far away in the stove-house humidity of all around. With shirt and trousers completely wet through, sweat pouring down one's neck and off one's forehead, and few thoughts farther ahead of one than the next shower, there came the need for some extravagant experience worthy of this torrid heat. For the orchids of Sumatra and Borneo could flourish in this climate, and the plants with painted leaves beloved of nineteenth-century botanical collectors. It was painful to walk in the ruins on this hot soil which burned through the soles of one's shoes. Where were gone the causeways and the stone giants, the dancing nagas and the stone bayadères upon the bas-reliefs? For they all seemed very far away. The only certainty was the great storm blowing up, and the marvellous knowledge one was in Angkor; that one was here where one would never come again. We must get away from the early brick buildings which could be anywhere upon earth to the fantastic structures that are of nature inhabiting this heat.

Like the storm, that experience must be coming soon. And it came, in little but telling foretaste of what was in store when we got to the shrine, rather than temple of Neak Pean. This is one of the smaller fantasies which prove the wonder of Angkor is not only in its scale. It is not all pantomime splendour, and imagination at work with the largest company of actors. Here are no elephants in procession, no sprites or demons, and no harlequinade. Neak Pean is indeed little larger than the Victorian drinking fountains of which, absurdly, it reminds one; and I am thinking in particular of that one which stands in Hyde Park near the railings of Bayswater Road, and of another near the bronze statesmen in Parliament Square. They are very typical things of their age. Certainly the shrine of Neak Pean is nearly as big as the Albert Memorial, or the Scott Monument on Princes Street in Edinburgh, the two leviathans of their cusped, granite race. Whether, as in the Hyde Park instance, built by an Indian Rajah for horses to drink from, having lost thereby any present utility it ever had, or, as with the other example, intended for human beings, they are two of the more curious monuments to be seen in London. That drinking fountains are still drunk from I know by watching the characters who pour libations for themselves at the wall fountain under the portico before entering to bury themselves in the Reading-Room of the British Museum.

One should not be thinking of such things only a few steps from the shrine of Neak Pean at Angkor but they obtrude, nevertheless, and it is because of the feverish degree of heat. This was now becoming exaggerated before the storm. Instead of remembering the Victorian drinking fountains which are as characteristic of their age and place as the vespasiennes along the Paris boulevards, even from the little we can see of it already Neak Pean should be reminding us of the Eleanor Crosses, and that of Geddington in particular, which is the most beautiful of them and in my home county. It will be recalled that King Edward I raised these crosses, eight of them in all, at each place where the body of Queen Eleanor rested on its way from Nottinghamshire, where she died in 1290, to her tomb in Westminster Abbey. The Eleanor Cross at Geddington is octagonal below, and raised on seven steps; the upper part of it is triangular in shape. Under the canopies above, carried on slender shafts, are three figures of the Queen. 'Sparrows have built their nests on the Queen's shoulders, sprays of slender grasses rise at the base of the figures, and the stone is tinged with yellow lichen.' The top portion of this skewer-shaped monument looks as if it were telescopic and its pinnacled top storeys would close and fit into each other as with the marvellous late Gothic font-cover at Ufford in Suffolk, a wonder which even Dowsing, the Puritan iconoclast, spared and wrote of it: 'There is a glorious cover over the font, like a Pope's triple crown, a pelican on top picking its breast, all gilt over with gold.' Our diversion is not inapposite, for it is of such things of their age and sort that this little shrine speaks to us from out the sacred park of Angkor.

'A floating shrine, built on an island . . . From a central basin rises this small oratory of stone, carved in the likeness of a lotus blossom; but since the whole of the upper part has been consumed by the roots of a giant tree, it is now possible only to distinguish the shape and carving of the base.' So my brother wrote of Neak Pean in 1937, adding that the water was only present in the wet season. When we saw it there was little water in the basin. Since he was there, the banyan tree has been extricated from the summit, and now the lotus is visible for the top of it is clearly intended for a lotus blossom. Not only that, but the circular steps or plinth are lotiform; not like a lotus flower but a lotus leaf. The shrine stands on this lotiform stone island in the middle of a square basin, with a causeway leading to it from one side, and a rim of stone steps round its four edges. In fact the stone band which is nearest to the water is meant for the body of a naga, or a pair of nagas, for there are two heads to it, so that from whatever angle you see it one or both serpents lift their hoods of stone. Four smaller tanks are at the four cardinal points so that in plan the sum of its five squares has twenty sides. The water-tanks with the steps down into them were intended for ritual ablution, as shown by the little chapel-like structures along the steps, but the little shrine on the island with its false stone doors has no interior at all. As beautiful as either, or both of the Gothic monuments mentioned in the last paragraph, Neak Pean is of the same date as the Eleanor Cross at Geddington, and contemporary therefore to the red chapels of Banteai Srei.

But, in reality, it is neither temple, shrine nor sanctuary, and but a lotus tower on a lotiform island in the middle of a square basin of water.

Its uses, of however high an order of invention, are entirely ornamental. It is a park ornament in a sacred park, no less no more, and this is only to be expected of a city which had 'eight hundred' (artificial) 'ponds within the municipal precincts' (Macdonald, *op. cit.*). Within the limits due to their never having found the secret of the true arch, and having therefore to have recourse to corbelling in order to roof over even a small hall or a narrow passage, the Khmers were the equals of any other race in building, and surpassed most others in the ornaments to their building. It could be said of them that no other race living in a tropical clime contrived an architecture that so expressed and fulfilled their climate. This it does to the extent that the greatest mediaeval works of Europe tell of their environment and are natural to the landscape in which they stand. The force of their dual religion, Hindu and Buddhist, must therefore have been as strong and fruitful as that which raised the mediaeval cathedrals in France, England and Spain. Or even, looked at from some angles, it was more forceful still for they must have known that there were secrets which eluded them, and yet in their fever for construction they continued and went on. The very extent of the causeway and covered galleries of Angkor Wat, and the endless repetition of the hieratic faces on the towers of the Bayon, could be interpreted as a virtual confession that neither was a building in the absolute meaning of the word and that such deficiences had to be covered up by the profusion of ornament and other devices to catch and hold the eye.

Their technical ability which only took them to a certain point, and no farther, must have been made clear to them in their greater ease with wooden buildings. For there is every reason to think their carpentry was more skilful than their masonry. Their present-day descendants at Phnom Penh, who have kept the one talent and lost the other, can still build wooden throne halls and pavilions of the greatest elegance. An idea of how picturesque this wooden architecture of Angkor may have been can be had from reading of the Royal Palace of King Thebaw at Mandalay which was only built after 1857, (and much damaged in the Second World War). It was protected by a moat 100 yards wide, crossed by five wooden bridges. Inside this was a wall with sides a mile and a quarter long; walls of red brick with thirteen peculiar and elegant watch-towers of Burman design to each side, built of teak and freely ornamented with gold. Within were numerous courts, the armoury, printing-press, mint, royal monastery, wooden pavilions occupied by the queens and princesses, and two walled gardens laid out with canals, artificial lakes and grottoes. But the chief feature was the hall of audience with the lion throne, a wooden hall 250 feet long, but only 45 feet deep (in fact another passage like the stone corridors of Angkor Wat). This was upheld on giant teak pillars and had over it a seven-storeyed gilded spire. If we think of this dragon-eaved and corruscating palace, 'peopled within living memory with a splendid Indo-Chinese royal Court,'[1] inside a moat which was covered with the pink or white flowers and broad leaves of the lotus, and had on its waters in King Thebaw's time several state barges, gilt from stem to stern, and propelled by as many as sixty rowers—adding to all this the many temples and pagodas all around, their roofs and spires inlaid with gold and Burmese lacquer, including the Glass Monastery with exterior and interior decorated with mosaic of cut glass (like the 'grande salle orné de miroirs, salle de conseil, d'audiences, ou mêmes des fêtes' above the Terrace of Elephants at Angkor Thom?)—it is to give that full meaning to the picturesque which was till lately manifest in the palace at Mandalay, is still eloquent in the Temple of the Emerald Buddha at Bangkok, but may have attained to its height of beauty with the wooden pavilions and pagodas superimposed upon the stone architecture of the Khmers at Angkor.

And we continue from Neak Pean, a lotus tower on its lotiform stone island, to the serious, more tragic ruins of Angkor, by which time the humidity was beyond anything I have ever experienced. Yet at the same time, not enervating, but conferring energy, though of spasmodic kind as if communicated by electric shock; sudden bouts of wishing to see everything, alternating with moments when it seemed impossible to walk another step. It was about half past five in the afternoon when we got to the temple of Ta Prohm. It is this temple that has been left untouched by the archaeologists, or almost so, in order to give an idea of how the forest trees are tearing the stones of Angkor apart. The guide book tells how the French sailors who came here with Commander Delaporte in 1868 only a few years

---

[1] H. G. Quaritch Wales, op. cit., p. 218. The palace of Mandalay is described in Notes on a Tour in Burma, by Dr Oertel, Government Press, Rangoon, 1893.

after the first reports of the temples reached home, one evening mistook the huge tree roots at Ta Prohm for 'prodigious serpents'. This is entirely credible. Ta Prohm should be among the natural wonders of the world; as a spectacle it must compare with the sea battles between the cachelots and giant decapods, squids with a pair of tentacles eighty, and the other ten tentacles forty feet long, that wrapped the whales in their coils and bore them down into the depths, as witnessed by Greenland whalers, and the source of not a few stories of the great sea-serpent.

For the descending limbs—as I have said, they seem to be poured down upon, not grown up out of the stones, indeed exactly as though squeezed out of a tube, or like guttering candle wax—have poured over the stones and have set and become solid. They were liquid and were spilt and poured down. But at the next stone porchway one can see they have caught the stones in a vice, and are pressing down with all their weight upon them. Ta Prohm is at first a succession of courts, one darker than another from the overhanging trees, with some fragments of naga-rails, but they are small, not giant serpents. It grows darker and darker at every corner as we clamber along over the stones of this sea bed, and look up at the towering trees above us. Now the stones have been hurled down in hopeless confusion. There are whole columns toppled over and wedged sideways, and broken bits of architrave. One can go no farther, and then another corner opens and we can see a few feet ahead, and turning round, an enormous buttress-trunk leaps up from over the doorway we have just come through.

We are now right in the middle of this huge debris, in the glaucous depths of the sacred wood, climbing over the serpent stems, and as though jumping from rock to rock of a ruined city on the sea-bottom. They are trees that must climb eighty to a hundred feet into the electric air, now shaking and shuddering before the storm. Next moment, a gate or gopuram stands in front of us, demonstrably Indian in style even in its ruin, but like a building in a sunken Atlantis on the sea bed such is its condition. Now we are in an enfilade of stone cells stretching for a long way ahead. There are carved lintels to the doors, and in one of the darkest of the cells a stone altar in full view still has a lingam, of unobtrusive size but it is impossible to mistake the purport. So endless is this enfilade of monks' cells that either it is a monastery of vast size, or it could be one monastery leading into another.[1] Perhaps only at Ta Prohm of all the temples of Angkor do the living-quarters leave any impression but, as always, no cloister, dormitory or refectory. Here one could be lost entirely only a few feet from one's companions, and wait into eternity for anything more to happen than the thunder of a falling tree.

And what was that? For now the kettle drums that have been playing all round in the distance are come suddenly nearer and are rolling and thundering in the near trees. In all directions at once, and there comes the white blink of lightning. As if too frightened to move till now the whole forest stirs in the rain. And now it peals and rattles right overhead. The rolling of the drums is for all the gods and demons of Angkor Wat and Angkor Thom to review their armies. The thunder was tremendous and not a little alarming, but it is among the sensations of a lifetime to have been in a great thunderstorm at Angkor; no less so than that other storm long years ago, in 'the corn ripe Argolide', at Agamemnon's Tomb. There were, at least, masks of gold and human bones in those beehive vaults at Mycenae. It called for description in another medium, that of poetry. This is a whole dead city, a vanished civilization in a sacred park. It seemed too big even for poetry while thunder boomed and rain poured down.

[1] A four-faced stone stela, dating from 1186, has a list of Ta Prohm's possessions upon it; 3,140 villages, and 79,365 persons, or, according to another account, 66,625 in all, including 1,800 priests, 2,740 deacons, and 2,230 assistants living in the precincts, of whom 615 were dancers; also 512 beds of silk and 523 parasols. Lest such numbers sound excessive, the Troitsa monastery, near Moscow, in 1764 had 104,000 male serfs alone attached to it.

Book Two

NEPAL

Chapter Eight

•◆•

KATMANDU

THE ONLY HINDU KINGDOM in the world is in the curious position of having been almost inaccessible till lately, though now by sudden reversal of policy it is thrown open to the cameras of all who care to go there. This sudden revelation of things long hidden can only be paralleled in this century by the flood of tourists landing on the island of Bali, the setting of another ancient Hindu civilization, in the years after 1925. In all other respects the 'island paradise' could not have less resemblance to this Himalayan Kingdom. But the protection of Bali had been distance and outside ignorance of what was going on there, while in the case of Nepal it was the physical difficulty of the journey and the refusal of all permission to approach it. In the result only a dozen or two Europeans have been there since the beginning of this century. There are few written accounts of it, and of those few not all draw attention to the buildings and works of art in Katmandu, Patan and Bhatgaon, the three cities of the valley of Nepal. These are of remarkable and very individual nature, though now glanced at carelessly by many who have neither time nor temperament to look at them in detail.

Nepal has an art of its own although India and Tibet are so near, and the three cities of the valley are nothing if they are not Nepalese. But in this there lies a contradiction. It is a mediaeval civilization akin to that of European countries in the fifteenth century, yet due not to the present Gurkha ruling race but to the Newars who preceded them. The Gurkhas only conquered the three cities in 1768-9, and it was the Newars who built the temples and old houses and made the sculptures and the carvings. The culture is therefore Newar and not Gurkha, and the Newars were the original inhabitants, of Mongolian and not Indian stock, nearer indeed to the Tibetans. The Gurkhas arrived in Nepal much later, and according to tradition had come

95

from Rajputana, though they are certainly now Mongolian of feature.

But everything to do with Nepal is exceptional as though it were destined from early times to be reserved and kept apart. What could be more peculiar than its geographical position; the 450 miles of frontier with Tibet, and by way of contrast the former British summer capital of Darjeeling only a few miles away over the mountains! The valley of Nepal is rather to the eastern end of the country and is only twenty miles long by fifteen wide. Until a few years ago access to this valley was by an eighty mile journey on foot, animal or human, from railhead at Naxaul, part of it through the steaming Terai jungle where Nana Sahib of sinister name lay hid after the Mutiny. This natural barrier where malaria was rife had further protection by wild tigers, and could only be traversed during the cool months of the year. Even the parties of mountaineers who have been allowed to climb Everest and other Himalayan peaks in recent years have had to keep strictly to their permitted routes, and the western half of the country is still practically unknown. But there the Newars are not the predominant population and so it is unlikely that there are works of art. The rhododendron forests, the horned tragopans and other painted pheasants, the blue poppies, and the Tibetan-style lamaseries must be the interest.

It is still possible to make one's way on foot to Katmandu but such work-to-rule procedure on the part of the tourist would cause needless trouble, and there are daily aeroplanes from Delhi and Benares. The flight of three and a half hours from Delhi offers a stupendous panorama of mountains, one after the other, but the going is more often than not unpleasant owing to strong winds, and there is the knowledge that the airfield is only just long enough to make a landing. The air hostess, of that Hindu canon of beauty in which compliments and comparisons are drawn from the family of elephants, a young woman whom we were to meet over and over again in Indian aeroplanes, had stayed in her seat in sign of 'air turbulence'. But Nepalese time is a few minutes different from Indian which yields a bonus in the form of arrival over the valley a little earlier than expected, and there were no more than a few moments to look down at the green crops of the valley before we landed at Katmandu.

That it is another land and not India is at once apparent because there

21   Temple Court at Katmandu

22　A Temple Carving at Katmandu

are no turbans and the men are much smaller. It is early in March. We are 4,500 feet up, an agreeable height with no ill effects, and with the highest mountains in the world not far away. The air is marvellously cool and fresh, as if off the ice, after the blaze of Delhi. During a considerable wait at the airport the American tourists line up in hope of having Everest pointed out to them, but it is no more than an insignificant mark of snow far down the horizon. The drive into Katmandu is a disappointment for its outskirts are no different from those of many a mountain town in any part of the world. But we only see the suburbs and are soon passing huge walled domains which are the former Rana palaces, and arrive at the first of the two hotels where we were to stay for owing to a muddle our rooms had been cancelled in the first and never reserved at all in the second with the result that we were expected in neither and had to make do with the only accommodation available. For this first night we slept in the one and dined in the other in circumstances to be described later.

In the street in front of the hotel were bicycle-rickshaws of a type not met with before. A boy pedalled the bicycle, and the passenger was carried on two wheels behind him; satisfactory enough when on the down gradient into the town, but entailing a good deal of panting and blowing on the way back. So after a Chinese meal in the first of the hotels, whose proprietor has given up his bedroom in a house across the road for one of us, we set off to see the town. It was not a long way to the corner of the Tundikhel, or parade-ground, where is one of the line of Rana statues to be noticed in more detail on another day, and thence down a long new street into the old town where after a 100 yards or so we are in the Middle Ages. It is a mountain town to be known at once as such by anyone who has seen old cities in the German or Austrian Alps, or Basque villages in the Pyrenees. This is because it is in part a wooden architecture, and for the reason that the mountain light is the same. But there the resemblance stops and what is uniquely Nepalese takes over. The houses have a prodigious amount of woodcarving on windows and balconies, and as the streets get narrower the buildings to each side show the extension of the window cornice, the prolongation, so to speak, of its eyebrows, which is a characteristic of Newar building and is their excuse for still more carving. This is often the case, too, below the windows, and wooden window frames or balconies treated in this manner are the main idiosyncrasy of Newar building.

G

But now, as we get into the heart of the city and crowds are jostling us on every side, we come to something that is entirely un-expected. Immediately in front of us in the middle of the street is a three-tiered pagoda on a high stepped base, unlike anything to be seen in India and in fact reminiscent of the pagodas of Nikko in Japan. Those are earlier in date but they must have had a common prototype. Nothing of the kind is left in India in spite of the argu-ment that Nepal is a survival of ancient India with no trace of Moslem influence. Certainly it is a surprise to find this Far Eastern-looking pagoda in the middle of a street in Katmandu. It is a winter or spring town with a mountain 'touch' to the buildings and no feeling of summer or autumn about it. The red colour of many of the houses darkens the streets still further, as does the almost black wood of the carvings. There are overhanging balconies of the richest work imaginable and giving the effect of intricately carved cages set into the walls. As there is no view except up and down the street, one may think, and rightly, that the intention is that processions should be watched from them. Certain houses which must be temples have a most curious contrivance almost like a puppet stage over the door so that one waits to hear the squeaking voices of the marionettes. More-over, the same gilded or brass animals and birds we shall see later on the crestings of temples or above the 'golden doors' of Bhatgaon and Patan adorn these open balconies. To make it more puzzling there are always one or two men or children sitting there, looking down.

A few yards farther on there is a loud clashing of drums and cymbals and a crowd pouring into the courtyard of a temple. Their cheeks and foreheads are all daubed with red powder of paint-like consistency. How much they would relish that virulent, almost blinding red which has only appeared for a few years in the posters on our hoardings, with the equally virulent yellow and green that go with it, colours that have appeared, too, in the ankle socks of teen-agers in our midland cities! But this chalky, sticky vermilion makes them a little obscene and menacing in expression. Women are squatting in circles on the wet, uneven stones, chanting, as one picks one's way through the black mire of the pavement. The smearing with red or yellow paint is a Hindu custom, but Hindus and Buddhists are so muddled up together in Nepal that this festival, whatever it was, probably pertained to both religions. There were certainly Buddhist monks in the crowd which was clearly made up of the six or seven different tribes or races inhabiting the valley. A strange, shuffling person with clasped hands and something peculiar about him, stood, watching us. His head in a knitted cap was too big for his body, and but for his slow, lethargic way of walking he could have been a masker of the festival. Then we saw his bloodless face and ashen skin. He was an albino, and the most entire albino ever seen; ill perhaps, as well, we thought, with sleeping-sickness (*encephalitis lethargica*), and we remembered that albinos are regarded as lucky and half-sacred by the Hindus. But the clash of cymbals and the loud, pounding drums made nasty mental association with the albino, and none too certain of how much our presence was liked we soon came out again into the street.

And wandering on, with the bicycle-rickshaws following a few yards behind, there are pagodas and temples in every direction and we are in the Durbar Square. It is a sensation of no mean order, and to a lover of mediaeval architecture as we know it in Europe I would compare it to that moment of first seeing the tombs of Can Grande della Scala, and others of the Scaligers, in the open piazza surrounded by the old churches and palaces of Verona. The Durbar Square of Katmandu is as full of incident as that, the equestrian statues under their pyramidal canopies giving much the same excitement as these painted pagodas, though we did not on this first occasion climb their steps and look at them in detail. Hanuman Doka, the temple-palace where the Kings of Nepal are crowned, is the huge lamasery-like red building at the end of the square. The statue of the monkey-god Hanuman, sticky with the reddened ghee painted on it, and swarming with flies, is at the door. But sated with what we had seen already we were pedalled back to the hotel.

We had to remove from this after the one night because there were no rooms, and were constrained therefore to form an assault party upon the other hotel. This is one of the Rana palaces, its Russian proprietor being the best known character in Katmandu, which is understood by anyone who has seen the long line of poor persons fed by him every day at the back door of the hotel. We had only to mention Diaghilev's name to be promised somewhere to sleep for the following night, and be asked to a party that very same evening. He had been a member of Diaghilev's famous company, and with talk of 'Sergei Pavlovitch', food and drink all the more palatable to those emerged from India's 'vast' (and dry) 'sub-continent', Gypsy and

Cossack songs, and every symptom of Russian hospitality, evening merged into the early hours of morning.

The Rana palace was vast, and all on the first floor. It was an impressive token of the riches enjoyed during the century after 1848 by the Rana family of hereditary prime ministers, a situation analagous to that of the Shoguns of Japan. All the riches of Nepal ran through their hands; and it could be said that their palaces give out the impression that their owners had been wherever they liked in Europe, while scarcely a European had been to Nepal. Harem accommodation is on a comprehensive scale, as in, one imagines, the palaces of Arabian oil sheikhs; and the air of vapidity and of ignorant, total boredom is quite terrible to breathe. All this has been largely dissipated by the voices of air tourists, and the remaining traces of the Ranas are the grand stairs and a room of portraits. These, some dozen in number, are in astonishing variation upon the theme of state robes and orders, with wide choice of beard and whisker added. But, also, there is a further particularity to note about their head-dresses for all wear bird of paradise plumes in their jewelled helmets. The present King Mahendra of Nepal has a magnificent diamond-encrusted helm of this description, and the chief nobles and the field marshals of the army wear bird of paradise plumes as part of their insignia. During the hundred years of Rana rule many more of the head-dresses must have been in evidence. They are all made of the plumes of the same bird of paradise (*Paradisea Papuana*; the lesser bird of paradise), and in the Rana portraits and in their equestrian statues it looks as if the head-dresses were all made by the same jeweller. The export of bird of paradise plumes has long been forbidden from New Guinea. One wonders whence the inspiration for these head-dresses came to Nepal, and for how much longer the wearing of them will continue. Already owing to the mere number of Ranas wearing them in that hall of portraits, they seem to belong to a past age.

The equestrian statues of the Rana prime ministers are no less curious. There is a line of them along the road at the edge of the parade-ground. They are bronze equestrian figures, five of them in all, reined in or curvetting, on high mettled steeds, in field marshals' uniform, with the bird of paradise plumes in their helms. All the statues, which show a considerable degree of technical skill for a figure on horseback is no easy problem for the sculptor, could be by the same hand. Were they commissioned, one after the other, from the same sculptor? Where were they cast? Still more, how were they brought to Katmandu through the jungle and over the mountain passes? The farthest away of them or last down the line, is perhaps the most spirited. They all depict small men of Gurkha physique, and this particular warrior, the famous Jang Bahadur, turns in his saddle and is about to cut down an enemy with his sword. In general, the Rana equestrian statues are among the minor curiosities of sculpture. At least they are curious, but not ridiculous, as are the statues of Kings Victor Emmanuel II and Humbert I that disfigure the streets and squares in Italian towns.

The air of Katmandu was a delight to breathe after the heat of Delhi. But, also, it was a relief to have escaped from that swarming population. Not that the capital of Nepal is any cleaner than the Indian towns, or the inhabitants less poor or prone to illness. That they are of tougher physique being of mountain stock may be true, but the beggars are no less pitiful. Emaciated mothers, not averse to revealing a shrunken breast, will follow a stranger half-way across the town, and there are children who look as if they cannot survive. More than a few babes and adults can have little hope other than to crawl into some hole and die. One does not like to think of their sufferings in the long winter at that altitude. But in spite of the dirt and squalor it is the freshness of air in this mountain valley that stays in the memory every time we set out to explore the town, and before long we are once more in the Durbar Square. So sudden has been its revelation, and that of the older and still finer Durbar Squares in Patan and Bhatgaon, and so little has it been preluded by any previous descriptions, that it is as yet little appreciated that this is the sub-Tibetan, quasi-Indian equivalent of a surviving, unspoilt mediaeval town. Though we call it half-Tibetan, or in part Indian, it is not to detract from its being wholly Newar or Nepalese; but, also, the monuments and piazzas of a mediaeval Italian town such as Verona were mentioned a little way back, and that does compare to the 'incident' of the Durbar Square at Katmandu. It is as full of action as that, in terms of carving and architecture, and certainly the squares of the two other towns when we come to them are not inferior in interest and in technique of craftsmanship to what one would note in looking about one in a mediaeval square in an Italian town.

But now it is necessary to describe the sub-Alpine, or, rather, sub-Himalayan buildings. 'A good red brick flashed with a kind of half-glaze, and bound with beams of *sal* timber' is the comment upon them by about the only experienced English writer who has approached the Durbar Square, but his description applies more strictly to the older squares in the two other towns, as is evident when he praises 'an exceptionally good quality of clay . . . and a masonry which seems to defy all weathers by means of a system of firing which produced a hard, smooth, shell-like surface.'[1] His remarks indicate that he is thinking more of Patan and Bhatgaon than of Katmandu. The majority of the temples and houses in Katmandu, were built by Newar craftsmen for their Gurkha conquerors, and not for themselves, a difference which is soon felt in the older towns. But, in fact, the date of scarcely a single building is known for certain in any of the three towns. I would hazard the opinion that the pagodas which are so marked a feature of them, and for scandalous reasons, are hardly more than a hundred years old. Few, if any of the other buildings date from before the Gurkha conquest of the town in 1786; nevertheless, the houses and temples are in Newar, not in Gurkha style.

What is exceptional in these towns is the technique in wood carving, and where it is a matter of working in bronze the combination of hammering and casting in metal. For not only are there wonderfully intricate bronze surrounds to doors, and bronze utensils of every sort, but, also, in the Durbar Square there are bronze portrait statues. They stand on stone columns upon lotus capitals; while some of the temple doors are guarded by pairs of huge kylins, and at least one temple has giant rats on stone pillars at its door. It is evident that the seventeenth-century Newars had a technical mastery over sculpture in metal that had died out in India by the time of the Moslem invasions, while the fact that the Middle Ages in Nepal are so recent in date has preserved things which elsewhere would have been destroyed long ago. They did not excel however, at stone carving. It is a brick architecture with fantastically elaborate wooden windows and balconies, and the human and animal forms in the sculpture give to the Durbar Squares that richness of incident which reminds one of Italy. It is something never anticipated of this remote Himalayan valley.

The richness comes in part from the variety of pagodas, there being three large, and eight or ten lesser ones in the Durbar Square at

[1] *Picturesque Nepal*, by Percy Brown, A. & C. Black, London, 1912.

Katmandu. These are of different form, according to whether they are in wood or stone. The ordinary, two- or three-tiered wooden pagoda is varied by having its quadrilateral roof elaborated into an octagon, and there is a tendency to build three or four of the pagodas together, but out of line, so as to give an enfilade of their roof-lines at every height and at all angles. It is the roof-struts supporting the great overhanging eaves of this type of pagoda that are carved into figures of Hindu deities with many arms, caryatids, more often than not, of obscene intent. These are at the corners, while the wooden jambs of all the lesser intermediate roof-struts are carved with over-lively scenes of a like import. They form the sensation and the shock of Katmandu; and of the two older towns as well. It is this form of pagoda that I find it difficult to believe is much over a hundred years old.

The stone pagodas are more intricate and more Indian in appearance. One type is pyramidal in shape and much turreted, of pepperbox affinity, and raised on pillars, more a small monument than a temple, and in fact persons climb its steps and sit there under its arches. Another type is more elaborate with maybe three floors of open colonnades and a pyramid tower over them, but the inner core to such buildings is thin indeed. It is to be remarked that in the towns of the valley there are always persons climbing and sitting about in the pagodas, and that this gives them animation. There are eight or even sixteen-sided buildings of this nature, more kiosque than temple for they seem to have no interior except a stair. What rites, if any, they perform, they conduct in secret for one cannot see them. Then, looking round, there is a stone elephant at our elbow; or a tall and strange, open belfry with huge bronze bell hanging from it, but the steps up to it, and the beam over it, are as a ceremonial gallows.

So little has been written about Nepal that the erotic carvings on the wooden pagodas are still a topic for conversation among tourists rather than a theme for serious literature. No one has yet attempted an iconography of these scenes, or compared them to their parent body in India at the temples of Khajuraho and the Black Pagoda of Konarak. Two or three of the pagodas stand on their stone platforms with children playing underneath them in front of Hanuman Doka, the coronation temple-palace in the Durbar Square of Katmandu. But after the first shock of seeing them, one soon loses any sense of embarrasment and finds oneself climbing the steps and walking round the sides of the pagoda looking up at the crudely coloured orgiastic groups on the roof-struts and at the four corners only just above one's head. A small boy may point to a particular scene, or some young men watch derisively for a moment or two, but the inhabitants are inured from childhood to the mimed saturnalia below the eaves of their pagodas and take little notice of a foreigner's reactions.

Hanuman Doka has sentries at the gate and door-keepers who tell one each day to come back on the morrow. But after an attempt or two we were allowed inside past the idol of Genesh, the elephant god, in bas-relief on the left-hand wall, and inches thick in reddened ghee. The high white walls of the inner court with wooden cage-balconies projecting from them produce an effect of counterfeit snow as though there were snow upon the ground, making it look much like what one imagines the court of a Tibetan lamasery must be. It could be the setting for a devil's dance in dragon robes and ferocious masks, or for the butter festival when the lamas fashion life-size figures out of coloured butter. But this half-secular, half-religious structure, mingling the sacred and profane, has erotic scenes high up on the painted brackets like those on the pagodas just outside. It becomes more and more difficult to reconcile these blatant contradictions in one's mind, or think of a phschological background for their aberrant fancies. The interior of Hanuman Doka, so far as we saw it, is a warren of stairs and long narrow passages, but there must be more courts and inner buildings which we did not see.

That afternoon there was a grand procession. Crowds had been collecting since midday, and every balcony was crowded, particularly those two or three in the houses of mystery which have the openings like puppet stages over their doors. Children, presumably acolytes, had been sitting there for hours in the front seats. The Nepalese are as fond of processions and religious festivals as the inhabitants of Naples or Seville, and as it is a repertory with only limited possibilities all processions granted they are of a certain standard tend to be much the same. There were the usual delays with no sign of anything happening, while we took the chance that the crowd were looking away and had their backs turned to walk once more round the pagodas and examine their 'Pompeian' carvings. There were drums beating which came nearer and nearer by slow stages and at long interval, also distant sounds of chanting.

At last, after an hour at least, something was coming. It was moving at the level of the tops of the houses, coming very slowly, halting, then moving forward a few feet at a time. It in fact resembled the 'guglia' of the religious processions in Southern Italy, portable towers of wood and pasteboard which are carried through the streets; but this was made of bamboo and straw and branches, and looked very highly combustible as though it would flare up from a single match or lighted cigarette end. It swayed dangerously, and was carried forward by short rushes with much shouting and singing. At this moment a jeep with short and alert looking Gurkha officers in khaki uniforms pressed through the crowd and managed to pass the procession at a corner. It meant further delay while they reformed ranks and got moving again, taking ten minutes or more to advance double that number of yards, with the tower or 'guglia' now toppling and even touching one of the balconies. It was freed with much shaking and lurched forward again only to be stuck once more between two overhanging houses. Here it seemed likely to fall over completely and injure people with its tumbling, but once more it righted itself and came on again. In order to get a better view of it we turned and hurried down a side street where it would pass the corner in a few moments. There it stopped again right in front of us where we could see its flimsy structure and that there were persons sitting on the lower part of it, just as they do on the 'guglia' in processions in Italy. The same teams of men, too, were carrying it, except for their Mongol features and for the fact of their coming not from the image-full churches of Nola or Benevento, but the Hindu temples of Katmandu.

As it came forward men ran through the crowd in front of it beating drums and blowing horns in a way one associates for ever afterwards with Hindu festivals. Next day we were to hear the same discordant trumpeting as of conch-shells from within the temple at Pashupatinat where, also, there was exciting drum-beating from mysterious places up the steps above the river. The days of the Juggernaut procession in its glory at Puri, when the image of the god in his rath or chariot, forty-five feet high, with sixteen wheels each seven feet in diameter, was drawn forward by relays from 4,200 devotees along a broad processional road through the centre of the town from his temple to his garden house amid 100,000 pilgrims, must have been the loudest instance of this cacophany. We were hearing that din a little in Katmandu, but what made it more curious was the passage through the crowd of a Buddhist lama, a huge man in red skirt and toga and red crested hat, typical of Tibet and yet those red or yellow head-dresses have a classical air about them for their outline is that of the helms of the Greek heroes. He seemed to join in the festival with as much enthusiasm as any of the rest of the crowd, showing the duality of religions in Nepal where you may find Buddhist images in a Hindu temple, or the smeared images of Ganesh or Hanuman outside a Buddhist fane. This red hat lama came probably from one of the lamaseries under Everest and the great peaks among the rhododendron forests and the snows.

One never tires of the Durbar Square at Katmandu, and soon gets to know other and more hidden old houses and their courtyards, in the side streets leading from it. In the towns of the valley there is a distinct palace architecture, and palaces with as much right to the name as in old, but remote towns in Italy or Spain. There are better examples in Patan and Bhatgaon, but the few in Katmandu remain in the memory, and among them one in particular which we had often admired for its beautiful proportion, fine cornice and beautifully carved windows and massive doors. In some small Italian mountain town in the Abruzzi a glance at its shape and size before one was near enough to look at it in detail might suggest that it was late fifteenth century in date but in fact this little palace is certainly no earlier than the eighteenth, and may well be more recent than that in this retarded valley. It is a place where the old forms lingered almost till within living memory. In Italy there would be a shop or two on its ground floor, a blacksmith might be hammering at his forge, or it could be a wine shop, or they would be selling pots and pans. The upper floors would be offices with, maybe, the family of the owner still living in some corner. But this little Renaissance palace as one came to regard it, passing it every day, was an entity still and must be devoted to one purpose. People were living in it, and it belonged to them and had no other uses.

It was after admiring this building for a day or two that we read of a living goddess in Katmandu who is carried in a litter in processions and lives 'in a beautifully carved house which is believed to be over five hundred years old'. She is 'the living goddess Kumari, who is about nine years old', and we set out to see her, or, at least, the house where she was living. We were taken through the Durbar Square,

and straight to the house we had so much admired. The heavy old
door was open, and we went in to a court the floor of which was half
an inch thick in mud. There was a colonnade round its sides, filled
with heavy rubbish of the sort one finds in lumber rooms and barn-
yards. It was necessary to step over this in order to get into the courtyard. The inner wall opposite had finely carved windows like those
on the outside, unglazed, of course, and with wooden shutters to
keep out the cold. Now a man about forty years old came towards
us, who was a good deal taller than most Nepalese. He was the
father of the living goddess. Our guide spoke to him, and asked if
we could see his daughter. He bowed and smiled, and pointed to the
middle window.

This experience of seeing a living goddess in her palace was so
unusual that we welcomed the few moments of waiting while she
was got ready. For it was explained to us that her mother was
dressing her. According to what we could learn of her, the printed
description of her as being 'about nine years old' is three years out of
date. The living goddess Kumari is now twelve years old. Her parents
are peasants from a country village, and the children playing in the
courtyard were her brothers and sisters. She was twelve or thirteen
years old, and might at any moment now drop her incarnation and
cease to be a goddess. This would happen as soon as she received a
cut or knock of any kind, and lost a drop of blood; or, with her age
in question, at her first signs of menstruation. Then, her family must
pack up and go back to their village, taking her with them. Moreover
no one would marry her. She would become an outcast; a shell once
inhabited by the goddess, and now deserted. Another child would be
found somewhere by divination, and would be installed in her place.
No one in Katmandu would tell us for how long this had been
practised. Could it be that this palace of the living goddess was after
all 'over five hundred years old', and that we were mistaken about it?
But there is no building in Katmandu as old as that. It must be the
priests or Brahmans who set out and know where to find her; but the
living incarnations are a feature of Tibetan lamaism, beginning with
the Dalai Lama, himself, and continuing into Buddhist Mongolia
with the Chutuktu Khan of Urga and the living gods of lamaseries
on the steppe. That there should be a living goddess in the capital of
Nepal was·unexpected.

Then we looked up, for the little goddess Kumari was showing herself at the window. We could see her mother or elder sister putting her in place, and leaving her. She wore a golden skull-cap, and the corners of her eyes were painted, giving her a more than alluring appearance. It was wonderfully, and a little pruriently exciting. 'An instant later, two or three girls of the palace raise the curtains with their little fingers . . . and the King with his sword in his hand appears at the window.' That was the Khmer Emperor in the Chinese pilgrim's account of Angkor eight hundred years ago. But in the very act of looking at this seductive nymphet-goddess in her gold cap, her rouged cheeks and darkened, slanting eyes and eye-shadows, to no 'sound of distant music, or blowing of conches', she stood up and was gone. She came and went, to no music, but like a puppet at the window; and we made a small present to the father of the goddess and, also, came away.

✦✦✦✦✦✦✦✦✦✦✦✦✦✦✦✦✦✦✦✦

Chapter Nine

TWO OLD TOWNS:
PATAN AND BHATGAON

THE ROAD TO PATAN takes one along the line of Rana statues cur-vetting on their horses, and over a rushing river through the green fields of the valley, to where the brick houses begin again three or four miles away. It is a growing excitement, past buildings one would like to get out and look at, and so into the Durbar Square where the first sensation is that it can hardly be true. Nothing in India has prepared one for this museum of living incident, which could be an exhibition put on by a scene-painter and producer of genius, of a calibre that has not yet appeared. No talents, of however high an order, could have achieved the realism, that is, also, the reassurance of this dirt and squalor. The side lanes leading from the square are one entire gutter, like the contents of a septic tank spread thick upon the cobbles. In the square itself, stalls of apples and of dangerously fresh green vegetables with the contaminated water still upon them are almost touching on the miry pavement. An apple rolls off and into that black mud, and a child, who, we must hope, has some inherited immunity in his blood, picks it up and not bothering to wipe the black off its green skin, takes a bite at it. There are baskets of carrots that being root vegetables should be equivalent to a signed certificate of future illness, with trays of radishes, that if anything, must be more dangerous still. At least, no oysters or other shellfish are on sale in Patan or Katmandu, and bouillabaisse is not on the menu in either of the hotels.

The squalor is the reassurance, and but for that the Durbar Square is so old and unspoilt that it could be new. That is to say, it is as new in the dirt and squalor of diurnal use. I think it is dirtier than any town I have ever seen, to include the industrial north of England and the new, but old Haarlem of Notting Hill. Moroccan towns like Fez or Meknes, as they were in 1927, were different because they were Semitic, and some aroma of the cypress beams of King Solomon's Temple still clung about the fondouks and the stalactite medersas. But this is Himalayan and compound of Hindu and Buddhist with, it could be said, the brick tea with rancid butter of the Tibetan lamaseries not far away. Tribesmen who had never washed in their lives, with curved kukris in their belts, rubbed shoulders with ablution-loving Hindus and sadhus smeared with ashes. Women from the hills, wearing enormous nose-ornaments, were marketing at the same stall as country women of the valley in wide black skirts with red flowers in their hair. Their skirts are tucked up at the back to reveal their tattooed calves. Both times we were in Patan the same group of youths in the pages' caps of mediaeval Perugia with long sticks in their hands stood or sat about on the steps of an octagonal, it may even have been a sixteen-sided stone pagoda of many columns and little cupolas that ended in a cone or rounded pyramid. Here, how many thousands of miles from Italy, they suggested the popinjays of Umbrian hill towns, or partisans of Guelph and Ghibelline. Nor did the buildings in the background detract from the picture, except that the architecture was neither Classical nor Christian but wholly fanciful and capricious as a setting.

There was a bronze head on a kind of platform, as fine a sculpture as in any market-place in Italy, but mysterious, and of undefined purpose. Indeed, I never knew for certain if it was male or female; but it is the sculptures, and the absence of any inhibition against the portrayal of human or animal form, that makes the Durbar Squares of Nepal different from any square in front of a mosque, and invites comparison with a square in Italy or Spain. Hindu sculptures in India are in or on their temples; seldom, if ever, are their sculptures in the round. There are no monuments in Hindu cities in our sense of the word. There are temples covered with sculptures, but no statues. As those are only seen in Classical or Christian sites, the immediate comparison on seeing one of the Durbar Squares is to some Mediterranean city, in whatever remoteness of Alps or Apennines. The Durbar Square of Patan must be one of the most difficult places in the world of which to make an accurate plan. The Temple of the Emerald Buddha that seems so full of quirks and turns of incident is simple by contrast; probably because it is really haphazard with only one or two dazzling tricks to play on the spectator, while this has a bigger and truer repertory of forms with which to work. As at Katmandu there is a large old royal palace in red brick to one side of the square, and some dozen or more pagodas of widely different shapes scattered about like chessmen after, or before play. One temple stands out by reason of its gilt ornaments; and another, where the ragged popinjay youths stand all day, for its stone colonnade. But, in general, as has been said before, the temples only consist of a small cell to house the sacred images. They are not halls for worship, or ritual; but the temples, themselves, are objects of worship and held sacred which, again, explains the multitude of pagodas in a Durbar Square.

Patan is a Buddhist stronghold and has, it is said, more than a hundred Buddhist monasteries, few of which, if this be true, can contain more than one or two monks for they are rarely met with in its littered streets. But it has been a sacred place for more than two millenniums owing to legends that the Buddha came here, which is far from improbable since he was born on the borders of Nepal. Asoka, the Indian Emperor of the third century B.C. who was converted to Buddhism, and went on pilgrimage to all the places visited by the Buddha, paid particular attention to Patan and built five stupas here, one in the middle of the town and the others at its four corners. They are mounds of brick, grown over with grass, and only of historical interest as showing that Patan is one of the holy places of Buddhism. But this is not to be anticipated in the Durbar Square where the pagodas bespeak Hinduism, and that, to judge from the carvings on them, in one of its more extreme forms.

Before we come to those, how much there is to admire here in this square. It is among the most picturesque groups of buildings in the world, yet until a few years ago it could only be seen by special permission to be got with difficulty. A writer, whose book has only been published in translation in 1959, mentions how 'later', he 'managed to obtain permission to visit Patan and Bhatgaon'.[1] We are viewing things which were forbidden, but which, contrary to the usual rule in such matters are of the first order. This is not the case where other 'forbidden cities' are concerned. It could be said, beyond fear of contradiction, that there must be more and better works of art in

---

[1] *Window on Nepal*, by Tibor Sekelj, translated by Marjorie Boulton, Robert Hale Ltd., London, 1959.

Patan alone than in the Ka'aba Square at Mecca and the great mosque
adjoining, put together. But that has for long been an object of
declining curiosity whereas the Durbar Squares of Nepal are wholly
new to knowledge. They have appeared in tourists' snapshots before
learned authority has had time to write of them.

Beginning to walk down the side of the square next to the Royal
palace, there is another of the huge bells hanging from its gallows-
frame near to that mysterious bronze head, and a little after that a
bronze statue on a tall stone pillar of one of the Newar Kings of
Patan. It is figures such as these that relate Nepal to fifteenth-century
Italy even if the statues in question date from three hundred years
later. The Newar sculptors and casters of metal had inherited the
technique from classical India; or it could be that it was their own
tradition. If pagodas are a Newar invention taken thence to China
and Japan there is no reason in point of inventiveness why their
sculpture, too, should not be indigenous and native to Nepal. It is the
bronze Kings on pillars and the enfilade of pagodas that are unique in
the Durbar Squares and that would be the puzzle could one be
dropped here in the early hours of a summer morning before anyone
is about. A huge three-tiered pagoda rises on the wall of the palace
and overshadows the street, and diminishing into the distance on the
left hand there are the roofs of four or five more of them, starting
from that stone pagoda where the youths wait about all day. But
going down to the end of the street among the red brick houses there
is a public washing-place and drinking fountain of which the bronze
spouts are another instance of the Newar artistry in bronze-casting.
It is a public fountain worthy of an Italian city. There are these places
for ablution in all the towns of the valley, and their variety of metal
forms and beautiful detail call for a book to themselves.

Down in that direction the town dwindles to an end, which
seems unlikely in a town with a hundred thousand inhabitants, but
coming up again into the square, and making to the left from the top
corner of it in search of a local industry of Patan that is the making
of small boxes of turquoise and coral inlaid in metal, the street of
little promise where the boxes are made has dark alleys, more like
tunnels, leading off it. One of these, entered while waiting for a few
moments outside the shop, opens out of its darkness into a small
brick court in the middle of which stands one of the oldest pagodas
in Patan, said to date from eight centuries ago. It is a beautiful example

23 A strolling Musician
    at Bodnath

24 The Durbar Square at
    Patan

25   Pagoda of the Hanuman Dhoka at Katmandu

of brickwork, and there must be many more such surprises down the dark alleys of Patan.

The Mahavihara or Great Monastery, down another side street, is altogether more magnificent in scale, so far, that is to say, as one is allowed to see it. Its gate has huge kylin-like lions, seated dog-like, front paws on ground, but they are as big as hippopotami, which makes the more improbable their Pekinese heads and chests of swollen scale. It was only possible to look past these and into the courtyard where stands the three-tiered pagoda glittering with gold and containing, we were told, the best works of art in Patan. Farther than that, the door-keepers were unwilling to let us go. The endless subtlety of the brick buildings is the fascination of Patan, that, and the flowering of bronze at the hands of the Newar craftsmen so that it is in a horrid phrase an 'art city', in a sense that applies to no city in India, not even Fatehpur Sikhri. It is in the temples and old houses hidden away in the side streets of Patan that it appears in its true light as a Buddhist city, and one more full of old buildings than any other this side of Kyoto in Japan. But it is an exterior architecture; there is scarcely an interior worth the trouble to get inside.

The brick courts and temples of the side streets are a corrective to the Hindu elements of the Durbar Square, from which one could come away convinced it is a Hindu city, the mystery apart of why there should be pagodas here of a sort one would expect only to find in China or Japan. But are they a Newar invention, as has been argued from the admiration expressed by the seventh-century Chinese Buddhist pilgrim Hsüan-tsang for a seven-tiered pagoda in the King of Nepal's palace, implying that there was nothing of the kind in China? Or are they an imitation of classical Indian forms long since vanished? On his pilgrimage to India Hsüan-tsang visited the famous old abbey of Nālandā, one of the holy places of the world, near Patna, which is not far from Nepal. He stayed there two years, and describes it thus: 'The whole monastery is surrounded by a red wall, which encloses the entire convent from without . . . The richly adorned towers, and the fairy-like turrets, like pointed hilltops, are congregated together. The observatories seem to be lost in the vapours of the morning, and the upper rooms tower above the clouds. There is a water clock, and deep translucent ponds for bathing, or for lilies. The cloisters are endless, and the courts of many floors. The storeys have dragon projections and coloured eaves, and

H

the pearl-red pillars carved and ornamented, and the roofs covered
with tiles that reflect the light in a thousand shades, these things make
the beauty of the scene.' It would seem that the monastic skyscrapers
—written of by Hsüan-tsang as if he were a contemporary writer
admiring the Glass Towers of Mies van der Rohe at Chicago, or his
Seagram Building at New York, but with a sanctity missing from
those—were pagodas. If this is so, we get something considered
typical of the Far East, which did not exist there in the seventh
century A.D., and is really Indian, though found no more in India. At
least, and on all acounts, it is Buddhist, and not Hindu. But in Nepal,
as we shall see, the Hindus have taken over the pagoda and adapted it
to tenets that have no place in Buddhism, but are specifically and
essentially Hindu, and pertain only to one esoteric sect of that, which
is, itself, remote and alien to most Hindus.

For the strange and extraordinary carvings on the wooden struts of
the pagodas are, it has been said, the sensation and the shock of
Katmandu. And how much more so in Patan and Bhatgaon, cities
that have a deeper patina of antiquity, that seem distant and venerable
and to have come out of a remote past. Perhaps the incongruity is
more marked at Patan for this very reason. The attitude of the
inhabitants towards these carvings is one of the unexplained mysteries
of human psychology. For the carvings are not allowed to obliterate
themselves in the dust and dirt of ages. Much to the contrary, they
are continually repainted; and this had last taken place only a few
weeks before we saw them in honour of a Royal visit. No sense of
shame attaches to them in either official or sacerdotal eyes; and where
the portrayal in sculpture of like subjects in the Indian temples is for
the most part hidden away in remote places in the country, here in
the three cities of the valley of Nepal they are in full view just above
eye level of a tallish person with, as we have said, children playing
underneath them.[1]

The explanation of these scenes is to be found in the sixty-four
books of the *Tantra* which go back to the classical age of India more
than a thousand years ago, and which besides magical formula contain advice and instruction about every form of sexual pleasure; with,
in supplement as it were, the *Kama Sutra* of Vatsyayana, the latter
being a veritable encyclopedia of sex education. But the theme of

[1] Murray (1905 ed: p. 48), describing Benares, writes of 'the Nepalese temple, a picturesque
object, but disfigured by indecent carvings; it does not resemble in the least the Hindu
temples'.

Tantrism, and of Shaktism which is the parallel form of Buddhism, is made no simpler by a learned authority who refers the reader anxious to know more of Tantrism 'to the Vasanta Vitasa, the doctrine of Parakiya Rasa, and the poetry of Chandi Das, Vidyapati, and Jayadeva'. In order to effect any understanding of Tantrism at all it is necessary to accept certain concepts and not to be surprised at them. As for instance: 'None of these scenes' (this refers to precisely similar subjects portrayed on the famous, or some would think infamous Indian temples of Khajuraho) 'could however have got on to the walls without universal acceptance of initiation ceremonies of young Hindu brides as part of the ritual of marriage, of the acceptance of union between the male and female as the height of spiritual sensitiveness, and of the extension of the pleasure of the body as the vehicle of the soul in the warm, lush universe, where people came to drink the amrit of energy from the temple . . . as the mating of lingam and yoni,'[1] symbols which have in fact followed us here all the way from the temples of Angkor. The traveller in Hindu lands soon gets to recognize this stone symbol for the combination of the male and female sex-organs, which is visible enough at Angkor, but in plenitude when we come to Pashupatinat, the holy place of the Hindus in Nepal.

'It is the custom for parents to send for priests to deflower their little girls; if they are the daughters of rich people, this occurs between the ages of seven and nine, if of poor, sometimes not before they are eleven. A Buddhist or a Brahman priest is employed, according to which temple is nearer, but certain priests have a regular clientele, and a regular tariff, consisting of presents of wine, rice, silk, arecanut, and silver plate. In case of poor families, some priests refuse money. The priest may only deflower one girl a year, and when once he has been engaged for her, must refuse all other requests. On the night in question, the parents give a great banquet with music, to their neighbours, and then, with palanquins, parasols, and a band, they all go to find the priest and lead him back. Two pavilions are made of different coloured silks, and in one of them sits the young girl, and in the other, the priest. It is impossible to tell what they are saying. The sound of music is deafening, for on this night you are allowed to make as much noise as you like . . . When day dawns, the priest is led home again, with palanquins, parasols, and music. And

[1] *Kama Kala*, by Mulk Raj Anand, Nagel Publishers, Geneva, 1958, p. 34.

the young girl has to be bought back from him, with presents of stuffs and silks, or else she will always be his property and will not be allowed to marry anyone else . . . Sometimes in a single street as many as ten families have this ceremony on the same night: often their processions meet, and there is no quarter of the town where one can be sure of being spared this appalling din.' This is the Chinese traveller Chou Ta-kuan writing of Angkor eight hundred years ago, a city of a million inhabitants where family life was as sacrosanct as in mediaeval London or Paris. These initiation ceremonies brought from India to Cambodia were practised to an even greater degree in Hindu India itself, as witness the Hindu author from whom we have quoted.

But Tantrism was the ritual saturnalia of the creed carried to excess. Not for nothing were the Tantric temples constructed in remote places. The Black Pagoda of Konarak, another Indian centre of the cult, is on the lonely sea-shore for the purpose, it has been suggested, that their rites should be practised near the temple in the open air. The temple represents the chariot of the sun-god, so that it has twelve huge stone wheels under its platform, and there were gigantic statues of horses in front of it as though taking off with the chariot of the god behind them into the clouds of the sky. Here, under a pyramidal spire that, if completed, would have been 200 feet high, and below a frieze of statues of women musicians blowing into shawns, clashing cymbals, and beating drums, are figures of amorous couples, 'some of them of a definitely perverse nature', while the spokes of the great stone wheels are carved with like subjects.[1] One must be aware of writing of the Black Pagoda of Konarak as though it were a Venetian ceiling painting. This is a temptation because of its imagery as a chariot of the sun, but there is no doubt that this temple must be one of the more extraordinary architectural conceptions in the world. Its date is about the middle of the thirteenth century.

But with the carvings of the pagodas we have in front of us still in mind it is profitable to divert for another moment to 'the culmination of the Indo-Aryan genius in architecture', (Benjamin Rowland, *op. cit.*) which is at the temples of Khajuraho, not far from Benares. Here, on the turreted bases that rise up like buttresses or clustered organ-

---

[1] 'the function of these endlessly repeated pairs in dalliance must have had something to do with actual orgiastic rites conducted in association with a special cult of the sun as universal fructifying force . . . the feeling of movement, as well as the marvellous suggestion of the participants melting with love, transcends the character of the action'. *The Art and Architecture of India*, by Benjamin Rowland, Penguin Books, 1959, p. 162.

pipes at one of the temples, the provocation is in the form of a beauty chorus or triple tier of naked apsaras in poses that display 'a languid and calculating eroticism', varied on the corner piers with what the Hindus choose to call 'ritualistic embraces'. As to the beauty of these scenes there can be no two minds, and they come into a curious half-sanctity of their own at the thought that they are nearly a thousand years old. The apsaras of Khajuraho are of an extreme sophistication compared to their peasant sisters on the bas-reliefs of Angkor, where these scenes are never suggested, let alone fulfilled. Perhaps the more alluring are those with their backs turned, looking round at us, and unloosening the wisp of muslim round her hips. All have towering, high head-dresses like mitres or tiaras of flowers. But the 'ritual embraces', and this is less pleasant, include what must be initiation ceremonies between very young girls, probably nine or ten years old, and bearded men who are the priests or sadhus. It should be added that the convention of these bands of apsaras, one above the other at Khajuraho, establishes a fixed physical type in its portrayal of slim, supple bodies, their bee-black hair, delicate hands, and heavy-lidded eyes.[1] Perhaps no more excuse is needed for this divergence than its contingency to the pagoda carvings of Nepal. For Khajuraho and the Black Pagoda are among the stranger yet more authentic wonders of the Orient; the pursuit of which should include the holy city of Bhunaveshwar, and continue in the same vein as far as the great temple of Madurai in Southern India.

Compared to those, the pagoda carvings of Patan do not qualify as works of art. They are but comic strip cartoons of unpleasant nature, though the very same scenes are to be recognized as in photographs of the Black Pagoda and Khajuraho so they must all derive from the same Tantrist sources. On the corner struts of the roofs of Nepalese pagodas are to be seen one or other of the mother goddesses of the Hindus; Kumari on her peacock, Brahmani on a goose, Kali on a demon, and so forth, in all the transformations of their religious mythology; Kali for instance being another incarnation of Parvati, the wife of Shiva, but it requires a clear head to venture far into the 'lush universe' of Hindu lore. In any case a very particularized knowledge of the Tantric books would be needed in order to identify these subjects. Every form of known and unknown perversion excepting

---

[1] One writer draws attention to the absence of this physical type at the present time, and is even inclined to attribute this to past excesses.

for direct homosexuality is depicted, either on the corner posts or in the square panels of carving below the wooden struts. In many panels four or six persons are engaged, often with donkeys, goats or other animals thrown in, with a total effect which before long becomes merely laughable and comic, but which leaves one for ever afterwards with a prurient suspicion of most Hindu temple sculpture.

The crude colouring makes these scenes more farcical still. The painted beards and moustaches of the participants and their ludicrous facial expressions soon reduce the whole experience to the level of seeing dogs copulating in the street. But it does nothing to explain the manifestation. That cult of which there are signs in the ruins of Pompeii and in the Museum of Naples, as, likewise, on the paintings in any collection of Greek vases, and which portended, we are told, the fall of Greece and Rome and the necessary and natural advent of Christianity, is here displayed if not with pride, certainly without shame, and is even flaunted before the eyes of the beholder. Nor are there the signs of decadence in the population. But, on the contrary, they are remarked as a smiling people, more genial than the Indians, and the Gurkha regiments are famous as being among the finest soldiers in the world.

No authority seems to have made up his mind as to the date of these carvings, but they may be no more than a hundred years old. This would postulate that there was a large Tantrist following here no longer ago than that. But in order to understand this one would have to know more about the 'right-hand' and 'left-hand' Shaktists and their cult for, respectively, the 'white' and the 'black' manifestations of Shiva and his consort. It is the sect of the 'left-hand' Shaktists who held the ritual orgies and whose precepts are portrayed on the pagodas, and it is the truth that little or nothing is known about them. That they should have conducted their secret practises behind closed doors in three populous towns only separated from each other by a few miles is in a sense even more curious than that they built their temples a thousand years ago in remote and far off places. On the pagodas of Patan and Bhatgaon we have the decadence of what was sensually the most beautiful sculpture there has ever been for nowhere else are there bas-reliefs to match the three rows of naked apsaras of Khajuraho. They are the aesthetic antithesis to the hairy anchorites of the Thebaid, and no one could fail to be moved by their display of sensual activity and the massed orchestration of so many emotions. If they are indeed 'entertainers in the reconstructed heaven' that the structure of the temple itself suggests, and creatures 'not made of gross flesh, but constituted rather of the air and of the movements that compose their heavenly dances',[1] then their tergiversations are but a spectacle and no more our concern. But the descent in scale from when these subjects were works of art, as at the hands of the sculptures of a millennium ago, to when they have become crude carvings even more rudely coloured, is the measure of their present ugliness and squalor. What is extraordinary is that they should be as visible and even conspicuous as film-posters or newspaper placards. Perhaps the lack of inhibition concerning them is in sign of the strength and security of the inhabitants of Nepal who face up to the future without fear or shame of the past.

Bhatgaon, another former capital which we would expect to find not much different from Patan, lies out in another direction, about eight miles from Katmandu. On the way there we pass the green spring fields, and come by houses where cow dung in flat cakes is drying on the walls for fuel, in sign, we may like to think, that the yak herds of Tibet are not far away. Some tastes prefer Bhatgaon to Patan on the plea that it has better buildings, but its Durbar Square is much less effective than the Durbar Square at Patan, and indeed the prime sensation of Nepal is the square at Katmandu. Nothing can ever efface that first impression for one is not prepared for it, and had little or no idea that anything of the kind existed in this Himalayan Kingdom. Or that it should be only and specifically Nepalese, with but as much of India to it as was inevitable by reason of propinquity. That there is much of Tibet in Nepal is more evident, and the accounts by mountaineering expeditions attempting Everest or other peaks suggest a landscape and inhabitants that could be across the watershed and over the other side of the frontier. It cannot be as Tibetan as Ladakh where there was till recent years a lama-king, and where a traveller saw wild pale blue roses growing, one of the most unnoticed secrets of professional horticulture for no one paid any attention to his account which could prepare the way to the blue rose.[2] Ladakh is within the Indian frontier, but by a freak of geo-

---

[1] Benjamin Rowland, *op. cit.*

[2] 'From a bleak, barren mountainside we descended to the town of Pannamik, where the air was warm and still, and the land was covered with small, wild, blue roses . . . it was a lovely flower, with petals of true sky-blue.' *The Fire Ox and Other Years*, by Suydam Cutting, Charles Scribner's Sons, New York, 1947, pp. 11, 12.

graphy lies far to the north of all Tibet and even on a level with Chinese Turkestan.

There were country women with red flowers in their hair walking to market at Bhatgaon, to remind one that this Himalayan vale with the belt of malarial tiger-infested jungle guarding it has not only the highest snow peaks in the world, but, also, groves of mango trees and that hot, teeming India is not far away. The dual religions had come up to Nepal out of that glare of heat. Once away from the towns of the valley with their mountain roofs and mountain balconies to remind one inevitably of Brigue, of Domodossola, towns at either end of the Simplon Tunnel, or of any town in the French, Austrian, German, Italian, Swiss Alps, there is the hint of India, and with that a suggestion of the four hundred and fifty millions of the plain. This must be at its strongest and most violent when the tens of thousands of Hindu pilgrims come up from India for the religious festivals of their holy week and all but naked sadhus are to be seen stepping down from aeroplanes, for they have quickly taken to air travel like Catholic priests and nuns.

Bhatgaon had flower-decked women on the road to it but was older, deader then Patan. The way into it was dusty, and its brick buildings are yellower, dustier than in the two other towns. There is not mud in its streets, but dust and dirt. There is a long way to go, too, before it comes to life, and the feeling that it will dwindle and die away before anything happens. It is weaker and older, and there can be little left of it compared to the ant-hill life of Katmandu. But once in the Durbar Square there are those same elements that make its sister squares unique so far as the Orient is concerned, and that compare inevitably to mediaeval squares in Italy.

As in the other towns there is an old royal palace with a heavy, frowning cornice such as might really be found, in, say, Piacenza or Cremona, a notion which is immediately contradicted by the shapes of three or four pagodas of the typical form and a tall, pyramidal, stone *lingam* temple rising just to the right of them on a high stone base. In a moment it has become as rich of incident as the squares of Patan and Katmandu; but in front of the palace and standing out against the outline of all the pagodas is the truly splendid statue of Raja Bhupatindra, one of the Kings of Bhatgaon. He sits on a stone pillar some twenty-five feet tall; a column with a lotus capital and a serpent encircling the lotus stalk. One can see from far off that the palms of his hands are pressed together in the gesture of salutation with which Indians and Nepalese greet each other. He is bowing to his successors and, therefore, to future ages, much in the manner of an actor taking a curtain call and bowing to his audience, almost as though he were asking their approbation. At the same time it is clearly contrived by the sculptor that he is throned on his lotus column and, therefore, in majesty and reigning. At the back of him as at a durbar is his parasol of state. This bronze figure which has the patina of gold on it could compare favourably with almost any public statue in the world. In the Orient where so few things of the kind exist it is unique, its only rivals being the other statues in other Durbar Squares in Nepal. In this land of ancient and continual Buddhist association the statue only dates from about 1700, but its traditional form descends direct from the lion-pillars set up by the Buddhist Emperor Asoka in various parts of his kingdom in about 250 B.C.

The King's statue faces the door of the palace which is called the 'Golden Gate', the cynosure of all cameras, and the most famous single object in the kingdom, enough to condemn it according to some tastes. But it is a beautifully wrought piece of bronze work, with something about the frieze of animals upon its cornice which is unmistakably, irrevocably Newari, a term that has to be enlarged at such moments into Nepalese. They are the same bronze creatures that are to be seen over the balconies that look like puppet-theatres in Katmandu, and are divine elements or symbols of the mixed Hindu-Buddhist faith. It is reasonable to suppose there is a considerable proportion of gold in the alloy of the metal, and it has certainly a gleaming, golden effect which justifies the name.

But this is not the only square in Bhatgaon. There is another, leading down into itself, and also crowded with buildings. It has one temple in particular, which was undergoing restoration, and there-fore, enmeshed and almost invisible behind a palisade of bamboo scaffolding. This is the temple which has carved figures sitting on its steps; a rather senseless legend explaining that the lowest pair of them are two gigantic retainers of the King, ten times stronger than anyone else; that the lions above them are ten times stronger still, the elephants that much more muscular, and so on up the steps, a compe-tition in which the sculptor's art has but small part to play. In fact they are stone figures, and the Newari sculptors never excelled in those. But their reputation is retrieved in the bronzes of the ablution fountain just below, the spouts being absolute models of their kind such as would not be out of place in an arcaded square in Bologna.

It is on looking up from this lowest part of Bhatgaon that one can recapitulate what has been seen so far in Nepal, and realize how much higher it has reached than would be anticipated but for the evidence of one's own eyes. In what other unknown land in the Orient would one be reminded continually of Italy or Spain? It is the work entirely of the Newari craftsmen, a race of whom it is not mere general ignorance scarcely to have heard mention of before. The pagoda sculpture is here again, if less obstrusive than at Patan and Katmandu. Perhaps the Newari sculptors are not authors of that; their hand was so much more skilful. For proof of which it is but necessary to look once more at this fountain, and leaving that, ascend again into the Durbar Square towards the golden statue on its lotus column. That has the peace and majesty of art, and imposes the past on to the present in the way only a great sculptor can achieve. What is left of many, many more famous kings? His is but a name, but it is a presence; and the Golden Gate in front of him becomes a part of that, as if the thoughts of this king on his lotus throne were that he had once lived and reigned, and would not be forgotten. Coming away, one thinks again of his seated figure, hands pressed together, in his tall turban; he reigned before the plumes of birds of paradise came to Nepal for kingly head-dresses, in earlier, unbroken tradition coming down from classical India of which the only living evidence is in the Durbar Squares of Nepal.

Chapter Ten

❖❖❖❖❖❖❖❖❖❖❖❖❖❖❖

THE BUDDHIST SHRINES OF SWAYAMBUNAT AND BODNATH

THE ATTITUDE OF THE FOREIGNER on being admitted into Nepal and allowed to see its holy places should not be one of patronizing condescension. If we think of the spiritual recreations of, say, a mining town in the East-Midlands of England, add the places of pilgrimage we are about to visit which are in the annual programme of the Nepalese, and take away the dog-racing, filling in of football pools, and television-watching of our own countrymen, it is no more a quandary as whom to envy, whom to pity. The inhabitants of Nepal have certain spiritual things that have not been taken away from them, and long may they continue to enjoy those before they are condemned to the factory-bench and the same pleasures as their 'betters' in more civilized parts of the world.

A gentle and idyllic haunt of the inhabitants of the capital is the park of Balaju, calling it that in default of a better word for it is a little difficult to explain just what it is. Balaju lies in an idyllic landscape only a mile or two from the town, where the woods begin. The Royal family used to hunt and have their picnics here, and because of this it is kept tidier than the religious purlieus. It is nothing more than a large stone bordered tank with huge carp in it, and on the terrace below that, a fountain with a score or more jets of water spouting from it, at which devotees are making their ablutions, or, more prosaically, women are attending to their laundry. Another terrace runs along at right-angles under the trees. But the clue to this place is the water-statue of Narayan, or Vishnu, which we may even have walked past without noticing, for it rests in a smaller tank of water to itself. The god lies just under the water on a bed of snakes; the significance of the statue in this particular garden of kingly association being that the King is himself an incarnation of Vishnu. One writer says of this statue that 'the water rippling over it gives the effect of breathing'; and this is true, but, also, it gives life to the nagas (cobras) he is lying on. The water-statue is a beautiful and original invention which would have had appeal to Vignola and the sculptors at Villa Lante, that most poetical of Italian Renaissance gardens, where there is so much play with water but the conception of a statue lying in water had not dawned upon them. All in all, Balaju is to be remembered for its quiet and restfulness.

It is a sacred park of the Hindus, but if we have already seen the temples of Patan we will be expecting to find more signs of Buddhism in Nepal, and owing to recent happenings the Buddhist holy places have many Tibetan refugees. During even a first walk in Katmandu it is easy to pick out Tibetans in the crowd. They are taller than the Nepalese by several inches, are more Mongolian of feature, and are to be known at once by their dark or reddish-brown homespun clothes and bright coloured felt boots. But, also, alas! because they are thin and half-starved being no longer pilgrims, but refugees. More cheerful evidence of Tibet was visible in the first hotel we stayed at in Katmandu for the proprietor had many Tibetan apso terriers in a variety of colours, white, cream, golden, silvery gun-metal, and particoloured. They were finer, smaller dogs than those of their race to be seen in England or the United States, and he bought them from Tibetan officers who had tried to bring anything valuable with them out of the country on their flight. They came, he said, from a western province of Tibet of which he could not remember the name. He was willing to sell the puppies, and it was probably a unique opportunity of buying first-rate dogs of this breed. Their gay friendliness and delicate colours were most charming.

As though what we have already seen in Katmandu is not interesting enough there are two Buddhist places of pilgrimage to visit which are the introduction to an entirely new, but immensely old world of experience. It is exciting to be climbing to one of the holy place of Buddhism, even if accounts of the ascent are exaggerated and a road goes half-way up the hill. It is the temple of Swayambunat on a hill that legend says was climbed by 'the Lord Buddha', and beyond argument it is a holy place. The long flight of steps near the top have huge old trees of venerable shape hanging over them, and it is about here that the monkeys begin. They are the ordinary small monkeys of every monkey-drawing or monkey figure, but there is something inherently nasty and vicious the nearer that they approximate to human beings. If they are half-human they should be by that much the better for it, but this is not so. The more human, the worse they are. Naturally there is something a little touching about an infant monkey with its mother, but they are soon in our bad graces again by their hoppings and scratchings and nasty little wizened faces. The more human a dog, the more we love it because it is so dog-like. But a monkey is hateful because it is so human. Even the curs and scavenger dogs of the East have their tender moments and may respond to kindness. But the monkeys have the manners and bearing of early man and are the caricatures of humanity, demonstrating how bad were our beginnings and how much worse we may become. If we want to have the certainty of this in our own consciences we have only to compare the deer in a deer park to the monkeys in so many of the Indian temples. Deer are creatures of innocence, by contrast, and monkeys are imitative and evil.

One expects to find them in Hindu temples because their antics seem natural beside the prolix carvings, as though both are emanations of the humid heat. But monkeys at a Buddhist temple are more unexpected, and the calm of this other religion gives them another meaning as if they are lost souls. They are lingering on and must not be hurt or injured. It was strange to find monkeys at Swayambunat, and then look to the snowy mountains from end to end of the horizon. This we will be able to do in a few moments for the steps now go under a gate in the postern wall, and we are on the hilltop and inside the temple precincts. The immediate impression is of a bazaar or fair held round the perimeter or circle of a gasometer. The open space between the outer ring of buildings and the chaitya or circular mound in the middle is crowded with pilgrims, out of whose number a young man in a ragged khaki uniform attaches himself to us, saluting with idiot persistence whenever he can catch our eyes. This ghost of Albuhera Barracks, Aldershot, from the winter of 1918, kept with us all the afternoon and no subterfuge would shake him off. But, at least, it is in every folk-tale that there should be a soldier at the fair. He apart, nothing could be remoter or more far away from all experience. There were little knots and circles of people sitting round braziers, and holding services or making incantation on their own. It looked as if they were to spend the night there, but it is probable they sleep in the low circle of buildings on the outer ring after praying and chanting half-night through. One supposes they spend some days there before they come down from the hilltop.

But, also, the open space round the chaitya is hugely cluttered up with objects, mostly of bronze. There is a great gilded affair, as long as an ancient cannon, which is the thunderbolt or dorje of Indra, the Hindu god, a confusing object to find at a Buddhist temple, but it is an emblem of the Himayana or Great Vehicle sect of the Buddhists, and yet another sign of the intermingling of the two religions in Nepal. Walking round the chaitya entails jumping over all manner of stones and wooden beams with the white mass of it in front of one all the way round. It has, too, a curious jack-in-the-box quality, for being painted white it is like moonrise with an immensely distended moon, as can happen on autumn evenings, and jumping out of it is a square golden tower that has a pair of eyes and eyebrows painted on each of its sides. The four whites of the eyes to each side of the pupils have an odd staring effect. One cannot but think it is some play upon the 'man-in-the-moon', but its real meaning is the all-seeing eye of the supreme Buddha which is no profound change of imagery from the eternal face upon the earth's satellite. But, also, it is a face rising out of a tumulus for the shape of the thing is like a burial mound, whitened and made lunar. Above are thirteen gilded rings, one smaller than the other, perhaps intended for parasols, and over them a real parasol of metal. Working round the outer circle of buildings, there are a pair of platforms with wooden structures on them, and the wall is left free in places so as to get the view of the valley below and the far off snow peaks.

The prayer-wheels along the lower wall of the shrine itself are the confirmation that Tibet is not far away. One has read about prayer-wheels but probably not seen them before. They are cylinders of copper with prayers and magical formulas inside them, and all that it is necessary to do is to turn them as though it is a game of chance in some casino. Overhead are hundreds of prayer-flags to add to the excitement of this fair-like place of pilgrimage. In the meantime monkeys are leaping about and making off with the pilgrim's offerings. No place is sacred to them, and they will make a flying jump to the head of a sacred image, and leap from shrine to shrine. They have the measure of the pilgrims, and look on them with contempt as easy victims. How different is a dog's attitude, which even from the corner of its eye looks on all persons as superior beings, even while sneaking off with something! But the monkey that knows it is made in our image has a right to everything, and its only aim is to run off as quick as possible, and rob again.

Making the full round of the circle we are back again at the most crowded part of the perimeter. It is even noisier than before with what must be a wedding party. There could be many here from distant villages in Nepal who have not previously seen a European. They could have come here from 200 miles to the east of Katmandu, or 300 miles to the west. Some among them are likely to have been on pilgrimage to Muktinat, near the Tibetan border, and beyond or on the far side of the snows of Dhaulgiri and Annapurna, a pair of 26,000 feet Himalayan peaks only little lower than Everest. Muktinat must indeed be beyond the mountains. There is no road leading to it upon the maps. Yet thousands of pilgrims go there from India and Tibet, as well as all parts of Nepal. Some of the pilgrims, here at Swayambunat, had the broad cheek-bones and dark snow-burnt skins of Tibetans. Heaven knows where they can have come from, and if informed, one would not be able to find it on the map. The Tibetans, at least, one could tell were Tibetan by their height and dark-brown clothes, and above all by their boots; and there were women wearing whole trays of heavy jewellery on their persons, enormous necklaces and bracelets, nose-ornaments, and box-like ear-rings the shape and size of the pomanders of the Elizabethans. They were of enamel, and showed an obsession with turquoise, and some were almost as big as prayer-wheels. The dresses were in bright colours, but obviously for wear in howling winds, and as they were never changed had become a part of the wearer, as much so as the pelt of some fur-bearing animal. Among them were mothers who cannot have been more than twelve or fourteen years old.

It was the contrast between these wind-break females—accoutred to resist gales blowing from the aching, empty distance and the snow squalls off the mountains—and the monkeys of Swayambunat that so much struck the imagination. And how ugly, incidentally, is the race of monkeys when it develops from the basic ape to gorilla and orang-outang, or flaunts the posterior colours of the mandrill! How does their designing instinct then compare to that of the artists of genius residing in the humming-birds or birds of paradise! Here, at least, are ordinary, workaday monkeys without frills or fancies; even if the older of them have coats as mangy as that of the ghostly soldier who still followed us round, saluting. In half-idiot manner he treated them as a joke that could be turned on and off, like the music in a juke-box. They were always there, but could be sent scampering away, though like mosquitoes, like bluebottles, like persistent monkeys they came back again. There could not be many other holy places with monkeys so near to the snows. Are there monkeys at Muktinat? It seems improbable the farther side of those tremendous peaks.

As we were leaving Swayambunat, two Tibetan monks in wine-coloured togas came round the corner. They were thin and emaciate, and tall enough to be Tibetan, for one must remember that most of the monks met with in Nepal are from Nepalese lamaseries. Not long before leaving England I had copied down in my notebook from a Sunday newspaper that there were yeti scalps, so called, in the monasteries of Pangboche, Khamjung and Nemche Bazaar, and yeti hair at Thyangboche. These were lamaseries right upon the route of the mountaineering parties among the rhododendrons and the snows. One had to think again to realize one was in Nepal, and that the monks were either Tibetan or Nepalese. But one of the monks in the wine-red toga was evidently in great pain. He was not begging, but put his hand on his side when he saw us looking at him. Probably he had an ulcerated stomach, the result of the long retreat into exile. And what hope was there of his ever getting better? There is dreadful poverty and suffering among the refugees. A friend who had worked among them in India with the 'Save the Children Fund' told us of the cheerfulness of the Tibetan children, and of how they were in rags and had not enough to eat. She had formed a high opinion of the Dalai Lama, and was convinced he was a holy person. We were to see more and more Tibetans on the following day, but the ill monk made a noble and sad impression. He was in need of medicine, not money.

The other Buddhist place of pilgrimage in the valley of Nepal is Bodnath, a little farther out of the town and not in the same direction. But, also, it seems much farther away in another sense. There is nothing Indian about it, and only the shape of the chaitya is Nepalese. If indeed this is especial to Nepal, but one would need to know much more about the great lamaseries in Mongolia in order to be certain of this. Bodnath does not seem to resemble Tibetan lamaseries or places

26   Monkeys at Swayambunat

27   Chaitya at Swayambunat

of pilgrimage as those appear in photographs. What does seem to be typically Nepalese are the eyes of Buddha again on the square box or tower coming out of the top of the chaitya, as at Swayambunat. It has the same jack-in-the-box, man-in-the-moon effect, and you expect it any moment to be looking at you from a little lower down with perhaps only its eyebrows showing, and then to go down entirely and you will be told you have seen the moon setting. Only with something a little peculiar about it, as can happen on a transcendental evening.

The half-sunk, gasometer look of the chaitya is more pronounced than at Swayambunat, probably because it is bigger in diameter, and flatter. Impossible not to be reminded of passing the gas-works on a day when the tanks, if that is the right word for them, are low down. Why they sink, or rise, I confess I know not, but assume they are full when they are at the top of the cage and fill the whole of it. At Bodnath it is, so to speak, a permanently low pressure of gas and the balloon or the full moon is just above the horizon. Indeed, coming to think of it, this is moonrise more than moonset. But the jack-in-the-box is never going to show any farther out of his tower. The eyes are looking perpetually from all four directions, and it is the exaggerated moment. The more so, because whereas the chaitya at Swayambunat is at the top of its hill and therefore somewhat of a natural phenomena, as it might be the fiery crater of a volcano, or a lake filling the volcano, at Bodnath the chaitya is in the open country and seen from a long way away. It is as when in the daylight of an October evening the moon comes up out of the fields or from behind some trees and appears so large and luminous that one might think it had landed here and wonder what will happen next. If a square tower were to lift out of it with pairs of eyes painted on its four corners, then indeed, as now in this valley between India and Tibet we are in the land of bucolic comedies and it is the kingdom of Cockayne.

At Bodnath there is a slightly different form to the chaitya for it ends in a stepped pyramid, and there is a staircase up the whitened hemisphere, making it more than ever like a lunar satellite or interplanetary projectile of some kind. A stair of shallow treads for six or eight-legged passengers issuing from the hemisphere? But this detail was left unnoticed in the excitement of arrival under or past one or two archways of fanciful design. It is easy to believe that this chaitya is the biggest in existence, no difficult feat of construction because it is

I

but a whitened mound with nothing inside it. Stupa mounds, such as this, are as old in origin as the tumulus. What else is this but the whitened sister to Silbury Hill, Blue Man's Bower, or other 'British' earthwork? There is a ring of houses round it, most of which are nothing more nor less than unfurnished lodgings where pilgrims move in during winter. Bodnath is a place of pilgrimage, and is, or was, to some little extent a Tibetan winter resort. That is to say, Tibetans came here in their thousands, and from great distances, in order to escape the winter snows compared to which the valley of Nepal must be a Riviera or Costa Brava. Also, the streets and shops of Katmandu must be an attraction, not to mention Swayambunat and other Buddhist holy places. We were told that during the winter months Bodnath is full of Tibetans who pitch their tents in the fields. They would in normal circumstances have returned home by the time we were there which was in March, but some have stayed on and in addition there are a number of refugees.

Bodnath in fact is to be considered as a Tibetan holy place, and probably among the last ones left now Tibet has been 'liberated', not, of course, at the request of its inhabitants. At Bodnath we are on the edge, on the outer periphery of something extending all the way for 2,000 miles from here to the lama temple built by the Chinese Emperor Ch'ien Lung in Tibetan style in his hunting palace at Jehol, near Peking. The Abbé Huc, who never went to them in person, is almost the only witness if he can be called that, to the great lamaseries. If his account of them is not written at first hand it at least does more to fix them as a picture in our minds than the snapshots and sparse accounts of modern travellers. From Lhasa in Tibet to Urga in Mongolia is now a closed part of the world. The grand lamas, the living incarnations, the Hutukhtus, are gone, never to return. That is what makes the living goddess Kumari of such interest in her palace in Katmandu. A list of the living incarnations of only a few years ago would make curious reading, and a book that could never be written might have for subject the great lamaseries; the huge Tashi Llunpo, outside Shigatse, where lived the Panchen Lama; Natung, another lamasery near by; Drepung, which had 7,500 lamas; Sera which is bigger still, both near Lhasa; and countless others across the Gobi desert into Mongolia. It is evident that the Tibetans had a natural gift for building.

Although Bodnath in Nepal takes rank as a holy place of the

Tibetans it has no architecture. Leaving the Potala of Lhasa out of the comparison for that is obviously among the world's more impressive buildings, there is nothing at Bodnath to compare with the chorten or shrine of Shigatse, the second city of Tibet. This is a building of five painted terraces of wavering cornices, with an interior, at least, unlike this whitened mound, and the top part of it does in fact a little resemble the top parts of both Swayambunat and Bodnath, but without the painted eyes which we now see looking at us again headlong down one of the side alleys of Bodnath, the more curiously for having been these few moments out of mind. In fact the moon is rising out of the end of the street, where there is an elaborate and rather pretty archway leading to it, though it seems in some way tied down and tethered, and has strings of prayer-flags that go from its cupola to the surrounding houses. We are near enough now to see that they are rather like an owl's eyes, and there is even the suspicion of a nose or beak. But back again to the eyes and the eyebrows over them for one cannot look away for long.

There are prayer-wheels in bronze cylinders all round the mound. And now coming round the side of it we meet a band of musicians. Or they are lying in wait for us, knowing we would end up at the house of the Chini Lama. But more of him later, for we have enough at the moment with the musicians. There are three of them playing some sort of primitive stringed music, a broken down, poor relation of the violin, that has never known better times, and has hope only in the slum streets in Central Asia. Some attention has lately been paid to the folk music of Nepal, and the two tunes they played certainly stayed in the memory, though we were told their theme was Indian film songs. This was borne out in the antics of a dreadful small boy, perhaps three years old, who waggled his hips, snapped his fingers, and strutted along at a snail's pace in front of them in parody, we imagined, of a belly-dancer. It was impossible to dispense with this child. He knew we would be spending an hour or more in the circle of Bodnath, looking at the chaitya and the Tibetans, and calling upon the Chini Lama, and he was ours for all that time. There were no other foreigners. If we looked round only for an instant they would start up one of their tunes and he would begin wriggling round the ring again.

But there was a stranger character with them who was the singer. We did not see him at first. He must have come out of one of the houses. He had a very high, thin falsetto voice, and his physical frame could not have been more suited to that. The whole of him, voice, style, manner, clothes, person, were in some strange way lunatically southern, in the sense that he could have been a street singer in some southern town like Catania or Syracuse. Impossible to think he had not somehow or other crept into the gallery of an opera house, and was imitating the singers. But he was like a beggar or street singer of a hundred years ago, not today, and I could see him in some poverty-stricken town in the Two Sicilies.

His broad-brimmed hat was of the day of Fra Diavolo and Masaniello, but on the operatic stage, and not in life. He wore some-one's cast off coat several sizes too big for him, and a goatherd's white baggy trousers—as I remember them driving their herds with clanking goat bells through the streets, and stopping to sell milk at the doors of houses, in Sicilian towns. The long stick in his hand was a shepherd or a goatherd's stick. The only touch of the Orient was his ragged and filthy cummerbund. He had trachoma, or some other eye disease, and the poor creature was nearly blind. It gave a blank or empty expression to his eyes. But, worse than that, was his perpetual smile which was in parody of the 'sunshine of the south', as you can hear that in Neapolitan songs and in their singers. It is this they are 'selling' in their songs. What could all this have to do with Tibetan pilgrims in Nepal? What indeed! For all his trade was with nomads come down from the snows. Having seen and heard him, what else can one say but that it was there. I can always see him somewhere in that ring of houses round the whitened, lunar mound.

Of course, the strategic point in that circle is the house of the Chini Lama. In fact the musicians were playing just at his door. The Chini Lama is the chief priest of Bodnath. According to the leaflet in the hotel, 'this stupa is cared for by the Chini Lama who is reckoned to be the representative of the Dalai Lama', and that announcement in itself is enough to make him interesting. In a way it is equivalent to visiting the Russian monastery of the old régime on Mount Athos, except that beyond contradiction this is more remote and far off. Both in one, it is a relic of old Tibet and China; and not so old, at that, because Tibet, now gone irrevocably and beyond recall, was a 'going concern' only three or four years ago. It appears that he is called the Chini Lama simply because his grandfather came from China, let us suppose seventy or eighty years ago. Again, the Nepalese know him as the Chini Lama, with the 'is' pronounced like double 'ees', and one did not know it was the same word in Nepalese. His grandfather must have become a lama, and eventually chief priest or abbot of Bodnath, though the only other monks we saw were obvious Tibetan refugees. But the Chini Lama must have his place in the Tibetan hierarchy, though the emphasis seems to be on his having come here from China as if that were something unusual and extra-ordinary.

We asked for an interview and were allowed in to see him. The Chini Lama lives in one of the three-storeyed houses in the ring, and several charming looking young women of his family stood at the windows while we were waiting. We were ushered upstairs into a room furnished a little like the salone in some small hotel in Italy. Gilt-framed mirrors, that is to say, and sofas and chairs with fringes and bobbles hanging from them. There was a brightly flowered carpet on the floor. A man about thirty years old received us who was the Chini Lama's son. He wore ordinary European clothes, and talked in broken English till a pretty young woman came and joined in the conversation. She is the Chini Lama's daughter. The talk was of Tibet and the plight of the refugees. But the Chini Lama is not a poor man. He owns several farms between Katmandu and the mountains where he spends part of each year. As representative of the defunct Ecclesiastical authorities in Lhasa he must be in some danger of being overwhelmed by the demands of refugees. Perhaps, to listen to the local gossip concerning him, he is too clever to be taken in in this way. Whether the farms are his own, or monastery property, their income would not last long if shared out and the days of the lamasery and the chief lama would be numbered.

Then the Chini Lama appeared in person, wearing a compromise between Chinese and European clothes. He is clean shaven, in horn-rimmed spectacles, and speaks a few words of a score of languages. One has the impression that his house must be one of the most com-fortable in Katmandu. The rather desultory conversation about the refugees went on, and it appeared he was hearing continually from the Dalai Lama in exile in India. He had often been to Lhasa in the past. And now that is another world vanished in favour of, so called, new and brave horizons. But there must be many besides myself who prefer lama-owned to collective holdings. The fate of Tibet has been a terrible tragedy. The world is poorer for its lost incident, and a civilization as interesting as that of the Incas has perished under our eyes. It is a duller day with the Potala of Lhasa without its Dalai Lama than that of most other emptinesses that were once inhabited. The Chini Lama, having now offered to be photographed in his robes, went out of the room for a few moments; and it was impossible not to think during that interval of the dying world of which he was part. More than one writer has described the Potala of Lhasa as among the most imposing buildings in the world, and although lost and gone it is by now familiar from photographs. We know the look of it from afar; the towering lines of windows, the staircase leading up to it, and even the gleam of gold from the tombs or shrines of seven dead Dalai Lamas on its flat roof. In the same way it could be said that we know by sight, even by sonorous sound, the nine-foot long bronze trumpets of the lamas, and the racks that hold them and are like the bronze pedestals of early astronomical instruments. What one would have wished to see perhaps were the houses of the disposers of the dead, which were made of the horns of slaughtered animals. And in another vein altogether, the gold lacquered hats of the shapés, and the aristocratic Tibetan ladies in their brocaded dresses, aprons in lateral stripes of brilliant colours, and horned head-dresses—one form worn in the capital, and another at Shigatse—like the pikehorn head-dresses brought to the court of Richard II by Elizabeth of Bohemia and still to be seen on mediaeval tombs in England.

From there my thoughts went to the lamas who had themselves walled up alive. One has read accounts by travellers who were present when a novice had himself bricked up for an initial period of seven years in utter darkness; or having emerged after years, had himself returned to it. They took a trumpet made of a human thigh-bone with them into the sempiternal night. But how much of this was genuine? Did any traveller have the curiosity to examine the backs of their cells and look for any other opening? They had no light with them in their cells, and sat in darkness. Food was passed to them through a little opening. Were they never given a renewal of clothing? The purpose of their immurement cannot have been contemplation so much as negation, and withdrawal into absolute vacuity. This will have been achieved after a very few weeks of incarceration. Would not blindness, dumbness, deafness, follow after a few years? Yet there are accounts of conversations with lamas who have undergone this experience, and were willing to return to it again.

How many of these extreme votaries were there at any one time? In some of the lamaseries there was a row of the stone cells. One would like to read a report by a competent doctor on one of these emerged ascetics. In *The Fire Ox and Other Years*[1] there is an account of a visit to a gompa (lamasery) near Gyantse. Here were lamas who had themselves walled up 'for periods lasting from a month to a life-time'. The author saw and photographed one monk who had spent seven years in darkness, was partially blind from it, and had a permanent bump on his forehead from his continual prostrations in prayer. He was then taken to the outside of one of the cells where the monk escorting him, although it was not the hour when buttered tea would ordinarily be passed through the opening, 'knocked on a movable board and then removed it. Slowly a hand encased in a huge glove emerged and wavered in the air as if it led an independent existence'. Apparently the very size of the glove was to prevent more than that amount of him from being seen. The hand in the glove felt slowly round the stone sill and then removed itself. There is a horrifying photograph of the huge hand feeling round the stone slab which is raised on other stones, and is a little like a primitive altar. The young lama said; 'He's been in there many years. One day there will be no answer when I knock with the buttered tea.'

Now the door opened, and in came the Chini Lama in his robe of Imperial Chinese gold brocade of the sort that was worn formerly in Lhasa. We talked for a little longer. Various objects were for sale. There were pairs of the Tibetan boots of coloured felt, and prayer-wheels. Indeed, almost everything except the drum made of two human skulls which the Chini Lama told us he performed upon during sacred dances. My son bought a trumpet made of a human thigh-bone which he intended for use at home as a dinner gong. There were several of the thigh-bones, and we wondered where was their source of supply. Then we came out into the thin sunlight, and the Chini Lama posed for us in his gold robe, wearing a golden, but not lacquered cap, and holding a cup and a rosary and some other insignia in both hands. The street musicians looked on in silence, but when his back was turned began their song again. And the zany in the wide brimmed hat, dressed like a goatherd, was still smiling with eyes that watered as he sang of the false south.

[1] Suydam Cutting, *op. cit.*, pp. 194, 195.

Chapter Eleven

❖❖❖❖❖❖❖❖❖❖❖❖❖❖❖❖❖❖❖❖❖❖❖

PASHUPATINAT

DESPITE THESE INCURSIONS INTO Buddhism at least the valley of Nepal is predominantly Hindu, and the proof of it is a visit to Pashupatinat. On one occasion we went there from Bhatgaon, crossing a river near a wooded hill where the trees had what looked like carobs or other heavy fruit hanging from the branches, but they were flying-foxes. The animals were asleep head downwards, clinging to the boughs with their claws, and with furled sails, which is to say, wings folded like a grasshopper's wings along their sides. It was only a pity we did not see them when they stir and begin to wake, and start to glide from tree to tree. For, of course, they are gliders more than flyers. They cannot rise to more than a certain height, and then make long, swooping trajectories, but never for more than a few yards. How many millions of years must they have taken to evolve even this limited degree of flying! There was a time when there were no winged creatures of the air. What little truth there is in inherited physical traits should enable the hybridists, were it worth their while, to further trim or hoist their leathern sails, curtail their flight, or give it greater soaring power.

The flying-foxes in their oddity were a prelude to Pashupatinat. But it is even better to go by the ordinary road from Katmandu, because then we have a taste of the idyllic delights of the place as extolled by devout Hindus. It is as holy as Benares, and on the sacred river Bagmati that flows into the Ganges. All a Hindu desires is to die here, if it can be done, with his feet in the holy water of the river. Here are the burning ghats; but till now we are only in the holy woods and glades. There are ecstatic accounts of these, for it was here that the god Shiva escaped from a hunting party by transforming himself into a gazelle. One adept, whose account I read, describes the rapture of walking at dawn in these holy places. That was after first

bathing in the river, but we are not as far as that; we are but nearing
Pashupatinat, and admiring its old trees and green mounds and dells
for it has some little of the character of a sacred park.

It was here that we met with a sage walking along the road among
the trees. For a first meeting with one of the holy men of the East it
could not have been more auspicious. It was indeed the sadhus of the
Indian sub-continent who were the magnet drawing us in this direction. There are, as we must know, many classes and kinds of holy
men, but it is as well to begin with this one. His robe was neither
orange, nor saffron, but very clean and of a dark velvety dahlia red.
He must be, not a sadhu but a swami, we were told by the friend
accompanying us who lived in Katmandu. The swami had dark-
brown hair and beard, and a beautiful and kindly face, not disfigured
by being smeared with ashes, by having simian white horizontal
stripes down cheeks and forehead, or being daubed with red or
yellow paint. So benign and beautiful was his appearance that,
although he was walking away from Pashupatinat while we were
being driven towards it, we could not let him pass and see him but for
that moment. It was of no use offering him a lift as we were making
for opposite directions, and the only stratagem was for my son to get
out and run after him, and ask to be allowed to take his photograph.
The sage agreed, and coming up after that to the window of the car
slowly wrote out his name and address for us in capital letters, for he
would like a copy of the photograph for his pupils. He was on
pilgrimage here and came from Southern India. This swami left a
beautiful impression, and how often have I thought of our brief
meeting with him under those holy trees!

Looking back, we saw him turn round and wave his hand. In a
moment more he was gone behind the rocks as the road curved and
we were in Pashupatinat, to my taste and mind the most interesting
of the holy places of Nepal, and so I make two or more visits there
coalesce in order to form one long account of them. Already, by the
end of this sentence, we are entirely surrounded by beggars, old and
young, and of all degrees of mental alertness. If a window of the car is
lowered ten or a dozen hands are inside at once, and their piteous
faces are but an inch or two away. We shall see, too, that the monkeys
are in competition with them. But not for the moment. The beggars
have the town as far as the river bank to themselves. Down there,
and on the other bank it is another matter. But even in this short

time a sadhu is in sight, and a disappointing one, with too much in him of 'Prince Monolulu', the Jamaican racing tipster of Ascot and the Derby, all black face and ostrich feathers. In fact he is more clothed than most sadhus, in a dirty shift reaching to his knees. But his conical hat is completely covered over or encrusted with small round objects like conkers, or, at least, they are some form of tree fruit, and he has a treble necklace of the same reaching to below his waist. In short, no ostrich plumes, but the manner of the tipster, and we decide in our collection of sadhus to give him a miss.

We go down a curving street to the river with all the beggars of Pashupatinat after us, and a good few in front of us as well, and decide there is too much incident to take it in all at once, and halt therefore at the bridge. The sacred groves of the swami now seem far away, and we are in the midst of every form of rascality, and worse. One or two beggars of a playful blend of idiocy are the holy innocents of the place, and they are continually tweaking our elbows and looking at us with pitiful and pleading eyes. Others are more guileful, offering to lead us up the steps on the other side, and inferring by their manner that this excursion of a few minutes will be equivalent to crossing the Himalayas with an experienced guide. It is midday and very hot indeed, though nothing to the heat in Delhi, and all the time there is beating of drums on the far bank and sinister trumpeting behind us in the purlieus of the temple.

With only a glance at the burning ghats below us on the left-hand side we go back over the bridge towards the temple. Another sadhu is coming towards us down the street and he, too, is delighted to have his photograph taken. It is not so with all of them. There are some who bitterly resent the liberty, and from their gestures of refusal seem likely to provoke a riot. But the sadhu in front of us is of mild sort though his long hair and beard are those of a Rumanian Gypsy. But the Ciganjes of the horse fairs never go hatless. Or so they were in the past before the Nazis killed most of them. They could make all the effect in the world out of a battered felt hat. This sadhu, too, was almost certainly an Indian, to make one more sure in one's mind than ever that the Gypsies were in origin an Indian tribe. The hair, the beard, the look in the eye, the walk above everything else, are unmistakable evidence. We were to have more proofs of this later in the bear-leaders we passed on the road between Agra and Fatehpur Sikri, and in the Gypsy-like poorer classes of Rajputana, particularly at

Jaipur where perhaps the most beautiful dresses in the world are worn. Farewell to them till then, now we are in a town of sadhus and holy men!

Most of those we have seen until now in this sacred place in Nepal are Indian, and it has been calculated that in the whole of India there are not fewer than five millions of them. A large proportion are pure ruffian, but in the quest for picturesqueness, not holiness, rascality is no criterion. Some are tall naked fellows, of clothing all but invisible, who walk firm and fast with strong tread, their iron trident to denote they are followers of Shiva in one hand. They are of derisive manner, often, and walk ahead, laughing, defiant in their ruffiancy. Others are naked, almost, but rubbed all over with ashes;[1] their hair matted with dust and hanging in long twists; and with the red or yellow circle of paint in the middle of their foreheads. When thinking of their wild and ferocious picturesqueness even today, we must remember the thirty centuries of experience behind them, and that what we can see now is as nothing to what they have been before. If a procession or march past of, say, the five hundred most extreme in their different categories from all over India could be arranged to take place, we must conceive of another, over and above that, of all the most extreme there have ever been. Then, indeed, we would see un-imaginable sights and it would be the most astounding spectacle in the history of human religions.

It is not only in the prolixity of ornament that the Hindus are in-exhaustible. Their repertoire of religious appearances is unlimited, and has room for the swami of this morning who could have come from and been going back to Blake's 'House of the Interpreter' and the ferocious athletes of the banks of Ganges, fanatics of centuries gone by who would look over the river into the sun until their sight left them, and still they gazed with sightless eyes, or those more

[1] 'The skin is usually rubbed over with ashes, prepared by some ascetics with the greatest of care, being sifted repeatedly through folds of cotton cloth till it is quite as impalpable as any toilet powder. The application of the greyish-white powder to a dark skin gives a peculiar effect, which, I believe, is not without attractiveness in Indian eyes.' *The Mystics, Ascetics and Saints of India*, by J. C. Oman, 1903, p. 37. The sadhus who wear their hair coiled up carefully on their heads are jhuttedarees; those who wear their hair falling in disorder about their face are bhouveeahs. Foreheads painted with a central line, or shaven heads, denote followers of Vishnu; the others are followers of Siva and Brahma. One extreme cult paint their foreheads with vermilion dissolved in oil. Most often met with is the trifala—three lines drawn upwards from near the meeting of the eyebrows; central line white—others red, painted with roli, a preparation of turmeric and lime—the white lines are painted with gopichandana, a calcareous clay procured from Dwarka, out of a pool in which according to the Krishna legend, the gopis (milkmaids) drowned themselves on hearing of the death of their lover, the divine Krishna. Dwarka is in the peninsula of Kathiawar, and was till lately in the dominions of the Gaekwar of Baroda.

familiar in story who raise an arm, or even both arms into the air, and do not lower them till they are fixed for ever. J. C. Oman, in his *Mystics, Ascetics and Saints of India*, describes meeting an ascetic of this sort who had held both arms in the air for eight years, and hoped to do so for another four years before lowering them. The arms were held in the most uncomfortable position, making it difficult for the ascetic to get any sleep. H. H. Wilson, in his *Religion of the Hindus*; London 1862 (p. 234) describes this particular sect 'who extend one or both arms above their heads, till they remain of themselves thus elevated. They also close the fist, and the nails being necessarily suffered to grow, make their way between the metacarpal bones, and completely perforate the hand.'[1] Another sect hold up their faces to the sky, till the muscles of the back of the neck become contracted, and retain it in that position; while J. C. Bhattacharya (*op. cit.*) identifies these sects with uplifted hands, another who always remain in a standing-posture, and yet another who with their feet attached to the bough of a tree, keep their heads hanging downwards. J. C. Oman saw, and even photographed, one of these latter, swinging head downwards on occasion over a fire. To spend their lives reclining on a bed of nails was no unusual luxury, and this is still in common practice though we did not come across it. But the men of the trident were in plenty at Pashupatinat that morning, if in nothing like their number on days of festival.

It had been our intention to try and get inside the main temple which glitters and sparkles with its golden roofs on this hither side of the river. The view of it could scarcely be more exciting, owing as usual to the absence of any preconceived plan, and made more thrilling by the incessant blowing of trumpets to the extent, nearly, that it could be a trumpet factory. We tried at the little door on to the street, but were refused entry and led by our escort of beggars round the corner to the main door through which one could just see a huge, reclining golden bull. This is Nandi, the bull of Siva, and at that moment the trumpets rang out louder than ever, and for once in

---

[1] 'Among the curiosities of Sounaghut' (in Bundelkund) 'I must not omit to mention a fakir whom I saw one day. He was a goussain or religious beggar. Upon his face was tattooed in red the trident of Neptune; his hair, tied in a knot, was rolled above his head, forming a sort of pointed mitre; and his body, which was very lean and quite naked, was besmeared with ashes. But the most revolting thing about him was his left arm, which, withered and quite stiff, stood out perpendicularly from his shoulder. Through the closed hand, bound round with strips of linen, the nails had worked their way, and were growing out upon the other side; and the hollow of this hand, which had been filled with earth, served as a flowerpot for a small myrtle bush. The outstretched and stiffened arm made this wretched being look like a prophet of evil.' J. Rousselet, *India and its Native Princes*, 1876, pp: 323, 324

unison, with a brassiness to match the golden statue. We were to learn later in more than one place in India that this stray and apparently haphazard blowing of horns and trumpets which makes so strong an impression, is the work of no more than the legendary 'old man and a boy'. It was probably so in this instance but the trumpets seemed to ring out from every corner of the building. That brass bull, gleaming like gold, and lying out in the middle of the temple compound in the blaze of heat, as though ruminating in a gilded meadow and chewing the cud perhaps of golden lilies, and the ascetics striding along with their iron tridents were, it could be, his cowherds or his shepherds!

Quite obviously there was no admission, as, in fact, is nearly always the case in Hindu, but not in Jain temples. And we walked round again in order to come down to the river, passing the little side door and taking a last look through it as we went by. It was then, that, taking just one step inside the porch, and looking to the right into the darkness of what could have been the porter's lodge, we found that extraordinary person sitting, cross-legged, in the little brick cell. He never moved from that posture during the time we saw him on two consecutive days. If we were surprised to see him, he behaved almost as though he were expecting us, and certainly all the powers of bringing about astonishment belonged to him and were on his side. He wore a short blue coat of European cut, and his skirt or dhoti was of chequered cotton. His hands were on his knees. His staff was against the brick wall. He began talking in English immediately he saw us: 'I poor man. I hungry. I cold. I always hungry. I eat nothing. I have no clothes,' and so on, in a kind of parrot jargon, starting it over and over again, as though he had learnt it by ear, and did not understand what it meant. But he was not begging, and would not take money. It seemed more as if he were making excuses for being found here in his little cell in such poor clothes. 'I sleep here. I live here. I poor man. I never go outside.'

But the oddest and most telling thing about him was his features. His hair, grey with ashes, was piled up in a topknot on top of his head. There was a curious white disc on his forehead with a wisp of hair apparently going through it, the upper part of the forehead was painted yellow, and there was a gash of red paint in the middle of it, and running down it. But the surprise of surprises; below all that holy paint, as opposed to war-paint, he had blue eyes and, I thought, a decidedly European cast of face. In fact, a long oval face and white, even teeth. He was, most of the time, half-smiling. Again and again one returned to his European-looking face and blue eyes, that one could see by making some excuse to peer closer at him in his cell, leaning forward to examine his wooden staff, and so forth. Our companion asked him in his own language where he came from, and he answered from a distant part of western Nepal. Whenever we saw him he was talking with animation to a group of small children who evidently found nothing in the least peculiar about him. From their point of view he was a perfectly normal human being exercising a quite ordinary profession, and they even seemed to be in some sense his pupils.

Did he ever move out of that cell? I had the vision of him moving round the temple in the early morning mist. There was no sign in his cell of any form of lighting, and that is why I conclude he went to bed and got up with the sun. Nor any means of cooking, from which one assumes he went elsewhere for his food and perhaps ate in common with other temple sadhus. There were one or two thicknesses of matting on his floor so he spent the day and slept there. I even wished we could call at some time when he was not at home, could wait for him and see him walking back and getting down to work again, as when the bus-driver climbs into his seat, or the instrumentalists file back into their places and the show begins, the last metaphor coming into my mind because there was something of the actor in him. He had an actor's features against a bare brick curtain. Since seeing him, I have often woken up and wondered if he was sitting there, cross-legged, in the darkness. Or does he stretch out to sleep across his cell? I have the feeling that even in the middle of the night, at three or four o'clock tomorrow morning, if I looked into his cell, he would not be surprised to see me, but would begin again: 'I poor man. I here all day and night. I go hungry.'

But our collective interviews with him are at an end, and we walk away from him down the hill towards the river. And now we find at the foot of the bridge in rapid juxtaposition next to each other, as though of intent, one of the little pagodas not nearly as big as a bandstand with, I thought, more than usually obscene carvings on its wooden struts, and what must have been some half of all the monkey population of Pashupatinat. Two or three children were sitting on the ramp, and one could have wondered if the carvings were for their edification or that of the apes, but neither the young humans nor their imitation were in the least interested. One of the bronze bells, but in much smaller version than usual, hung below it on its scaffold. And we walked on to the bridge with the monkeys after us more than the children, and stood in the middle of it and looked to either side.

First of all back to the temple from which we had just come, of which one could see the double pagoda roof of bronze, and conjecture what might be the subjects of the carvings below its eaves, on the side facing the golden bull-calf and nearest to the sadhu in his lodge. The temple had a balustraded wall in front of it, and steps down to the river, with three little bell-shaped buildings like shrines, or bathing-huts upon the embankment. But there was a vast number of exactly similar buildings, row after row of them, upon the opposite bank. They are all temples of Siva, our friend told us, with a lingam in each of them: but in lingam-yoni form which is a stone phallic pillar with a hole and an incision on one side to symbolize the male and female genital organs combined together. It represents Siva as god of fertility and reproduction, and the crudity of the symbolism no longer disturbs the educated Hindu mind. What an extraordinary religion it is that can encompass and embrace within its folds the swami we met with walking under the trees, the door-keeper sadhu, and the trident-bearing fanatics of vigorous tread, all no farther afield than the banks of the Bagmati at Pashupatinat.

But this was no moment for general reflection because so much is going on within only a few feet of the bridge on which we are standing. While we are intent on looking down to either side, the monkeys of the place now become in mind little more than immensely magnified, stingless, but thieving mosquitoes, a sort of human parasite, worrying incessantly, and in minuscule human shape. It is indeed their being in duodecimo version of ourselves, being coated with fur, and having such tiny skulls and bald monkey faces that is wrong with them, and makes them less pitiful than other creatures. If one put anything down on the parapet they would be off with it in an instant.[1]

On one side of the bridge are the bathing places for lustration in the holy water, and on the other are the burning ghats, both on the same bank of the river. On the far bank are the lingam-yoni temples, a hundredfold of them; and we may take our choice whether we prefer

[1] According to a recent book the United Provinces of India, now known as Uttar Pradesh, has a population of twenty-three million monkeys, that consume almost as much food (including what they destroy) as the human population. The State authorities would like to see their number reduced but the people are very averse to their destruction.' *In Search of a Yogi*, by Dom Denys Rutledge, Routledge & Kegan Paul Ltd., 1962, p. 177.

to think that the devout with the pagoda carvings constantly under their eyes and a notable specimen, as we have mentioned, at the foot of the bridge only a few feet away, do really apprehend their meaning, or that, as another writer merrily suggests, the stone objects in constant repetition have no more meaning for them than the maypole on a village green. It is at the back of, and above the lingam-yonis that there is perpetual and mysterious beating of drums in answer to the blowing of trumpets from across the river, and it is here we surmise the priests' cells are situated and the one-room homes of the trident-bearers.

But to the burning ghats which entails coming off the bridge again, and down to the river! In respect of which Pashupatinat is a miniature, but a *very* miniature Benares. On a plan of the latter city I have just counted seventeen of the ghats, all on the left bank of the Ganges (and many more than that described in the text),[1] and in the account of that city beside much mention of lingams, my eyes fall on the description of the Durga or 'Monkey Temple', so called from the number of monkeys in the large trees near it, and which contains a 'band room' where the priests 'beat a large drum three times a day', from all of which it is apparent that Benares and Pashupatinat have much in common. Incidentally, are the 'staff-bearing ascetics called Dandi Pants,' of one of the Benares ghats, the same as our trident-bearers? But the ghats here at Pashupatinat are on a very small scale. There are only some half-dozen of the little platforms standing out into the water. Both times we were there, business was very quiet. Only on one of the platforms, there were a few burning cinders, and that was all. However, it is not difficult to imagine it with every fire burning.

Along the river beside the ghats is a low range of building with arches under it, where the attendants and stokers of the holy fires rest in the shade. There is no air of solemnity. The corpses are, one assumes, impregnated with unguents that catch fire easily. It is kindled by the son. or another male relative, who sets fire to a piece of wood in the corpse's mouth with a torch. There are varying accounts as to whether the intestines or the skull take the longest time to consume away, but in any event it is a process of three or four hours during which time the relatives keep watch on it before the ashes are taken up and thrown into the river. I have never seen a

---

[1] Along the whole length of the left bank of the river there are about fifty principal ghats at Benares.

28 Sadhu Porter at Pashupatinat

29 The Chini Lama out-
side his Palace at
Bognat

30 Gilded Statue of Rajah
Bhupatinda at Bhat

statement of how many bodies are consumed in a year at the burning
ghats in Benares, but it must run into many tens of thousands. At
Pashupatinat it may not amount to more than a few hundreds, yet the
waters of the holy river must be clogged and polluted with ashes. Nor
do I know if the custom of suttee was prevalent in Nepal; perhaps in
view of the strong Buddhist influence this is unlikely. This burning
alive of widows which is one of the horrors of religion seems merci-
fully not to have been widespread, but to have been confined to a few
instances, though in places as beautiful as Udaipur apprehension is
roused on passing the chhatris or cenotaphs of the Maharanas and
other ladies in the Mahasati or Royal place of cremation which is
enclosed by a high wall.

As we looked at the burning platform a particularly arrogant sadhu,
almost naked, but leprous with ashes, strode by, exchanging a ribald
jest with other hirsute ruffians lolling under the arches. A joke is a
joke in any language, and this was no mere comment on the weather.
Murray's *Guide to India*, (1905 ed:) says of Benares that it was visited
in a year by a million pilgrims, while the number of Brahmans
residing in the place was over thirty thousand. Did this include sadhus
and other holy men? Perhaps it is a safe calculation to cut off the
thousands at Pashupatinat and say there are thirty resident sadhus.
Most of them are certainly Indian. Apparently passport formalities
are waived, in the official phrase, in the case of holy men from India.
One would like to know more of the procedure. Do they attach
themselves to the temple on arrival? Or are they freelances, coming
and going as they please? They carry no recommendation, one
opines, as surely as they have no luggage with them. They are indeed
holy tramps or vagabonds.[1] They hitchhike or come on buses, perhaps travelling in a modicum of clothing and throwing it off on
arrival, as do tourists on reaching a beach upon the Mediterranean

---

[1] 'The necklace of little gleaming stones and the "golden flies" tells of far wanderings to
the shrine of Kali at Hingalaj, in distant Baluchistan' (those who have visited this shrine adorn
their hair with metallic beads having the appearance and lustre of gold and called Swarna
Makshi or 'golden fly'); 'the white conch-shell on the wrist tells of a visit to Rameshwar in
the far south; while rude armlets of iron, brass or copper are well-known badges of visits to
the lofty Himalayan monasteries of Pashupatinat, Kedarnath or Badrinath.' Ramesvaram
is a temple above a freshwater lake on an island on Adam's Bridge, the neck of land pointing
from India towards Ceylon. It is famous for its 4,000 feet of monotonous carved corridors,
and has by way of palladium the lingam placed here by Rama. This is daily washed with
Ganges water, which is then sold to pilgrims. I have been unable to discover any further
particulars about the two other 'lofty Himalayan monasteries of Kedarnath and Badrinath;'
and have been no more fortunate with regard to 'the shrine of Kali at Hingalaj, in distant
Baluchistan', though L. Rousselet *op. cit.*, describes 'the Baloochees', in a picturesque phrase,
with 'their red-brick faces and tawny hair waving like a lion's mane'.

K

shore. Presumably they sleep 'rough', in the open air or under a wall. But this is no privation, as all know who have seen the streets covered with sleeping bodies in Calcutta or Bombay. Those have some part of a white garment over their faces, and are as though ready for burial in white sheets. But the sadhus do not even have the white sheets.

They are, also, to some extent migrant, moving round from shrine to shrine. In the old days an observant eye might see the same fanatic more than once in a lifetime, at, say, one of the temples of Benares, and years later in the south at Madurai, beside the 'Tank of the Golden Lilies' (euphemistic phrase!) or at the Temple of the Juggernaut at Puri. Yet, so great is their number, there could not be as much chance of this as of recognizing the same taxi-driver in London. Many of course must have died in the great epidemics. At Puri, where a hundred thousand pilgrims at a time collected for the Juggernaut festival, the 'annual mortality used to amount to many thousands, and a spread of cholera constantly followed their dispersal'. What one would most like to have seen would be the gurus and sadhus of a thousand years ago, at the great ephoch of Hindu temple building when Khajuraho and the Black Pagoda and the temples of the south were in their prime. But perhaps some distillation of those wonders is till to be savoured in Nepal where, in this, or other small areas, are gathered sadhus from all over India.

One is filled with curiosity about this strange place. If one appeared at night and knocked on that side door would the sadhu-porter in his cell come, stumbling from his sleep, and open a few inches? Would there be anyone awake down at the burning ghats? But we had not the luck of another writer, and looked in vain for what he saw: a sadhu 'sitting on a kind of veranda facing the river. He sits on a tiger-skin, with legs crossed, resting his arms on a T-shaped branch. This man, not more than thirty, his body covered with ashes, his brown hair combed into disorder, and his eyes glassily expressionless, spends his life sitting in Pashupatinat, or in Benares or other sacred places, meditating . . . This ascetic was a follower of the well-known ascetic Aghori Baba, and he himself told me that, according to the rules of his sect, he was obliged to eat human flesh at least four times a month.' When asked where he obtained this delicacy, he explained that many Hindus and Buddhists could not afford the wood for cremation, and so were obliged to bury their dead. 'Then he would dig them up and have his feast. But the disciple of Agori Baba', he continues, 'must have particular cannibalistic instincts, for the place where he sits is almost constantly veiled in thick smoke and the penetrating, horrible smell of burning human flesh.'[1] But alas! he was not there on either occasion.

This extreme fanatic must be a member of the sect of Aghori Panthis, now nearly extinct though it is not impossible that some few addicts of it may still be found. A Hindu author,[2] writing of the Aghoris as lately as 1896, says of them that they eat human flesh, 'and profess to carry the pantheistic philosophy of the Vedanta to its logical consequence, and even to look upon faecal matter in the same light as the fragrant paste prepared by the trituration of sandalwood.' He quotes the *Statesman* of March 7, 1893 as saying: 'The race however is not yet quite extinct. The headquarters of the Aghori Panthis appear to have been always at Mount Abu and Girnar' (in Kathiawar). 'They have such an evil reputation at Girnar that the authorities do not like Europeans to go there without an escort. At Benares these objectionable people live at the burning ghats, and are supposed to number between one hundred and two hundred.'

The Hindu author continues that the Aghoris are a very ancient sect, mentioned even in a Sanskrit drama, 'and in that extraordinary Persian work, the *Dabistan, or School of Manners*', written probably about the middle of the sixteenth century, where a clear description of the Aghoris is given, and an account of one of them 'singing the customary song, and seated upon a corpse which he ate when it became putrid'. He, then, quotes from two French authors: M. d'Anville who alludes to the Aghoris as *une espèce de monstre*, and the more famous traveller M. Thevenot, who in 1665 'alludes apparently to a community of these cannibals, established at a place in Baroda,' a statement corroborated by a local official who ascertained that there is a tradition still extant among the people that a colony of cannibals did exist in the village of Walwad, a century or two ago.

The Hindu writer, reminding his readers that parallel abominations existed among the early Christians with the sects of the Marcianites and the Carpocrations, castigated by Gibbon in *The Decline and Fall*, resumes his account of the Aghori Panthis. 'In Benares many old men state that they have seen Aghori Panthis eating dead men's flesh, and affirm that the custom yet prevails, especially among drunken men, who will seize upon corpses floating in the water and bite off the

[1] *Window on Nepal*, by Tibor Sekelj, translated by Marjorie Boulton, Robert Hale Ltd., London, 1959, pp. 39, 40.
[2] *Hindu Castes and Sects*, by J. C. Bhattacharya, Calcutta, 1896, pp. 391, *et seq.*

flesh.' His account of these cannibal sadhus tallies with another mention of them in Moor's *Hindu Pantheon*, where it is said: 'One sect, at least, eat human flesh. They do not kill human subjects to eat, but they eat such as they find about the Ganges and other rivers, and near Benares they are not unusually seen floating down the river on a corpse, and feeding upon its flesh; and the human brain is judged by these epicurean cannibals to be the most delicious morsel of their unsocial banquet.' He, further, adds that: 'Women known as aghorinis are often associated with these ghouls, and are as filthy and even more shameless than their male companions,' their purpose being that they hoped to gain alms by horrifying the people and not gaining their respect. Of such, then, may have been this figure at Pashupatinat, seated on a tiger-skin, resting his arms on a T-shaped branch.

The bathing-places are no less interesting than the burning-ghats, only a few yards away from them and, it is true, always tinged with acrid smoke. We cross the bridge once more, and stand on the topmost of a triple series of stone terraces which are really river embankments and supports or foundations for the lingam-yoni temples in row on row above them. From here we are within a few feet of the bathers. The river is no more than two or three feet deep in the middle and flowing slowly over shoals of blackish sand. In fact there are dry islands of that, and only an inch or two of water between them and the bank. But the purpose of the bathers is to get into midstream. The isles of sand are covered with litter, fruit rind, old tins, and it is only reasonable to think, some deposit from the oily, thick smoke of the cremations, not forgetting particles and shreds of ashes. This is all in accumulation on the sands, if, indeed, it has not conditioned and caused their blackness. The sands are shared with the bathers by the monkeys, who behave as though the sands were theirs, by right. They scavenge, and eat anything edible on the spot, though covered certainly with scum. It is disconcerting that they should be eating in this manner all the time when one knows what a chemical analysis of the water alone would prove.

For a long time we watched the bathers. Some disported themselves no differently than if they were on the beach, sitting in the sun. But there were others who, one could tell by their methodical procedure, made a daily practise of it. They will have been persons living in Pashupatinat, or near by. Bathing in the waters here is of great spiritual importance. There are those who paddle out into the river, knee deep, and pour the water over their heads and shoulders, and drink it. And some of the women lie down in it and wallow in the waters. They are awash in a few inches of it, and on regaining the shore have their own modest way of pulling on a dry sari while slipping off the wet one underneath it. Of this art they are masters, no doubt from the centuries of inherited skill behind them. All the while a monkey will be picking up and nibbling some pieces of garbage hardly an arm's length away, and on the shoal near by a whole family of monkeys is picnicking.

But sunrise is the propitious time when indeed the ashes of the cremations are no longer glowing. It is not difficult to imagine that there may be a kind of ecstasy in the coolness of that moment, for pilgrims from India especially. The hot nights are a part of the curse of India, and then comes that marvellous and dewy freshness which is only for a half-hour or so before the heat begins. But in those few moments one is in the company of the ancient gods, and in their youth. Theirs is a much more inhabited cosmogony than ours, fuller even than that of the gods and goddesses of the Greeks and Romans. To come up to this mountain valley out of swarming India is almost a purification in itself, and an easy communication with their gods. It is a part of their ancient world preserved to them without great crowds. There are others who prefer huge seething mobs and excitements as of the fairground, and of course on occasion large numbers must gather at Pashupatinat, but this can be as nothing compared to the tens of thousands at Benares, at Madurai, and at Puri. Regretfully we were unable to visit Changi-Narain, a Hindu temple on the top of a hill at the end of the valley, 'which is without doubt the richest of all the Nepalese pagodas in carving, colour, and embossed metal'.[1] Instead we went to Pashupatinat again for it is inexhaustibly fascinating, and a microcosm of ancient India set in the mountain air of Nepal.

For how much longer can it remain so? For like everything else in the world it is in danger, and the nation of eight hundred, soon to be a thousand millions is but a few miles away. A little 'rectification of a frontier' can be enough to bring it down. But the wonder of Nepal is not so much that it has kept its independence as that it has come out of limbo into the modern world with so much of its own that was not known before. Perhaps it is the last revelation of its kind there can be.

[1] Percy Brown, *op. cit.*

But the problem and the mystery are as to how much that is typical is really Nepalese; and how much, or how little of that is Indian. Are the pagodas, which it is such a surprise to find here with their Chinese or even Japanese outline—are they an invention of the Newars of Nepal which was taken hence to the Far East, or are they Indian in origin, but long since gone from India where no trace of them is left?

Perhaps the simple explanation is the true one; that in classical India there were wooden or even stone buildings of this shape, as in the Chinese pilgrim Hsüan-tsang's description of the abbey of Nālandā, that this ensued naturally in Nepal where the Newari had instinctive talent in the arts, and that it was carried thence overland to China, a shorter and a safer journey than from Indian harbours to ports upon the Yellow Sea. If we subtract what is Tibetan-inspired in Nepal, by which are meant Swayambunat and Bodnath, we are left with Bhatgaon and Patan, two Newari towns of the Middle Ages, and Pashupatinat, in some little sense a living Delphi, as it were, of classical or ancient India. It is the distillation, the triple essence of a half a dozen or a dozen holy places all over the sub-continent, but here present in the calm and freshness of the Himalayan air and in the Newari accent.

It is the Durbar Squares of Nepal that have something to give to the world which is both old and new. Nothing can efface the impression of first arriving in them; of walking between and among pagodas, under palaces with carved window frames and cornices, and below gilded statues on lotus-columns. Just as one feels a breath of Italy in the balconies and frescoed façades of old mountain towns in the Austrian or Bavarian Alps, so something has come up from great India into the Durbar Squares of Nepal. But it is something Indian that has been carried farther, and has left India behind. It is perhaps most nearly approached in Rajputana, where you may look for the same thing in Jaipur or in Udaipur, and not discover it. But we find ourselves drawn again by the drums and trumpets to the sacred river, as to some ceremony of Worship of the Golden Calf. We have a sight of the brazen image lying out in the sun. A hand holding an iron trident comes round the door, and a little later we see the sadhu's ashen, but painted face, his wild hair, and the garlands of flowers round his neck. The door-keeper with the face of an actor hobbles past from his cell. It is the hour of dawn at Pashupatinat, and dew is on the river which flows into the great Ganges.

Book Three

A LITTLE OF INDIA

Chapter Twelve

- -

DELHI, AGRA, FATEHPUR SIKHRI

THE DINING-ROOM OF THE hotel is nearly the size of the Albert Hall, and there are dozens and dozens of waiters in pink turbans with long ends trailing behind them over their shoulders as they flutter about, a little ineffectually, like moths. At the next table, an old Parsee gentleman in a tight buttoned frock-coat and black hat, in steel-rimmed spectacles, is going through his accounts with a secretary, and if anything is amiss it is the secretary's fault. Next to them, a Maharajah and his ladies are entertaining an English family. He is in khaki with many rows of medals, and the Englishman is obviously a soldier, too. Beyond them, the tables lose themselves into infinity, and one can hardly see the far side of the room.

But the sensation is the orchestra. The wall of the apse at the back of the players is frescoed with half the houris of paradise, though some are of mermaid sort; and the stage is crowded with musicians, perhaps thirty of them all told, and most of them playing strange instruments. The noise is loud and strident; and on the approach of a tune or 'hit number' the music seems to retreat with banners flying and lead off in a different direction again. The programme is Indian musical comedy and film music. Meanwhile, different sorts of curry, all tasting the same, are being eaten. Glasses of water or innocent lime juice are on every table; and by and large the Welsh sing-song accent is on the air.

Coming away from the dining-room there is almost a street of shops, selling saris and beautiful gold tissues; a 'lounge' like a lesser, domeless Albert Hall; air-line offices on one side of the hall, and on the other the 'reception' with quite a dozen turbaned clerks, where many an anxious hour is spent imploring for the hotel account to be ready in time to catch an early departing aeroplane, or inquiring for friends, seen in their room in the hotel the previous evening, who have been staying there for a week, but whose very existence is denied at the hotel desk. It is all kindly meant, misleading, and on occasion annoying.

The hotel passages are of huge length with turbaned characters waiting about who salute in military style. Each bedroom has its own refrigerator with old gin and whisky bottles filled with water, and breakfast of a slice of papaya and scrambled eggs and ham is the best meal of the day. Every room has a balcony with a vast view over to nowhere in particular, but with the dome of a mosque low down on the horizon from whichever side of the hotel you look out, it being one of the hotel's peculiarities that from whatever direction you approach it you have to be driven in almost a complete circle round it before you reach the front door, that being below a high brick tower full of perforated openings for ventilation. The hotel is a high red building; the air, the dust, the horizon, the very atmosphere is tinged with red, except at night when the air-conditioning can be turned off and the window opened on to the balcony to let in the moonlight and the chattering birds of an early Delhi morning. By then all is already looking red again. We walk past the desk later in the day, down the steps to where the giant Rajput warrior-porter waits with beard and turban, while a taxi is telephoned for and comes up with, not one, but a pair of Sikhs on the driver's seat. Usually they are brothers, and the younger one may be no more than fifteen years old, beard and all. Sitting behind them, you can see their sleek hair combed up into their turbans. Distances are so great in Delhi that there is ample time for this while we are on the way to Connaught Place.

We pass any number of white houses with pillared porticos and nice gardens, where the families of English officials can hardly have moved in before they had to move out again. It all has the air of a military cantonment with an improved Aldershot at the back of the planner's mind. But the fountains begin; and after a mile or two we are in Lutyens' Delhi and passing fountain basins of lotus pattern on a Roman scale, all built of reddish sandstone. The round Parliament House comes into view, and before that we pass the sunken roads of approach to the former Viceregal Palace. On the skyline above a massive building are the fountains placed on roofs that I remember Lutyens talking of to my father when I was a child; but we were told later that their purpose was doubtful and that they had never played.

All is on the grand scale; and we look down the Rajpath, the wide avenue leading from the President's (the former Viceregal) Palace to the Gate of India, a huge triumphal archway, and to the statue of George V as King-Emperor, a not unimposing piece of academical sculpture standing under a sandstone canopy. The statue has two unusual conceits to it; that the Imperial robe overlaps and flows over the plinth of the statue and is continued down its side, and that the King-Emperor's crown is bulbous in form and of Czarist-Russian, even of Imperial Ethiopian shape.

This last great conception in 'straight' architecture, and the parting gift, as it turned out to be, of the English to India, is impressive and wonderful, and we have said, of Roman grandeur. But, also, it has some excellent detail, as, for instance, the projecting piers of red sandstone on the flanking wall at the south side of the President's Palace which have been worked as formalized elephants. They are an ingenious and fanciful conception. A blot on the skyline is the ugly black cupola above the palace with the squat turrets at its corners, contrived like some kind of cork or stopper to the dome and much too flat in perspective. But the Mughal Gardens by Lutyens behind the palace are a masterpiece of garden design; and I saw it, wishing that my father with his genius for garden layout could have seen it. The handling of water-channels and fountains is masterly, as is the design of the parterres. The flowers are from English seed packets, culminating in an amphitheatre of nothing but flowering annuals. If it seemed haunted to me, as it may do to other visitors from England, the ghosts are the Edwardian voices that I remember from my childhood, that of the architect among them; and in the result one comes away from the Mughal Gardens of the former Viceregal Palace at Delhi feeling, at once, proud and a little sad.

Connaught Place confuses, at first, by the difficulty in assigning the right date to it in one's mind. It could be the child of Nash's Regent's Park till one remembers that Calcutta was the capital of British India and that Delhi was only given this importance in the reign of George V. Nevertheless, Connaught Place and the streets radiating off it are eloquent more of George IV than of George V, but this is because a shabbiness as of a whole century has settled on its shops and arcaded walks. In fact the shops are better along the radial roads than in Connaught Place which is interminable to walk round, and it is there that the striped Benares silks and cottons are to be bought and there are the jeweller's shops, all belonging to strictly vegetarian Jain families. Indian ladies wearing every form of their beautiful national dress are to be admired on the premises of the Indian Cottage Industries which is hereabouts. Saris, exquisite in colour and texture are to be seen, though the gold border in many of them detracts from the effect and, also, there is the beautiful Punjabi style of dress with narrowing muslin pantaloons and trailing sleeves. The sari, while achieving a classical effect, is so much more beautiful than the women's dresses on Greek vases because of the softer, gentler line and a truer effect of coolness than ever air-conditioning can give.

In Delhi dresses from all over Central and Northern India are to be seen, though more so in the old city than round Connaught Place or in Lutyens' Delhi. It is for this than for the more obvious reasons that the Red Fort stays in mind. For the Red Fort, to which biased accounts would ascribe almost the visual importance of the vanished Imperial Palace of the Byzantine Emperors at Instanbul, is a disappointment. The exterior walls are imposing enough, but we only approach them at ground level and they have nothing of the romantic expectation roused by the red walls of the Alhambra at Granada, when seen from below. Over to the left are the striped melon domes and minarets of the Jama Masjid standing high on their platform, and almost too Mughal Indian to be true. Expectations are raised again by the long vaulted passage leading from the gate into the Red Fort, but they fall rapidly at sight of the Diwan or Hall of Audience, to collapse still farther on climbing the steps.

Here the Peacock throne stood before it was looted by Nadir Shah, and of course we should people this other pavilion with the marvellous dresses of the Mughal court as they are to be seen in Mughal miniature paintings. Also, the Diwan is in bad repair and not improved by the way in which it has been treated until recent years. It still gives a shock to read in a footnote to Murray's *Hand-Book to India* (1905 ed., p. 198) that 'Lord Curzon has announced that the Mughal Palace buildings occupied by the military since 1858 will be shortly set free.' Up till that time the Rang Mahal or Painted Palace where the Chief Sultana had lived was in use as a mess-house, another hall was used as a prison, while other pavilions had become stables. But even making allowance for its degradation and the destruction of many of its buildings the Palace disappoints and stultifies. It has its full share, and more, of Oriental ennui, the reflection of the boring lives

IV   Dresses at Delhi

led by its inmates. The Royal Baths are prettier with their inlaid floors and walls and marble-traceried windows but the pietradura panels are uninspiring. Some air of the Durbar of 1911 still clings to the hall with a balcony on which the King-Emperor sat enthroned above the parade-ground. That it was considered then to be one of the most beautiful places in the world has left it infected and contaminated by that moment in time. It is Mughal *and* 1911, and it seems likely that it will end there and that nothing more will happen to it. The sightseers, every time we were at the Red Fort, were the chief interest. Particularly the Rajputanis with their Gypsy manner of walking and quasi-Gypsy dress. Set a little apart, there is one beautiful little building which is the Pearl Mosque, built by Aurangzeb in about 1660. It has a red wall round it, and a marble court at the end of which are the three white marble onion-domes with their gilt finials, and a host of little turrets too small for minarets and more like dove-cotes. The texture of the marble slabs with which the domes are covered gives the effect of the rind or skin of the onion, and the whole mosque is of miniature bijou size, and impossible not to look at it and be reminded of George IV's Brighton Pavilion because, here again, it is too typically Mughal Indian to be genuine.

As for the Jama Masjid, also the work of Aurangzeb, and always mentioned as one of the largest mosques in the world, anticipation had run high until one expected this mosque to be on a par with the finest and most impressive mosques of Cairo or Istanbul. It is true that it is on an Imperial scale and the work, manifestly, of the Grand Mogul. The three great stairs leading to as many gateways give a sense of the high terrace on which it stands. The great court of the mosque with the cloister round it and fountain in the middle is noble in scale. Even the awnings in that intense heat were noble and splendid. There are three white marble domes with their melon slices outlined by thin lines of black marble; and across that burning court there is a pavilion in its far corner with relics of the Prophet, and even a hair of his red beard. It completed a picture in one's mind to have been shown that, and then to look across again to the melon-like, but improbable marble domes.

There are scenes as Oriental as that playing at every moment along the Chandni Chowk, of wonderful name. A whole bullock cartload of persons, topped in best pyramidal-composition form by a gigantic man in a pale blue turban; or a wildly picturesque family, including several Gypsy-like women, apparently in the very act of migrating with all their belongings. A few old houses must date from the time when the Chandni Chowk was one of the famous streets of the world in Mughal days. The pawnshops, the fronts of temples, the cheap picture houses with their lurid posters, are still not unworthy of it; and at some point along its length is the eating-house with kitchens one may think, like those of a thousand years ago in Baghdad, where unleavened bread is baking in pits in the floor, while in the upper rooms tanduri chicken reddened by some process in cooking till it is redder than the sandstone buildings of Delhi, is eaten with the fingers.

It is nearly obligatory to drive out and see the Qutb Minar, of which Fergusson in a near ecstasy remarks that 'both in design and finish it far surpasses any building of its class in the whole world,' or, that compared to it, 'Giotto's Campanile at Florence, beautiful as it is, wants that poetry of design and exquisite finish of detail which marks every moulding of the Minar.' These seem strange things to say of a 'tower of victory' which in fact is wholly military in expression. The fluting of this huge structure up all the height of its five storeys and the balconies to each storey are its features, though again it is difficult to agree with Fergusson that the honeycomb work under the brackets of the first floor balcony 'differs in no perceptible degree from that in the Alhambra'. The material of the Qutb, as ever at Delhi, is white marble and red sandstone, and the mosque adjoining it has its cloister formed chiefly from pillars out of Jain temples, as is quickly apparent from their style of carving. The celebrated Iron Pillar with Sanskrit inscriptions stands in this court, and for all its two thousand years is quite exceptionally uninteresting. But the old fortress of Tughlakabad a few miles farther on is a fine place for climbing about in, and beyond that there are monkeys living in the trees along the road.

After the Qutb Minar the most famous building in Delhi is the Tomb of Humayun, approached through a huge portal and raised on a red sandstone platform. It is a domed chamber of red sandstone inlaid with panels of white marble, the dome being buttressed on four sides by octagon towers or side wings which uphold and support it above a long open gallery of the same red and white stone and marble. It has been the custom greatly to admire the Tomb of Humayun, but it is in fact dull and monotonous and broken awkwardly by the little umbrella-like canopies along the roof-line, while the interior of the tomb as always in this type of Mughal building is dull and uninteresting. The Tomb of Isa Khan, near by, stands in the midst of green lawns where there are always students lying reading, and is pleasantly cool with its open arcades, though in rough, unprofessional style and with, again, too many domelets on the perimeter of the dome itself. There are more of these tomb mosques in and around Delhi, some of them quite difficult to track down, but the most beautiful of all, far finer though it be heretical to say so than the Tomb of Humayun, is Safdar Jung. It is the latest of them all and only dates from the middle of the eighteenth century. The paved walk leading to it once had water running down it in Mughal-garden fashion; and the place is beautiful now with its flowers and flowering trees, and while we saw it the porcelain blue jacarandas coming into blossom were like an intake of the langorous Brazilian into the Indian air.

Such is Delhi; and as one of the capitals of the world it is a disappointment. Of its historic past not much is left. The mosques cannot compare with those of Istanbul. That city has four Imperial mosques; the city of the Grand Mogul has but one, the Jama Masjid; but neither can the Red Fort of the Mughal Emperors compare to the Old Seraglio of the Sultans. There is no mosque in Delhi to compare with those in Cairo or in Isfahan. In truth the best things in Delhi are the Lutyens buildings and his wide avenues and fountains. They approach what I believe he intended, which was the capital of India as that might have been planned by Hadrian, Septimius Severus, or other Roman Emperor who was a builder. His plans were continually reduced and cut down on grounds of economy, as I remember hearing him complain. That taken into account, his achievement is the more surprising. Distances in Delhi are great indeed, and Lutyens made them longer still. It is an Imperial capital that took thirty years in building, that changed hands, and is not finished yet. In its residential quarter among so many gardens, it is a curious sensation to hear wavering cries all night, lifting and falling, and be told in the morning that those were jackals howling.

While at Delhi it is unavoidable to go to Agra which is but an hour's flight away. The airfield there has only a shed by way of offices, giving the impression that Agra must be a small city. It has on the contrary half a million inhabitants, but one does not feel it, perhaps because there is nowhere from which you can see the whole town. It looks more like a country town than the capital of the Mughal Emperor, Akbar. The hotel, which has a pretty garden, and perhaps a nearer approach to good food than any hotel in India, panders to the tourist trade by admitting conjurors, a man with performing birds, and snake-charmers to ply their trade, but they are outstanding of their kind. At the time of our visit a large party of French people on a world tour had arrived. It was amusing to watch the alacrity with which they embarked on eating curry, and how soon they gave it up in despair, not bothering for a second time to try chutney, poppadums, Bombay duck, or any of the other little side dishes that go with curry. In the morning they were keenly interested in the English breakfast, were explaining 'le porridge' to each other, and venturing upon it rather as swimmers try the water before they take the plunge.

During the night there was noisy shunting on the railway line, and somehow this brought the British past before one's eyes. When was it built? Was the railway here before the Mutiny? The direct railway line from Agra to Delhi was only 'under construction' in 1905. And what enormous distances it covered! 842 miles from here to Calcutta; 849 miles to Bombay; and 779 to Peshawar. It must be farther still to Madras; and how far from here to Trichinoply, to Madurai, or to Cochin upon the Malabar Coast? They are in another world they are so far away. Several generations of our countrymen had come and gone from this hotel. It was a long white building with wide verandas; with birds which, as often in India, flew in and out of the dining-room. In the garden there were branch establishments of the two or three chief antique dealers, or, as they called themselves in more picturesque language, 'Shawl Merchants, Gold and Silver Embroidery, Soapstone and Inlaid Marble Work, etc.' We visited their headquarters in the town, as well, and saw for the first time the beautiful Mughal jewellery and enamel work, whether old and genuine, or copied, but of which we keep the description until we get to Jaipur. There were also saris of the greatest beauty, including less obvious ones, without the gold borders, but in sombre dark colours and magnificent patterns coming from Madurai. But the beautiful and novel experience was to sit on the veranda of the hotel from about five o'clock onwards watching the parrots. They had their nests in the trees in front of the hotel, and when the hen-bird was on her nest a smooth green head and a parrot beak and eye would look at one out of a hole in the tree-trunk, just filling the round opening. Or the whole flock of parrots would be manoeuvring in the branches; settling, and then flying off with a marvellous flashing of grass-green wings, and now and again the blue light from their tail-feathers or underneath their wings. I remembered how often one had admired green parrots in the borders of Mughal illuminated manuscripts. It was wonderful to have arrived in the world of those green masquers.

As it was already late in the morning we started sightseeing with a visit to the Mausoleum of Itimad-ud-Daula, keeping the Taj Mahal until the sunset hour. This entails driving down through the town and over the Jumna, through streets of old houses and past a temple which has painted fairground animals like the horses of a roundabout in its forecourt. The person buried in the mausoleum was a Persian fled from his country who rose to be treasurer and prime minister to Jahangir, whose daughter married that Emperor, and who was grandfather to Mumtaz Mahal, the lady buried in the Taj. As father and grandfather to Mughal Empresses no expense was spared, and his mausoleum is as large as a mosque. It has towers with open cupolas at its corners and a kind of open pavilion on its roof. In the many little side rooms are paintings of wine bowls and flower vases in niches, recalling bad illustrations to Fitzgerald's 'Omar Khayyám'; while the central chamber where are the tombs has the passage that goes round it lined with pierced lattices in marble of painstaking work-manship, and, withal, of light-shunning, cool effect. Little more can be said of this, except that the Mughal tomb-chambers, Humayun and Safdar Jung at Delhi, and even the Mausoleum of Akbar, at Sikandra, here in Agra, do suggest and give expression to the mono-tony of death. And one wondered, was the Taj Mahal to be but another of them? It is even an anxious moment to be approaching it at last.

The first view of the Taj Mahal, having on purpose looked away for fear of seeing it to disadvantage from the bridge over the Jumna, is at a turn of the road from underneath some trees. Better still to get down, and walk out to look at it from below the boughs. This most visual and photogenic of all buildings in the world floats, or is tethered, a little sideways and at angle to us as if, itself, unprepared and looking away. It is of surprising, pearly whiteness and bubble-like, with its four minarets from this angle spread out wide apart, and only a pair of the smaller, mamillary cupolas visible at this moment. One

L

should remember from the moment of first seeing it that white is the colour of the deepest mourning. It was begun by Shah Jehan in 1630 in memory of his favourite wife, who died bearing him their four-teenth child, eight sons and six daughters, which on reflection makes the Taj more extraordinary still.

But now we lose sight of it, and come down past other buildings to the great gateway built of the ubiquitous red sandstone, inlaid with texts and with ornaments in white marble, and with rows of little white cupolas over its main arches which are strung out on racks over the roof-line rather as though they are the keys of a glockenspiel, musical glasses, or the notes of a cymbalom. The vaulted interior however is very fine, and the whole gateway, even to someone who is no lover of red sandstone as building material, is of imposing scale. Framed within that archway is the Taj Mahal, a stereoscopic view of it which you may shift up or down in its frame by walking a pace or two backwards or forwards under the arch. And now we come nearer to this almost physically beautiful marble object, which grows bigger and taller as we get nearer still down the cypress-lined canal. Beautiful as it may be by moonlight, and beautiful as it was in the cool of that evening, to my own taste the Taj is more impressive in the heat of midday, when it is hard enough to climb up the stair on to its terrace and nearly intolerable to cross the dazzling whiteness into the shadow at its sides.

Those persons are really very silly indeed who profess not to admire the Taj. Certainly it is feminine, but it is feminine by intention and on purpose. It is sentimental, also, that is if it be sentimental to remember the dead. In design, it is a little hunched up with the shoulders too near the neck and the four 'lighthouse' minarets can be objected to because of the ugly white marble bricks of which they are built. But they had to be of white marble, and how else could it be done? The curve of the dome is a miracle of correct calculation, and so are the openings both of the deep bays and of the subsidiary arches on both storeys as you follow round the octagon and come back again to the main door. It is these that give the shadow to the body of the Taj, which it is now becoming difficult to think of save in terms of human anatomy. The interior, as one might have expected, is another disappointment. The perforated white marble trellis round the tombs of the Emperor and his wife is a tour de force, but would be no less so if carried out in sugar as decoration for a wedding cake. As for the

Florentine-looking pietra dura work in coloured marbles and semi-precious stones, and the marble flower panels both within and without the Taj with designs of lilies, of crown imperials, and fritillaries among other flowers, these have now by alchemy of time stayed Mughal, but become Florentine, and English, as well, with their echoings of William Morris and Walter Crane, as if derived at second hand from Botticelli and Filippino Lippi. It is the outside of the Taj which is one of the miracles of human hands; and no experience is more beautiful than to walk round it resting for a moment in its shade, which is like the shadow of a human, and a very feminine body, and satisfying, too, are the red sandstone mosques to either side. The best view of all must surely be from opposite, across the Jumna, whence you can see it spaced out on its high marble platform with those triple-domed buildings at its sides. But the garden of the Taj Mahal is lovely enough with its fountains and flowering trees, and all but those with no conscience must feel sad on looking at it for a last time under that high Indian arch, and walking away.

The tomb of Akbar is at Sikandra, a few miles outside the town, and approached once more through a huge gateway of red sandstone inlaid with white marble in carpet patterns, and with four ugly 'lighthouse' minarets of white marble at its corners. The mausoleum itself is a huge huddle of cardhouse frontispieces, colonnades and cupolas, all heaped on top of one another, with something of the aspect of an aircraft carrier with all its aeroplanes on board ready for a sortie. The building is immensely large, and Akbar's cenotaph is right above, as it were, on the top deck, on a marble platform in the midst of a cloister which has pierced windows of marble trellis work round all four sides. A foot or two away from it is a pedestal where the Koh-i-Noor diamond lay under a canopy of gold brocade. This tradition appears to be true; but diamond or no diamond, there are too many of the cupolas, and no reason for them, since no watch or look-out is to be kept. The tomb of Akbar though attaining to the Imperial style of the Mughal Emperors, is altogether too fussy and overcrowded with those unnecessary umbrella canopies.

The Fort, an unimaginative name bestowed by the military mind, does convey some intimation of the Mughal Court in its splendour. Compared to it, the Red Fort at Delhi is of little interest. It has high walls of red sandstone which from a distance look like mud walls and suggest the walls of Kano or Sokoto. They are essentially military and to that extent it is true to call it a fort, but there is palace after palace within the walls. The great gate facing Delhi is splendid in martial import and has its archway high enough for elephants to pass through, a new dimension or yard-measure which strikes the mind in India, elephants as engines of war and vehicles of state having to be a first consideration in the designing of fortress or city walls. The gate has two octagonal towers, side by side, like gun-turrets, that under which we enter having a fine domed hall inside it. Now we turn and come up a long ramp or inclined road overshadowed by the red sandstone, to surface at length on a flat space surrounded by buildings that are extremely confusing to find one's way about in.

A huge structure over to the right is the Jahangir Mahal, a red sandstone palace and Mughal-Hindu hybrid, for in the words of the guide 'it is a wonderful specimen of Mughal architecture clothed in the graceful adornments of Hindu art', followed inevitably by the sequel, 'there was hardly a square inch of the palace which was not painted in gold and colours'. Now there is nothing left of that but carved capitals and brackets in the red sandstone, and it has a haunted air. Murray's Hand-Book, (1905 ed:) says of it, 'There are many vaulted chambers underneath the palace, believed to have been used as places of retreat during the summer months. They were thoroughly explored during 1857, but as the air is very close, and snakes are numerous, they are seldom visited', which fits in with our mood for we would expect to meet the ghost of a red-jacket in a helmet with a handkerchief worn at the back of it, as by the young bloods of the racecourse in their top hats in Frith's Derby Day, and perhaps hear familiar four-letter words pronounced in an old, unfamiliar way. There were between three and four thousand British soldiers, women and children, in the Fort at Agra during the Mutiny, and one still feels and almost hears their presence.

We now go up a steep staircase in a wall and are in the court of the Moti Masjid or 'Pearl Mosque', built by Shah Jehan, all of white marble with a marble tank in the middle. The mosque itself, with three domes of impeccable outline and seven fretted archways under them, is beautiful and empty and cool within, but again disfigured with too many of the umbrella canopies on its skyline, and three more of them put unnecessarily upon its entrance gateway. The 'Pearl Mosque' is beautiful and ineffable with the perfection of one of the Mughal portrait miniatures, all beard and turban and pearl necklaces. Near to it is the little three-domed Naginah Masjid or 'Gem Mosque' of white marble, which was the mosque of the royal ladies, smaller, but interchangeable, so to speak, with the 'Pearl Mosque' of Aurangzeb in the Red Fort at Delhi. They are the 'gems' of Mughal architecture, but one look at them in their perfection is enough. There is no need to look again.

The Diwan-i-Am or Hall of Audience is very big indeed, and as monotonous without the dresses of the Mughal Court. The chunam or polished stucco with which it is coated conceals the red sandstone, but cannot make its fretted archways less repetitive and dull. But we are coming to the Khas Mahal which is the most beautiful part of the Fort, by way of enormous, empty courts and many stairways. The Samman Burj or 'Jasmine Tower' is an octagonal kiosque or pavilion built out on the walls, and next to another audience hall, 'a miracle of beauty', with its flowers in red cornelian, and other semi-precious stones, inlaid on the white marble, but it is dull and oppressive from emptiness. The 'Grape Garden' near by is attractive in thought, if the more so because of its soil which is said to have been brought from Kashmir. But the clou and finale, as it were to the Fort of Agra, we have said, is the Khas Mahal, a white marble pavilion with open arches, very evocative of the hidden, inner regions of a seraglio. To each side of it are the Golden Pavilions, with curving roof and spikes of gilded copper, each pavilion with three open Saracenic arches in the middle of it, and a little room to either side. It is through these arches that there is a last and perfect side view of the Taj Mahal, appearing over but not across the waters of the Jumna for it is on the same shore, but down a curve of the river. There it is, more ineffable and perfect than ever, and no wonder its physical beauty is resented.

There remains Fatehpur Sikhri which is rather more than twenty miles away. We were taken by a taxi-driver who on arrival had driven us from the air-office in the town of Agra as far as the hotel, a distance of hardly more than 200 yards, for nothing, and had thereby inveigled himself into our inmost confidences. About half-way there a diversion presented itself in the form of Gypsies and dancing bears. They came jumping up from the ditch, and in a moment were joined by others from the encampment beside the road. By the time we had stopped and got out of the car there were a dozen men and boys in the middle of the road and five performing bears. The action was extremely vigorous. There was nothing wooden and lumbering

about the bears. Because the bears were younger? And had not come
far from their native Himalayas? Or did they move more quickly
because they were more brutally treated? It was probably all three
reasons in one. Each bear-leader had a stout, ragged staff in his hand,
and the bears were on their hind legs jumping and dancing with a
rope tied to the same hand as the keeper's stick. They jumped up and
down while a man rattled a tambourine, and a boy wrestled with one
of them. The men began shouting for twelve rupees and became
abusive, and we got back into the car and drove on. It is an old
Gypsy trick with the Ursari of the Balkans to teach the bears to dance
by putting a red-hot tray under them to make them lift their feet, and
their lightning dance in the road hinted at this and other brutal ways.
The black, shaggy silhouette of the bears, and their mutual hatred,
man and beast, took over and obliterated for those few moments the
Mughal buildings we had seen.

Fatehpur Sikhri, when we got there, was of the same red sandstone
again, a building material which makes for monotony and of which
I am no lover, whether it be at Lichfield Cathedral, in the churches of
Nuremberg, or even at the red chapels of Banteai Srei. But Fatehpur
Sikhri to conventional tastes is the most beautiful thing in India after
the Taj Mahal, and the city built and then deserted by the great
Akbar deserves close attention. It is homogenous, built of one piece
and at the same time, and in the hybrid Muslim-Hindu style. By now,
we are within its red sandstone walls with eyes attuned to the red-
pinkish glare, in an immense court with buildings of the familiar
colour every way we look.

One of the first things we see is the Panch Mahal or 'Five Halls' a
curious, lop-sided structure of open porticos that diminish after the
second storey till on the fifth floor there is only a four-pillared
pavilion with a dome. It was 'probably built for the ladies of the
court as a pleasure resort', but their pleasures must have been of
simple kind. As to the fifty or sixty carved sandstone columns of the
first floor, it is enough to say that no two of them are alike, but this
does not spell gaiety or high spirits. The Hindu sculptors, inevitably,
have brought elephants into their ornament which, alone, makes it
unlike a Moslem building. Not an emptiness, here, as of other
Mughal interiors but a suffocating fullness is the mark of Fatehpur
Sikhri, and this in spite of the place having been deserted and left
empty more than three hundred years ago. Typical comments are

'not an inch is left free of ornament'; or, of another building, 'the whole of the interior, pilasters, recesses, walls, and cusp-arched door-ways, is elaborately and beautifully carved with geometrical patterns'. It is a peculiar feature of Fatehpur Sikhri that its ornament looks better drawn out in plan than on the spot. In the coloured drawings of the four volumes published at the end of the last century by the Archaeological Survey of the Government of India, the arabesques and patterns are of a dazzling brilliance. One can only conclude that it is the ubiquitous dark red sandstone for background that is at fault.

Another of the dark red chambers is the Diwan-i-Khas, with the huge corbelled pillar in the middle connecting by stone bridges to the four corners of the hall. Did Akbar really sit there in council with his four ministers in the corners? It seems no more likely than that he played chess or backgammon with slave girls as pawns or 'pieces to take the moves' on the paving stones outside. Another huge quad-rangle of buildings now comes into view and begins to impress by accumulation of effect. This is the palace of Jodh Bai, part of the harem, and 'entirely of red sandstone', with a high entrance arch and pair of projecting hooded balconies over it, and of course a pair of umbrella canopies on the roof above, all suggesting a frantic seeking for coolness and to make use of any breeze that blew. How much the Grand Mogul who was rich as Croesus, richer than any Arabian oil sheikh, would have appreciated air-conditioning! The so-called House of Mariam Zamani is in a far corner beyond this, and the House of Birbal in the corner opposite, both of them pavilions of the Zenana or harem, and covered all over with carving and faded paintings. Hours could be passed in wandering about here, in exploring the little rooms and looking at their ornament; or, with nothing better to do, going as far as the Emperor's Stables and counting the stalls for a hundred and two horses and 'nearly as many camels'.

But now a sudden and entire change comes over Fatehpur Sikhri, beginning from where we go into the third and last group of build-ings, where is the mosque. It suddenly becomes noisy, filthily dirty, and entirely full with crowds. We have come in all innocence on one of the days of the eight day fair. We are in a large court or quadrangle with the mosque at the far end of it, and the much longed for tomb of Shaikh Salim Chisti in an odd position out in the middle, but to the right of it. I write 'longed for' because I had hoped that with the little Moti Masjid or 'Pearl Mosque' in the Red Fort at Delhi and the little three-domed mosque in the Fort at Agra, it would prove to be one of the jewels of Mughal architecture. Even on a postcard the tomb of Shaikh Salim Chisti has an ivory-like quality. It is a low pavilion, not of ivory but white marble, with Hindu-looking bracketed columns to hold up its heavy, shade-giving cornice, but with its entire walls perforated into trellis or lattice-work screens of white marble. A little casque-like dome surmounts this, and the whole pavilion should be of a lightness and airiness beyond description. That may have been so on other days, but not today when the tomb looked like the enlargement of a bad ivory carving. It is supposed that Akbar's choice of Fatehpur Sikhri as the site for a royal city was because the saint lived here, venerated by both Moslems and Hindus. He was one of a family going back for several centuries since the first of the Chistis, called after a quarter of a town in Persia where they originated, died in 1235, while Shaikh Salim Chisti died here in Fatehpur Sikhri in 1571. There were at least six or seven saints in the family. Nor was Shaikh Salim the last of them for the big sandstone tomb near by is that of his grandson, and descendants of another saint of the family 'still reside at his tomb' at Gulbarga in the Deccan. It is more than probable there were descendants of Shaikh Salim Chisti at Fatehpur Sikhri that day. The village under Fatehpur Sikhri is said to be full of them.

But his tomb seemed dulled and polluted by the crowd who had made the quadrangle of the mosque into their encampment, while the cloisters were their open air latrines. There were arches under which it was not possible to walk, and the stench and the swarms of flies were quite horrible. Standing a little away from the tomb one saw it against the red sandstone cloister with some dozens of the umbrella canopies, more canapé than canopy, all along the skyline. It was at this moment that an utterly fantastic din started at the great gateway of the mosque (of which we had not yet seen the inside) and a full brass band began to march across the court, all playing their instruments fortissimo and sounding the first note that came. There was tremendous reverberation from the buildings as they marched through the mob to Shaikh Salim Chisti's tomb, in parody of the mounting of the guard, and seeming to imply that they performed this every day, that they were in garrison, the resident brass band attached to his tomb, perhaps even recruited from his descendants.

No doubt they were villagers from the plain below. There were some fifteen to twenty in the band, and the crowd marching along with them, before whom we retreated to the tomb of Islam Khan, the saint's grandson the floor of which is covered with tombstones, and then worked our way round to the mosque. It has a tall frontispiece, and consists of three high square halls with rows of tall columns of decidedly Hindu type so that it is difficult, momentarily, to think this is a mosque. The effect is very grand indeed looking out between their much faceted outline into the court, and then up into the high red vaults above.

With most of the mob collected round the tomb it was now possible to cross the court and go out through the Buland Darwaza or 'Gate of Victory' which, being more masculine than the Taj Mahal, may be the most splendid of all Mughal buildings. Coming out under it, we are at the top of a great flight of steps with a deep drop down to the villages and the plain below. The steps were crowded that day as for a fair, and a creature approached wearing a cinder-black skirt, and with its face whitened and a false tongue painted hanging out. It, or rather he, for it was male, presumably, had also a false third arm or hand, and wore a crown; and was one of the most horrid visions ever seen. 'A joke', the driver told us, but he was indeed very far from funny, and insinuated himself upon us again as we were leaving. He made it difficult to get past him and go down the steps in order to look back and up at the 'Gate of Victory'.

Seen from below it is the half of a hexagon, and stands forward with marvellous boldness at the top of its great stair, 160 feet high from the bottom of the steps to the 'glockenspiel' canopies strung out along its roof. The huge open arch has the other walls of the hexagon answering it from within, and the steps spread out fan-wise to give it greater height. The pair of side walls are in three storeys, the top arch the size of the lowest, and three smaller archways on the floor between. The columnar bindings or edges to all three sides, four of them in all, have something of Perpendicular Gothic in them, but are more warlike and masculine. It is often reproached of Mughal buildings, the Taj Mahal included, that they are provincial compared to the mosques of Cairo or of Isfahan. This may be true even of the Tomb of Akbar at Sikandra, but it cannot be said of the 'Gate of Victory'.

We saw it last, not first, but it must make a wonderful gateway into the empty, but not ruined city. Having seen the Imperial buildings of New Delhi which are in the same style, it has to be said of those that they are not inferior to Fatehpur Sikhri and that they mark the genius of the great architect who designed them, and was inspired by this last opportunity to do his finest work. New Delhi is the English architectural achievement of our century, and it is unlikely there will be another. One cannot but think of that among Akbar's palaces and mosques at Fatehpur Sikri. But Akbar's city, at least, has the advantage of position, and of having been deserted and left empty in his lifetime. It was unfortunate to have seen it swarming with that great crowd. The dust from their trampling feet came up from the plain below and was like red smoke within the archway. The crowd closed round us; the clown or 'joker' came up again with false tongue lolling out, holding a tray in front of him to collect alms. He is an unfortunate memory of Fatehpur Sikri which on other days of the year is deserted. It is empty but not bat-haunted like the temples of Further India. It belongs to a saner, more balanced civilization which is nearer to our own, and for this reason its idiom was nearly suited to modern purposes, if fallen back into the blatancy of that brass band. And at that moment it started up again. They were marching back from the tomb to the 'Gate of Victory', and we fled from Fatehpur Sikhri in the drizzling rain.

Chapter Thirteen

✦✦✦✦✦✦✦✦✦✦✦✦✦✦✦✦✦✦✦✦✦✦✦

RAJPUTANA: JAIPUR AND UDAIPUR

THE OLD CHIVALRIC INDIA of princely states that was Rajputana has suffered a slow change into Rajasthan, and is still to be seen in semi-desert background with its caparisoned elephants, its camels, and lovely costumes in great difference from that other India of the lush south. Jaipur is the first and nearest to Delhi of the former states, and Udaipur is about the farthest away. It is to Jaipur, therefore, that one goes drawn thither by report that it is the most beautiful city in India, a truism that in this sub-continent of four hundred and fifty million inhabitants it would need a lifetime of experience to contradict. There are hills and deserts round it as seen from the aeroplane, and a palace on a rocky hill which must be Amber; and then we are arrived at Jaipur after only an hour from Delhi, and the clean efficiency at the airfield, and the fire engines, must be due, one guesses, to personal intervention.

On the way into the town, with several hold ups at level-crossings, there are peacocks on the mud walls beside the road. This is something of traditional India experienced now for the first time. They are wild peacocks, and the wonder is how these creatures carry their tiaras and long trains unsullied by the dust. Even while marvelling at this, one of them lifts his head and gives his raucous cry, which in a garden in England speaks of huge India, and here is the authentic voice of the peacock in his native land. But the peacock alights in the ditch and goes on scavenging. One remembers now the white forms sleeping in the streets of Bombay and Calcutta, and only a moment ago we were seeing in imagination marble palaces beside a lake, and the pearls and emeralds of Golconda. Such is India, which is, and has always been, both extremes at once; as, too, the peacock displaying, one moment, spreading his tail and rattling sistrum-like, its quills, and the next, scavenging in the mud.

But we are not going as far as the city. We turn left at a certain point, and a little later go through a gate in a wall into a park-like enclosure, soon becoming a garden with flower-beds in every direction up to a large white palace in true Indian style. It is one of the former ruler's palaces turned into an hotel, and exactly as the palace of a maharajah should be. Long corridors with endless rooms opening off them, interior courts of vast size and to little purpose, halls with tiger-skins and bizarre portraits on the walls, massive furniture, and upstair rooms with latticed windows. But the rooms were notably cool, there was a bar with a fountain in the middle, and better food than can be found in Delhi. The gardens were beautiful and did credit to English seedsmen; there were peacocks, whether wild or not, while hoopoes with black and white barred wings and cinnamon breasts, their crests of cinnamon and black showing, were courting on the lawns. It was a restful and delightful place to stay at for a few days; all the more so because there is not much to see.

But only in the sense of sightseeing. In certain other respects Jaipur may be more picturesque than any other city in the world, and from all accounts decidedly more so than any other town in India. This is because of the dresses worn and the way the streets are laid out. Other Indian towns have a touch of horror as concomitant to their picturesqueness of which even it can be ingredient, but from Jaipur that is altogether lacking. There are neither moaning poverty nor appalling beggars, save for the former at a Gypsy-like encampment of lean-to tents of old sacks quite near to the Ram Bagh Palace. Its inhabitants who seemed to work as tinkers kept to themselves and did not come out upon the road.

At the first moment of entering the town it is seen to be all of rose-pink houses with latticed windows. The streets are laid out, not haphazard, but on a regular plan; and it may well be true that the Maharajah Jai Singh, from whom the late ruler is descended, and who was famous as a mathematician and astronomer, had studied the plans of European cities. In the event he laid the foundations of Jaipur in 1727 after consultation with his learned men and according to the ancient Hindu principles of town planning. So it is said; but in the absence of any other Indian town of the sort, it is safe to conclude that he consulted the astrologers but proceeded with his own ideas which were certainly influenced by Europe. The main streets are wider than any contemporary streets in London; and after the succession of one rose-pink house after another on both sides of the road they converge on to an open space where is the flower market, conspicuous when we saw it by reason of the huge baskets and great spilled over bunches of marigolds. Here, too, the flower garlands are strung together and nearly everyone, rich or poor, men and women alike, had a garland round their necks.

Thence, the rose-pink houses run on again with, on the left-hand side of the road, the house called the Hawa Mahal or 'Palace of the Winds', a beautiful and fantastic structure, as much 'one of Jai Singh's chefs d'oeuvres' (Murray's *Hand-Book*)[1] as it is utterly and entirely unlike any other building one has ever seen. It is in five storeys of hooded, overhanging casements, pressed close on one another, all latticed and semi-octagonal in shape, and in some way or other suggestive of the hooded camel-litters in which women were carried, repeated over and over again sixty or seventy times, which is its number of windows, and withal of astonishing lightness and delicacy of effect, painted, of course, rose-pink, and one guessed, again, only a few weeks previously for Queen Elizabeth's visit to Jaipur. It has been stated that the Hawa Mahal is 'in Persian style', but there is nothing like it in Tehran, Varamin, Qazvin, Meshed, or Qum, or Isfahan, or Shiraz, all of them towns in Iran which I have seen. It may be that in Southern Persia there are houses like this, but it looks to be an original invention, if not indeed due to Jai Singh. The interior is said to consist of many little rooms with mirrored and spangled mosaic work on walls and ceiling. Much work of this sort is to be seen in Jaipur, but we were unable to gain admission.

This curious and beautiful 'Palace of the Winds', a hybrid of bow-window and camel-litter, and painted rose-pink picked out in white, if it resembles anything at all has a little hint in it of the castle of Coca, near Segovia, in Spain, a castle built of rose-coloured brick in Mudéjar style in the fifteenth century by a Fonseca Archbishop of Seville. I have written elsewhere that 'this castle with its rose-coloured battlements and sham turrets recalls the palaces of Rajputana';[2] and

---

[1] The Hawa Mahal, according to some authorities, is later than the time of Jai Singh and was built by Maharajah Sawai Pratap Singh in 1799.

[2] *Spain*, B. T. Batsford Ltd., 1950, p. 132. The Hawa Mahal is in fact the only portion of the Maharajah's palace visible from the street. That there are varying opinions as to its merits can be gathered from an author who describes it as 'of a singularly vivid rose colour, rising in the form of a pyramid, bristling with a nine-storeyed façade composed of a hundred bell-turrets and sixty-five projecting windows, adorned with colonnettes and balconies, pierced in open-work with countless flowers cut in the stone . . . a vapoury, impossible construction . . . a mere mask of stucco, more fantastic than beautiful'. *Cities of India*, G. W. Forrest, 1903, p. 120. The

now having seen it with my own eyes I would describe it in fantasy as the town house of the same Fonseca Archbishop, not in Seville, nor Segovia, but in Jaipur. Just across the road from it is a temple, and the raised pavement outside this is in use as an open-air clubroom by the sadhus who sit, or, rather, recline there all day long, often with legs dangling over the edge as at a swimming-pool, an effect heightened by an almost entirely naked sadhu standing at the back who might be just about to plunge into the pool.

Their varying types from semi-sage to tramp-cyclist grew familiar after passing in front of them a few times. There was one sadhu, in particular, who was the perfect type of anchorite from the Thebaids of the Sketian and Nitrian deserts. We met him once, striding along, coming away from the clubroom, and asked permission to take his photograph. Most sadhus show human weakness in this respect, and cannot refuse. But he strode on, bowing his head with emphasis, and making sweeping, negative gestures with his right hand. It was as though we were offering him all the caviare and champagne in the world, or inviting him on board a yacht filled with filmstars. This ascetic would have been a leader of the anchorites who once stormed and sacked ancient Alexandria. Other of his confrères, with long ringlets matted with dust and the mark of the trident in white paint upon their foreheads, seemed more ribald as they lay talking outside the temple.

The City Palace now houses several museums in its many buildings. In one there is a display of costumes belonging to the Maharajah's forbears, one of whom must have been of gigantic girth. In another is a vast collection of painted manuscripts and miniatures, both in Mughal and in Rajput style. It is a place for specialist study of the forms and design of turbans, of textiles and of the elephant mystique in processions, in hunting parties, and at war. There are, as well, carpets, and elephant caparisons and howdahs; but on that hot morning we were more attracted by tremendous and discordant

same author writes of the houses of Jaipur, 'all of a pale pink or violet colour, pierced with small windows, filled in with slabs of perforated stone . . . mere scenery, and walls made to look like houses and painted pink . . . the fairyland of the Parisian opera, but not the Arabian Nights'. Another writer described the interior of the Hawa Mahal as having rooms 'of different coloured marbles, relieved by inlaid panels or gilding; while fountains adorn the centre of the rooms. The structure consists of six storeys, but the three last are only light kiosques, surrounded by innumerable belfreys, and the small gilt flags which flutter with every breath of wind have given to it its popular name of the Palace of the Winds.' Louis Rousselet, *India and its Native Princes*, London 1876; the author, a Frenchman, spent six years, 1864-1870, in India, and gives valuable accounts of the courts of Scindia, Holkar, the Gaekwar of Baroda, the Nizam, and the Begum of Bhopal, among others.

music, as of the mounting of the guard. I left one or other of the museums more than once in order to investigate. Each time it sounded nearer and louder, and we felt we were missing some glittering military spectacle. In the hot sun of midday it was always round the corner; and they would have stopped and it would be over just as we arrived. As it was becoming intolerable we realized it was not in some other court, but upstairs, and leaving the museums behind for good and all we climbed several flights of stairs at random looking for this military band at rehearsal, evidently, and found it at last in a tiny room, and consisting of two old men and a young boy who were making all the noise. After which anticlimax it was exciting to see Jai Singh's Observatory with its extraordinary stone instruments for observation and calculation of the stars, the point being that these six or seven apparent staircases or mounting blocks leading nowhere all have abstruse mathematical purpose. Thought took off from them into the empyrean, and it is curious that their very shape and form should suggest that. They are jumping off points, and they look it, but it is only strange that any branch of mathematical science should produce or necessitate forms that so much suggest its purposes.

However the abiding beauty at Jaipur is the dress, set off against the rose-petal buildings. One does not even look round now at green eau-de-Nil or pink Edinburgh rock turbans, of the sort flavoured with rose. Those are even worn bicycling. But in fact such are but rudimentary terms for their exquisite colourings. Now and again an old Rajput warrior will walk past with white beard parted down the middle and brushed up like his mustachios on both sides. He has a walking-stick, and quite likely a dagger or short sword as well, worn as our ancestors wore court swords in the eighteenth century. One cannot tell the social background of these old warriors. They must be very minor chieftains, landowners, and the equivalent of the Polish gentlemen-farmers of long ago. In order to see the Jaipur dresses at their best it is only necessary to spend a little time at the flower market. Almost every moment a woman wearing a beautiful dress walks past, or there is a whole family having a rest on the pavement near a great mound of marigolds. They will be poorer people, pro- bably peasants from near-by villages, but their clothes are flaunting and gorgeous in colouring. The ladies of rich families in the town are most beautiful in their saris which would look graceful and in good taste in the salons of Dior and Balenciaga. At this hour of the morning they are out shopping, often with a servant to carry their parcels. Jaipur must be the most beautifully dressed city in the world.

It is pleasant to watch the camels striding about in the midst of this with their awkward walk and their noses in the air. Crossing the road in front of one of them is a Gypsy-looking woman leading three children and with another in her arms. She has the Gypsy way of walking, as one gets to know that from any Spanish town where there are Gitanos. There are a whole lot of them sitting on the kerb; the nearest, holding her veil close to her nose-ornament, in a blue, blue skirt and the shawl is a soft yellow with a black binding. Next to her, with a child at the breast, a mother in a pink-geranium skirt and a marigold shawl; and beyond her another woman in geranium-red; and then a pair of women in the marigold shawls with red skirts and silver edgings. A group on the pavement with a little girl all in some dusty red material which is as thin as muslin; a child in white criss-crossed with huge bright yellow stripes in different shades, vertical and horizontal; and a hooded woman in poppy-red with a yellow edging. Next to them, a boy in a white Gandhi hat holding a yellow paper 'windmill', and women with heavy bangles on their wrists, gentian-blue shawls dotted with white, and deep red skirts; or veiled from head to foot in full marigold and carrying a melon-green bundle on the head.

But best of all are one or two families who must be of the original stock from which the Gypsies came to Europe. They are semi-nomads evidently; and the first family of them are sitting, three young women together, in their flamenco red skirts with apricot or marigold shawls of as many different shades veiling them and trailing out along the ground, and only a sight of spangled sleeves. This being key, as it were, to the second group who wear heavy silver bangles on their wrists, but their dresses are of cotton stuffs in horizontal stripes or bands of pattern but with no repeat, giving the richest effect imaginable of many colours, with patterned shawls that have the stripes running down the other way, vertically, down their heads and shoulders; and a woman with them, all in white with a scarlet fringe to her shawl.

More of the Gypsy-like clothing is to be seen on the country road that leads to Amber. For much of the way there are summer pavilions in ruins at both sides of this road. They are exceedingly picturesque from 100 yards away, would appear an impossible proposition from

31 Golden Pavilion in the Fort at Argra

32 Dresses at Jaipur

near to, and yet any one of them could emerge as a second Sezincote or a minor Brighton Pavilion from clever hands, so long, that is to say, as they are not more cemetery than summer pavilion for some of the domed buildings are surely tombs. But the road goes into a rocky gorge, runs beside a small lake above which rises the castle, and we are at Amber. As though nothing is to be lacking from the adventure we ride up to the castle on one of the Maharajah's elephants, but it is not so much a ride as an amble and the elephant has made the journey so often that if you shut your eyes in the strong sunlight it is like climbing from foreshore to esplanade in the hydraulic lift. We turn a corner or two and go through a gate, and are at the lift stop which is a high platform under a tree like that in a Rajput miniature painting.

The palace inside the castle must be Rajput architecture at its best; beautiful, but dull, as are all interiors where there were too many women and you get the reflection of the dullness of so many lives. But before we reach that inner part of the palace there is the Diwan or Hall of Audience with pillars of sandstone that have elephant brackets for capital. One of the nice things about Jaipur is that one can never forget this is tame elephant country with for that matter tiger country not far away. Gateways, here and at Udaipur, have been made high enough for elephants to pass through, and this is a change from the notices about so many feet of headroom for lorries under railway bridges at home in England.[1] The zenana or seraglio part of the palace at Amber has gardens in inner courts with pretty parterres; mirrored and spangled rooms; water-channels running along some of the floors in seventeenth-century foretaste of ice-box and air-conditioner; and of course doors of sandalwood inlaid with silver or ivory. There is a lovely view from some of the windows down to the lake and to the parterre that has been laid out on the embanked island down below. The elephant-lift down to the town again is more jolty; and only a moment or two after stepping ashore there are temples round the corner with statues of elephants at the door, and a Jain temple that one is allowed to enter which may be a first contact with an altogether different style of architecture.

Jains, in person, we had come across at Delhi and Agra where all the jewellers are Jain. One of the shopkeepers in the hotel at Jaipur was a Jain, and tried earnestly to convert us with the help of tracts.

---

[1] In the pre-Cadillac days of last century the Gaekwar of Baroda kept up a stud of a hundred elephants. His gold and silver State cannon with 280 lb. weight of solid gold to each, and drawn by milk-white bullocks, can have been for ornament only.

M

He must be one of the more extreme of the sect in his sympathies, at least, if not in personal achievement, for he talked of how their holy men or Tirthankars would not tread on an ant, and veiled their faces for fear of swallowing a mosquito or a fly, extreme measures which carry the Buddhist concern for animal life nearly into caricature. Orthodox Jains eat no meat or fish or eggs, and live on vegetables and cereals. They are a sect numbering several tens of millions, male and female, living on a diet stricter than that of Carthusians, and nearly as austere as that of Trappist monks.

The jewellers' shops at Jaipur are as delightful as the dresses along its streets. In fact in their category, which has nothing to do with that of the best shops in London, Paris, or New York, I would say they are the most attractive shops I have seen after those of Kyoto, in Japan. There are some four or five principal ones, but it so happened that we came last to the best of them so that the standard was maintained and they had not begun to pall before we left. This particular jeweller is entered through a court on a side street, and then up some stairs. Even then you must pick your steps across an upper court where some of the craftsmen are sitting cross-legged grading pearls, or, a still more specialized procedure, weighing turquoises on a tiny pair of scales. The shop, when reached at last, is in the hands of two or three generations of the same Jain family, and nearly all the work seems to be done upon the premises. This shop, then, can stand for the others which are on the main streets, the objects on sale being in any case much the same as in the jewellers' shops at Agra.

It is the Mughal jewellery and the copies of it, that are the attraction. But even granted that the Emperor Shah Jehan or Aurangzeb were richer than the Kings of England or France, which is the truth, and taking into account the nobles of the Mughal court and the Rajahs and Maharajahs of Rajputana, it is impossible to account for all the Mughal ear-rings and necklaces and pendants that one sees. Some, therefore, though not all of them, have been made upon the spot but the workmanship seems little, if at all inferior to the original. Jaipur has been famous for its enamel work for centuries. It may be thought doubtful indeed whether there are the craftsmen for this kind of work anywhere in Europe. Turquoise or ruby or emerald necklaces of Mughal seventeenth-century design, and even of that date, have enamel work at the back of the clasps; and there are dangling, pomander-like ear-rings, and even on occasion a long Mughal chain of jewels and enamel down to below the knees. The silk ribbons with threads of gold made here are things of beauty in themselves, and one can feast one's eyes upon the show-cases. A green parrot is one of the badges of a branch of the former ruling family; and one of the most satisfying ornaments was precisely a green enamel parrot with diamond and ruby eyes on a bed or base of ruby enamel that, old or new, would not be out of place among the treasures of the Medici, or in the Green Vaults at Dresden. Jaipur may be the only town in our times where such work can be done.

Udaipur is some 300 miles farther into Rajputana, so far indeed that it is not much farther to Bombay. It is only a short distance, not much more than 100 miles but across intractable country, to the mysterious Rann of Cutch where the flamingos breed in their rose-pink millions. The mere mention of which colour makes one sad to be leaving Jaipur in the conviction, which unfortunately proves true, that few other towns in India can be as pleasant. Udaipur is more beautiful in situation, beside a lake, but other considerations conspire together to make it difficult for a stay. It is a drive into the town over hills that must look spring-like in their short season, and past the chhatris or tombs of the Maharanas, none of them, one hopes, exhibiting that sign of a protruding hand and arm which means that the ashes it contains are those of a woman, who committed sati.[1] One sees little of the town coming into it this way, and is soon climbing a little hill to the hotel with lakes on every side. It has been heard said that this is yet another 'palace of the Arabian Nights' like that at Jaipur, but it is not so. The hotel has an unbelievably dreary dining-room, though hung with the biggest tiger-skins ever seen, and a still drearier sitting-room. The food is bad beyond description, and until these conditions are improved upon no one can be advised to go to Udaipur. We in fact lived while there on Indian sardines and tinned fruit bought in the town.

---

[1] As at Wadhwan, in Kathiawar, but, also, in other parts of India (Murray, p. 149). Mahuli between Poona and Goa, was 'a favourite place for the widow sacrifice of sati before it became illegal under Lord William Bentinck in 1829', (*Picturesque India*, by W. S. Caine, 1890.) The same author (p. 306), writing of Benares, says: 'the pairs of stones set up on end are monuments to widows who in time past were burnt alive with their husbands. Their suttee stones are to be found all along the whole range of the ghats'. It is unfortunately true that the Mahasati, or cremation place of the Ranas at Udaipur, is only too closely connected with this horrible rite, e.g. 'to this day the Rajpoot proudly calls the attention of the European visitor to the fact that five and twenty women were burnt on the funeral pyre of Rana Sangram Singh' (d. 1734), L. Rousselet, *op. cit.*, p. 172. On the wall of one of the gates of the Fort, at the near-by Rajput city of Jodhpore, are the imprints of the hands of fifteen wives of the Maharajahs who underwent sati at his death, (Murray, *op. cit.*, p. 134).

But there were two other consolations as well as the view. A small boy spent much of the morning in front of the hotel trying to sell pea-cock-feather fans, with no success, I am afraid. But one was deterred by the idea they were unlucky; and also, however satisfying the feel-ing that this was peacock country, a fan of peacock-feathers would so soon become dusty if brought home. The other interest was a magnifi-cent vulture or eagle perched on top of the flagpole on the roof. It had black wings with white tips to them, the trouser legs of its race, and an aquiline profile. Every now and again it gave a low staccato cry. Its mate kept circling round it, but at considerable height, soaring and gliding with black-slatted wings and their white edges, so much more masculine than the peacock of the stolen plumes.

It was while sipping a lukewarm aerated lemonade at foot of the dirty stairs, where was the bar—and the lemonade was lukewarm because one felt nervous of the ice—that we fell in with a party of Englishmen and their wives come up from Ahmedabad to spend the Easter holiday. Their business was the cotton industry; and more than one of them was of Yorkshire origin and knew Scarborough where I was born, in token of which we were invited to spend the afternoon with them upon the lake. In this manner we passed several pleasant hours on the waters of Lake Pichola. It is reached through the winding and narrow streets of the town which are wonderfully picturesque, and now again it is a pity that Udaipur is so uninviting to the visitor because, even the lake apart, it must be one of the most beautiful of Indian towns. Until a very few years ago Udaipur was a night journey by train from Jaipur, and it has kept its distance and remoteness from the modern world.

There are temples at the top of flights of steps with stone elephants at the door, and overarching trees with tropical leaves, and although the dresses are not in such soft and subtle colourings as at Jaipur, it is a journey of fascination to the lake, reached at last down a long line of wooden sheds, under an arch, and on to the jetty. Here the light and the water break upon the eyes, and there are marble palaces towering up behind us and in front. In fact one marble island is floating only a few yards offshore. It is a sight that Turner and the view painters of a hundred and thirty years ago would have delighted in, and in imagination one sees the engraved views of it in a landscape annual. Once we are embarked and pushed out from shore Lake Pichola is every bit as beautiful as the Italian lakes. Udaipur lies down at the narrow end of the lake as does the town of Como; but neither Como, nor Garda, nor Maggiore, has massed buildings towering up above its waters as, here, the Maharana's palace. To see more marble palaces floating out on the lake is nearly too good to be true. Lake Maggiore has, at least, Isola Bella like Armida's galleon moored a little below the other Borromean Islands; and this, too, but for the white peacocks and terraces of lemon trees is illusory on landing. But Isola Bella is Italian; we are in the Orient where there can be more mirage than reality, and we must expect nothing on disembarking at these marble palaces.

What a beautiful scene, though! The Maharana's palace is of immense length and of many storeys. It rises in a square mass at the end, and then comes a landing-stage with heavy trees to shade it, and another wing of the palace recessed behind that, after which it goes on again taller and more turreted; then another more level roof-line, and it becomes entirely of the Orient with row after row of vacuous openings for windows, senseless towers at its corners, a zigzag of ramps in front of it leading down to the lake, and ends soon after that for no particular reason. Again the hopeless boredom of the vanished inmates oppresses and weighs one down. But the lake is beautiful as it can be; and here we are at the first of the marble islands, climbing the water steps, and with the momentary and inevitable vision for that instant of the water-steps at Venice, a city where it is not just Italian and only façade, but where there is always something more to see. That is not so at this palace of Jag Mandir, although it goes as far back as the time of Prince Khurram, who took refuge here from his father Jahangir, before he became Emperor, himself, as Shah Jehan. There are shady mango trees and traces of garden courts, but the palace as a whole is stifling in its lack of interest. Workmen were repairing the floors and spangled walls, and the only fascinating object was a coal black female infant in a sun bonnet and necklace of silver bells. She seemed to find this marble island, as we did, dull indeed. A bedroom with iron bedsteads and a dreary collection of clocks could not make amends for so much money spent and so little to show for it.

Some twenty minutes later we were at the steps of the other marble island out in the middle of the lake. This is the Jag Niwas Palace with marble elephants trumpeting, circus fashion, trunk to forehead, at the landing-stage. From the shore, from the palace at

Udaipur, from the lake waters, from anywhere except on the island itself, it looks superbly beautiful. Marble ramparts all round, airy kiosques at various places on the walls, many trees, and a palace at one end, covering an island four or five acres in extent. We walked to the far end of it where was an ancient water-wheel worked with whining noise while a bullock dragged it round and round. Thence, through an orchard of mangoes and papayas, where a curious sight was a green parrot on the look-out, as in a conning-tower, at the very top of a dead palm tree where it had built its nest. The palm was swaying about dangerously and just the parrot's head showed out of the hole. Our friends had brought their bearers with them and we sat down to a tea of cakes and papayas under a marble colonnade.

After tea we went on farther until we must have been some miles from Udaipur. It was exciting to think there was big game in this country; bears and wild-boars and probably tiger not far away. We neared another island, or the point of a wooded promontory, where there had been a shoot during the Royal visit only a few weeks before, and there sure enough a log-like object just showing out of the water was a crocodile and it looked to be nine or ten feet long. On the way back on the far shore was pointed out to us where the Maharana had tiger and wild boar fights; and we came by a strange little marble island, no bigger than a tennis-court, all platform and protecting wall, where, we were assured, very private performances were given sometimes of an evening by the dancing girls. All the way we talked of Ahmedabad where our friends were living, were indeed the only Englishmen now in the town. Sir Thomas Roe, writing of it in 1615, says it was 'a goodly city as large as London'. We would have liked to see the Jain feeding places for birds, which look like pigeon-houses and are a feature of Ahmedabad; 'extremely picturesque, ornamented with carving, and often gaily painted'. There are innumerable mosques (Murray describes eleven of them); a Jain asylum for animals with a room where insects are fed; manufactures of kincobs (brocades of gold and silver); and the over careful window tracery of trees and palms in marble in the mosque of Sidi Sayyid. And to further beguile the time, our friend and leader of the party told us of Mount Abu, not much more than fifty miles from here but difficult to get at, where are the Dilwara temples of the Jains and the *sadhus* of the Digambara or sky-clad sect go completely naked.

But the landing-stage of Udaipur draws near again. The city of palaces shines and sparkles in the distance; a young woman with a beautiful back is bathing in the lake, and changes skilfully into another sari while we are looking at her; and an afternoon is over which we will never know again. Our kind friends from Ahmedabad even come with us to buy sardines and tinned fruit at the store. Night falls, and we spend some time drinking with them on the terrace before we open the tins and begin our evening meal. They are gone by six o'clock next morning for Easter is over and they must get back to work, and we will never see or hear of them again.

Quite early, for the days are beginning to get too hot, we go down to the town and visit the Maharana's palace. There are elephant gates and an enclosure where the creatures were made to fight, and on occasion trample criminals to death; and past innumerable buttresses capped with zenana windows we get to the gate where immediately we are made to take off our shoes and walk round the palace in stockinged feet. The palace, for all its being the residence of a Maharana 'descended from the Suryabansi, or Sun-stock, and the premier house of India in point of blue blood'—even perhaps because of that[1]—is of a suffocating ennui, there being nothing to remember about it beyond an open court with ugly mosaics of peacocks, and the beautiful vision of it we had yesterday from the lake. The little marble kiosques at the landing-stages, the trees shading them, and that line of palaces above the water; but nothing, nothing in the interior, and it would be wiser not to set foot inside it.

In disillusionment we gave the Victoria Hall Museum a miss, omitting, thereby, 'the turban of Prince Khurram, from which the present headgear of Mewar has evolved' (Udaipur is capital of the state of Mewar), and the turban of Shah Jehan the builder of the Taj Mahal may have been exceptional. Instead, we drove to a park or zoological garden where there were unhappy tigers in cages and a great variety of parrots, and then along an embankment beside the lake. It is in fact difficult to make out the shape of that; the lake below the hotel is another lake altogether, and an artificial one, connected with Lake Pichola by a canal. But our confidence was restored by seeing the Sarhelion-ki-Badi or 'Garden of the Maids of Honour', said to have been laid out for ladies given to the Maharana by the Emperor of Delhi. It is therefore a Mughal garden, and one of the

[1] Descended in direct line from Rama, the legendary hero of the Ramayana, from the Sasanian Kings of Persia, and the Roman Caesars, and representative of the Solar race.

few in existence, though much restored, original gardens of this period being as rare as 'Persian' gardens in Iran. Countless water jets are turned on, and an almost too Mughal-looking pavilion of white marble in the middle of the pool is subjected to a shower-bath pouring all over itself. The effect is cool and beautiful which is what was to be desired, and to one side of it there is a grove of dark, ilex-looking trees. The Sarhelion-ki-Badi is more of a bath than a garden; more white marble and water than roses and jasmine.

There are places of shadow all over Udaipur from its many trees, in which respect it differs from Jaipur which is more open and sandy. Jaipur seems nearer to the desert, and is indeed not far on the map from the Thar or Indian desert. It is to be noted that the next state of Rajputana to the west of it is Bikaner which 'lies deep in the Thar desert behind endless waves of sand dunes' and is famous for its Camel Corps. It is not a surprise to see camels in the streets of Jaipur; and what with its Hawa Mahal or 'Palace of the Winds', and one thing and another, though so typical of Rajputana, Jaipur seems to connect through the desert to Persia, whereas Udaipur is not of the desert, but semi-tropical, and therefore more Indian than Rajput. Jaipur is one of the beautiful cities of the world because of its rose-coloured houses and its dresses; Udaipur has more of the lines of beauty with its lake and palaces, but there is nothing within and the beauty palls and dies.

Chapter Fourteen

————————————————————————————

BOMBAY, AURANGABAD,
THE CAVES OF AJANTA

IT IS A LONG AND endless drive into Bombay, past shanty towns and along a narrow neck of land with a breath of the Indian Ocean and the masts of a great many fishing-boats on one side. We had to undertake it six times in all and this did not make it seem any shorter. But, rather, it got longer and longer, past the white gewgaw of a mosque to where the houses begin to have wooden verandas and balconies. Then comes mile after mile of this which is inevitable with a city of more than four and a half million inhabitants, perhaps twice the population there was in the whole of ancient Greece. The shops now begin, but very poor ones, and it is a long way still before they show any lift into more prosperous surroundings. When this happens at last they are ugly houses but the roads have English names, Arthur Road or Haines Road, and their subsidiaries, and we come out at last, at long last, on Marine Drive. There are more miles of this with buildings of a monotony unmatched outside the sea fronts of Alexandria or Havana, and then we turn left and into the town again to stop outside the air terminal. After a halt here we resume once more, and it is only a short distance to the hotel.

This is a grandiose building with a domed tower as though minded to declare itself another Imperial Institute, or play understudy to the Victoria and Albert Museum. There is a quadrangle in front of it where one can imagine students from the drawing schools sitting or lying out on the grass during the luncheon interval; and on the ground floor are flower shops and silk shops, and a bookstall where expensive and lavishly illustrated volumes on the sculptures of Khajuraho and other temples are substitute for the livelier film magazines. The dining-room upstairs has a cold table where something new to experience, but rather resembling brawn or calf's-head, offers itself under the name of 'hump'; not camel's hump, but the hump of a Brahma bullock, and why not? It is quite good, and lends variety to a meal that is due to end with bread and butter pudding. But it is on the floor above that fantasy has its fling. There is a grand staircase-well with four forbidding flights of stairs, and as you proceed to your room you are reminded of woodcuts of a Victorian model prison. For the floors are all of perforated cast iron, and the table and chair on the landing suggests that it has been designed so that a single warder can oversee a whole wing of the building. In spite of which the rooms are large and airy though electric light and fan and air-conditioning do not always work hand in hand.

But the hotel, at least, is in full gusto with the town. For it is here in Bombay that Victorian Gothic had its chance, and was given opportunities denied it in Manchester or Birmingham. We have, though their names and functions may now be changed, the Presidential Secretariat in Venetian Gothic, designer Colonel Wilkins, R.E.: and the University Hall in the French decorated style of the fifteenth century, designed by Sir Gilbert Scott, and called after Sir Cowasjee Jehangir Readymoney who gave a lakh of rupees for its erection. The Univeristy Library and Clock Tower are 'a grand pile' designed by Sir Gilbert Scott in the style of fourteenth-century Gothic, the tower being the most conspicuous building in Bombay; and there are the Courts of Justice, architect, General J. A. Fuller, R.E., in Early English Gothic; the Telegraph Office in 'modern Gothic' style; and the Post Office designed in the mediaeval style by Mr Trubshawe; near to which is the statue of Queen Victoria that at any rate in 1905, was 'an object of constant interest to the natives'.

Other buildings in the same mood are the chancel in the Cathedral which is 'a satisfactory specimen' of modern Early English, with the fountain in front of the building given by the same Sir Cowasjee Jehangir Readymoney; the Royal Alfred Sailors' Home, with sculpture in the front gable, of Neptune with nymphs and sea-horses in Bath stone by Mr Bolton of Cheltenham; the Elphinstone College in mediaeval style and, once again, called after Sir Cowasjee Jehangir Readymoney who gave two lakhs of rupees towards its construction;

the Victoria Station, architect F. W. Stevens, C.I.E., 'the finest railway station in India, if not in any country,'[1] in Italian Gothic, 'with
certain Oriental modifications in the Dome'; and the Municipal
Buildings, also by Mr Stevens, where 'the Oriental feeling intro-
duced into the Gothic architecture has a pleasing effect'; and the
Pestonji Kama Hospital for Women and Children, in the Gothic
style, with its obstetric ward 'due to the munificence of Mr Bomanjee
Eduljee Allbless.'

It will already be evident that much of this Gothic building fever
was assisted by Parsee gentlemen, and not the least curious feature of
Bombay is the statuary erected to them. One grows familiar with
their figures in bronze frock-coats and the black, sloping Parsee hats.
There is the statue of Sir Jamsetjee Jeejeebhoy, Bt., between the
circular stairs in the Town Hall; addresses Mazagon Castle, Bombay,
and Fountain Hall, Poona, first of a line of baronets created in the
momentous year of 1857. A copy of this statue is in the Jamsetjee
Jeejeebhoy Hospital which was founded in 1845, and this same
gentleman built the School of Art which was called after him, and,
as well, the Jamsetjee Jeejeebhoy Institute. More instances of this
public spirit are the Ruttonsee Mooljee Fountain outside St George's
General Hospital, and the drinking-fountain in the Central Hall of
the Crawford Market given by Sir Cowasjee Jehangir Readymoney;
while the fact that one-eighth of the cost of building the spire of
St John's Church was defrayed by Mr Cowasjee Jehangir Readymoney in 1864 was in the words of Murray's *Hand-Book*, 'a striking
instance of Parsee liberality and of good feeling between Parsee and
Europeans'. At which point, with respect to the odd and confusing
names of the Parsee families, names such as Allbless and Readymoney, more still, to names such as Cursetjee, Jamjetsee, Rustamjee,
Byramjee, Cowasjee, Nanabhoy, and so forth, which appear to work
as multiples in the Jeejeebhoy family[2]—as, too, names like Dinshaw,
Manockjee, and Dhunjibhoy in the families of Petit and Jehangir,
other Parsee baronets—it is at least a move towards greater simplicity
that by appropriate Acts of the Legislative Council of India, in all
three cases, all holders of the title relinquish their own name on
succession and assume those of the first baronet, becoming, thereby,

---

[1] It was from this station that the trains started for Calcutta 1,400 miles away in 1905, but
later the route was shortened to 1,220 miles.
[2] The reiterated aspirate in 'bhoy' imparting as it were, an extra note of Hibernian high
spirits to the name.

Sir Jamsetjee Jeejeebhoy, Bt., Sir Cowasjee Jehangir, Bt., and Sir Dinshaw Manockjee Petit, Bt.

More examples of statuary in Bombay are the statues of Mr David Sassoon by Woolner—the ex-Pre-Raphaelite and companion to D. G. Rossetti and Holman Hunt—in the Mechanics or Sassoon Institute; of Dr Blaney, Coroner of Bombay; and the statue of the Prince Consort in front of the former Victoria and Albert Museum, by Noble, given by Sir Albert Sassoon. It will be apparent that the great period in Bombay was between 1860 and 1890, and that its Gothic buildings are later in date than St Pancras Station and contemporary to Eaton Hall, Chester, and to the last outburst of the movement. As to their appropriateness, it is to be remarked that Calcutta which began its prosperity earlier has most of its buildings in the Classical style, though there are a few in Hindu-Gothic, or 'spurious Gothic modified to suit the climate of India', which substyle is, again, a different subject altogether. The colonnades of Classical architecture, of at least Mediterranean derivation, are somehow more appropriate to the Indian clime, and the wisdom is to be questioned of treating this city on the Indian Ocean as though it were Birmingham or Manchester.

It is a curious sensation to walk about in the heart of this city of a dozen Indian races with nearly as many South Kensington Natural History Museums on every side, and statues as at Parliament Square of Governors and Generals, but, also of rich Parsee merchants, in the midst of the traffic, or on any space of green.[1] It is only just after cockcrow and the ghosts have fled, but leaving this very tangible evidence behind them which it will take a long time to forget. There are whole streets like Northumberland Avenue; and that for communication with each other English is still the official language spoken in the Indian Parliament (at Delhi) does not lessen either the mystery or the wonder. At night it is another matter with the thousands sleeping in the streets. They, too in their pullulation are the results of British rule.

In this city of Gothic town halls and hospitals and institutes there are few cinemas, no fried-fish shops or public-houses, and one does

---

[1] In Moor's *Hindu Pantheon*, new edition by the Rev. W. O. Simpson, Madras, 1864, p. 316, it is comically stated that 'ascetics of the orthodox sect in the last stage of exaltation, disuse clothing. I have very seldom seen individuals *entirely* naked, except in Poona, where dozens sometimes of these brawny saints are seen lolling and sleeping in the streets, and on shop boards, as naked as they were born . . . I have known one of these *nudes*, now and then, come to Bombay; but he has been speedily admonished by the officers of police of the necessity of a more decent appearance, or of immediate departure.'

not have to be reminded that it is an Indian city. The licensing laws are particularly strigent in Bombay; in our huge hotel nothing so dangerous as a glass of beer is allowed and Europeans must be content with iced lime juice. The restaurants in consequence are more like tea-rooms. If it is true, as a person very prominent in Indian political life remarked to me, that no one can hope for a career in politics in India who is not an ascetic, or, at least, a vegetarian and teetotaller, it is equally true that they cannot hope to attract tourists to India without relaxing these absurd rules. Yet at the time of our visit the politicians were intent on making them absolute and enforcing complete and entire prohibition. That will certainly be the death-knell of the tourist trade.

After looking at the Gothic buildings and the statues one has only to visit the market to be assured one is in the semi-tropics. Pommelos and Alphonso mangoes are on sale; and the fish stalls are offering pomfret of which one soon tires on hotel menus, another fish with 'projecting knobs, like a flounder', as Murray has it, together with bommelo 'a glutinous fish', that has nothing whatever to do with the half-melon, half-grape-fruit pommelo, but after being left to decay and dry on the sea-shore makes another appearance as the Bombay duck eaten with curry. On the poultry stalls Murray mentions a bird called florican as 'excellent' but we never came across it, and it may have another name.

We passed through Bombay three times, on the way from Delhi to Ceylon, coming back from there and starting for Aurangabad, and returning thence in order to go back to Delhi. On each occasion, with a week or two in between, it had become even hotter. But there was a coolness and a kind of half-agreeable melancholy in wandering across the road to the Gateway of India, surely the last example of Hindu-Gothic for it was built to commemorate the landing here of King George V and Queen Mary on their way to Delhi for the Durbar of 1911. It is now used for ceremonial landings and departures, and it is true that in some curious way it suggests leaving more than arriving. This is where the English left India. I have read somewhere an account of the last British regiment marching down to the Gateway of India with drums playing and colours flying, and embarking at those water-steps for the journey home.

Our own first purpose in coming to Bombay was in order to visit the Caves of Ajanta, and still more the Kailasa of Ellora, and both places have to be seen from Aurangabad which is about 200 miles inland and in the territory of Hyderabad, in the former dominions therefore of the Nizam. It is now the easiest possible journey to get there as it only takes an hour so that Aurangabad is very much less remote then, say, Udaipur. But cities are distant, not only from each other, but from, and in, themselves; and in this sense Aurangabad feels very far away. The landscape round it is not unlike High Castile. We could be approaching some town like Soria, till the whiteness of the distant buildings resolves itself into domes and minarets. There is a remarkably good hotel outside the town built by Indian Railways before the British left, but the English manageress stayed on and is now the only European in Aurangabad. The flamboyants in the hotel garden were more brilliantly scarlet than any I have seen. It is, I think, well known that this flowering tree (*Poinciana regia*) differs very considerably in colour from place to place and according to season. Here it is of a lighter, shriller scarlet perhaps because of the sandy soil. It lifted one's spirits to look out on the flamboyants from the windows of the dining-room where, as ever in India, small birds were flying about. The colour of the scarlet trees was as a fanfare of trumpets.

But Aurangabad, itself, was more interesting than one had anticipated. Its name of course is of association with Aurangzeb who made use of it as his southern capital; though Murray has a sentence to the effect that the city was founded a little earlier than that by Malik Ambar, 'the head of the Abyssinian faction of the Ahmadnagar State'.[1] When Aurangzeb held his court here he was attended by more than fifty great princes, including the Maharajahs of Jaipur and Jodhpur from Rajputana, with thousands of armed retainers, so that some remains of magnificence are to be expected. Among them is the Panchakki or Water Mill where a Moslem saint, Baba Shah Musafir, is buried. He was friend and spiritual guide of Aurangzeb, and yet another member of the Chisti family of saints. The Panchakki is one of the three or four beautiful Mughal gardens, belonging, therefore, to a rare category. The Moslems for all their appreciation of flowers and blossoming trees and water have left so few gardens, all told. So few indeed that at the Panchakki one cannot but think of the Moorish garden of the Generalife, how many thousands of miles away at

---

[1] Malik Ambar, who founded the city in 1610, was originally an Abyssinian slave. The city was then called Fatehnagar.

Granada, and see in mind its cypresses and fountains, and its mirador giving on to the Gypsy caves of the Albaicín. And hearing the Panchakki only spoken of as the Water Mill we so nearly missed it altogether!

It is simple enough. Only a raised tank of water with a graceful colonnade at one end. This tank is full of fish which are held sacred. There is a second and larger tank with a vaulted hall under it looking on the river. This is described as a noble hall but is in fact nothing of the kind. What are beautiful at the Panchakki are the tanks of clear water, the lines of the garden, and that indefinable sense of peace of which only the Moslems are masters. There are buildings on two sides which are libraries, and the perfectly beautiful mosque—in its simplicity—or shrine of the saint,[1] dating from the time of Aurang-zeb, and a piece of Mughal architecture that could not be seen to more advantage, makes the third side. It is of light summer pavilion feeling, like the small mosques in the forts at Delhi and at Agra, but to be admired here without the crowds. How often in the teeming and overhot places of India one remembered the quiet and coolness of the Panchakki at Aurangabad!

It is still predominantly a Moslem city and the trades are carried on here in the Moslem fashion. We went to see the weaving of the hand-loom fabrics known as himroo which are peculiar to Aurangabad. Dozens of young apprentices were at work moving the shuttles and forming the patterns with incredible dexterity in the dark corners of a yard. The scene could have been Fez or Meshed, but the finished work was disappointing. Some of the women are still veiled at Aurangabad, and at the last moment just before it was too dark we remembered seeing from the balcony of the hotel a large white domed structure, and were taken to it. This is the Bibi-Ka-Maqbara where the wife of Aurangzeb is buried. It is not far inferior to the Taj Mahal in beauty, and much to be preferred on all accounts to the Tomb of Akbar at Sikandra—though this was the first time, I have to confess, that I have ever heard of it. True Aurangzeb had the example of his father Shah Jehan before him, but this is no reason to disparage the Bibi-Ka-Maqbara. It has a tall, imposing gateway, not so fine as

[1] Saints of the Chisti family were fortunate in their burial places. The most famous of them, Khwaja Muin-ud-Din Chisti, born in Afghanistan as early as 1143, is buried at Ajmer, in Rajputana. His mosque or dargah was built of the ubiquitous red sandstone by Akbar; while Shah Jehan added the Jama Masjid, a second mosque of white marble, and the tomb of the saint, a square domed chamber of white marble which looks to be among the little master-pieces of Mughal building.

at the Taj, but through it we see the mausoleum on a platform at the end of a long canal bordered with stone walls and with cypresses planted along it. The dome is not so breathtaking in its curve as that of the Taj, but the four minarets are less like lighthouses; and it is only when we climb on to the platform on which the mausoleum stands that we realize the whole enclosure is one huge garden, that we have only walked down one arm of it, and that the garden is continued on all four sides of the mausoleum which stands right in the middle. There are large mango trees in all four plots throwing their more than ilex shade, and as a garden this is more complete and less spoilt than the garden of the Taj Mahal. It is the version, in large, of those Mughal gardens in miniature on the tops of cabinets, with counterfeit flowers in the flower-beds, and canals represented by strips of mirrors, in one of which when it was brought to Europe late in the sixteenth century, the botanist Clusius recognized the first yellow rose. Here, at Aurangabad, these two things of which one has never been told before, the Panchakki and the Bibi-Ka-Maqbara are as beautiful as anything in Agra, and more beautiful than anything in Delhi.

But the prime purpose of coming here is in order to see the Caves of Ajanta which are, or should be, one of the sights of the world though the sad truth is that they are now too far gone with age to give pleasure. The paintings after all are fifteen hundred to two thousand years old; that is to say, they fluctuate in date between the frescoes of Pompeii and the mosaics of Ravenna. They are only paintings, they are not glass mosaics; and if we think that they go back as far in history as from the later Roman Emperors to the reign of Justinian it is not surprising that so little is left of them. But, also, they have been in desperate climatic conditions of both heat and damp, and the rigours of the climate are brought home to one on being advised to start for the Caves at six in the morning or earlier, owing to the great heat.

It is a drive of sixty to seventy miles through a desert landscape darkened after a time by the black ruins of Daulatabad, one of the most enormous fortified places in existence, incomparably more imposing and forbidding than the more famous fortress of Tughlakabad, near Delhi, with which it has close historical connection. Sultan Mohammed Tughlaq, who is buried in the place named after him in the middle of an artificial lake joined to the fortress by a causeway, made this great fortified town of Daulatabad his capital.

34   Jaina Masjid at Delhi

35   Hawa Mahal or 'Palace of the Wind' at Jaipur

Or, in the words of the local guide, this 'eccentric' Sultan—a mild term with which to describe this ferocious warrior—'was so much impressed with the maddening topography of old Deogiri that he deserted Delhi and made this his capital'. The same guide remarks that the rock of Daulatabad 'is smoothed so ingeniously, from the base of the fort to the level of the water, that even a snake or an ant could ascend it only with great difficulty', and this puts in a few words what it could have taken much longer to say. Blackened ruins, as though smoked with fire, reach all the way to the foot of the rock, with left-hand turns to meet the right-hand fire of the defenders', spiked gates in protection against assault by elephants, and even man-traps with iron coverings over them that could be made red hot. The rock, itself, has been dug round and given a perpendicular drop or scarp with sensational effect that can be seen from miles away. It is a terrifying fortress in which one might expect to hear ghostly bugles and trumpets blowing at any hour of night or day, the only historical fact that brings it near to one in a more human way being that the much read Arab traveller Ibn Batuta describes Daulatabad as he saw it seven hundred years ago.

It stays in sight for a long time as the road climbs and we can see the huge protruding rock and another angle of its escarpment, and then after a few miles more we come to 'the town of saints', a holy place of the Moslems called Khuldabad, where Aurangzeb is buried. There is a robe of the Prophet here, and hairs of the Prophet's beard, but the extreme orthodox beliefs of Aurangzeb, in reaction against the ostentation of his forebears, made it that he had himself given a pauper's funeral paid for by the sale of knitted caps that he had made. It is therefore rather the point of this holy place that there is little or nothing to see here. He is in fact buried in the open air under a flowering tree.

A mile or two beyond Khuldabad the road comes down into a rocky defile, and we are at Ajanta. We see a long line of openings in the rock, lose sight of them, and get out at the foot of a steep hill. Having up till now as a matter of principle refused all rickshaw or litter conveyance anywhere in the East, there now seems little reason not to be carried up this breakneck slope as the livelihood of the local inhabitants depends upon it, and so we are conveyed in this manner up the hill to where we come down the other side of it, and have the Caves of Ajanta stretching for half a mile along the curving side of

N

the rocky valley below us, along a path under the face of the cliff from cave to cave. Although it is only eight o'clock in the morning the heat is already something not to be imagined from any previous experience, even in the sultriness and thunder of Angkor, and there are twenty-nine caves to be seen. Not that the heat is any deterrent. On the contrary it can heighten appreciation, and I have found extreme heat a stimulant for sightseeing. I can say moreover in all honesty that I have wanted to see the frescoes in the Caves of Ajanta ever since the morning of enchantment when, at little more than twenty years old, I first looked at the books of coloured plates in the Reading Room of the British Museum. There are two of these; by J. Griffiths, published in 1896-7, and by Lady Henningham (1916), and in both cases owing to cost there are not nearly enough plates in colour, though Vol. II of J. Griffiths has many coloured reproductions of the decorative detail. We are seeing the Caves of Ajanta more than a hundred years too late. The only way of arriving at any idea of the frescoes of Ajanta in their prime is from copies of the paintings made in the last century. Since they were first discovered in 1819 there has been rapid deterioration owing in part to ill informed attempts to restore them. It would be true to say they have suffered more in the last hundred years than in the thousand years before that. There are the sculptured caves and the painted caves, but I refrain from any description of the caves which are carved out from the hill like chaityas, or, in fact, they quite resemble Roman basilicas, because I want to reserve this for the Indian masterpiece of masterpieces which is the Kailasa of Ellora.

Some of the most beautiful of the paintings at Ajanta are in the first cave one comes to. But the contrast between the darkness of the caves and their sudden and violent illumination with electric lamps is disconcerting because they cannot grow upon one and reveal themselves slowly and gradually as they were meant to do. But they are on the contrary switched on and off, as it were. Thus, the famous painting of the *Boddhisattva with the Blue Lotus* suddenly confronts us, larger than life, in his mitre of lotus and jasmine blossoms, and we are in fear of his being removed from us before we can remember him. For no photograph can do justice to this marvellous apparition. He is a being out of a forgotten world, with a young woman almost touching him, of darker skin, but with almost the identical mitre of flowers upon her head. She is the Boddhisattva's female spirit or emanation.

By now, the guide is moving his lamp so as to throw light upon the ceiling where are no fewer than four slightly varying versions of the same fresco, which depicts a feasting. The subject of these was for long thought to be the embassy sent to the King of the Deccan by the Persian Emperor, Chosroes II Parviz; but why, then, is it repeated four times? It has now been identified as the banquet of Kuvera, the god of riches; but beyond question there are Iranians portrayed in the painting. They are to be recognized by their paler skins, their typical physiognomy and their pointed caps.

All round these ceiling paintings are the conventionalized flower and vegetable motifs that are lavishly illustrated in J. Griffiths and that give so strong an impression of a long settled school of painting, more still, of age-long experience in the design of textile patternings. Such perfection in design is inconceivable without long practise at drawing the patterns out 'flat' to get the best effect and suit the techniques of dyeing. There would have to be many generations of art school practise to account for such experienced hands, for there were of course not one but several generations of craftsmen at work upon the decorative detail of this, and other ceilings. Their repertory here, and in the other caves, and extending over two or three centuries includes what we would call deer and humped cattle terms or torsos ending in scrolls of foliage or even mermaid tails; monkey, green parrot, and baby elephant motifs; cockfights; and patterns drawn from tropical flowers and flowering trees and tropical fruits, mangoes, and so forth, with the conspicuous absence of papayas or other fruits brought from Central and South America a thousand years later. All these subjects are drawn and made best use of as in the most experienced of art schools with the result that they approximate in effect to every other school of design that has attained the same degree of technical perfection—to all others, that is to say, but the pre-Inca Peruvian textiles that have different motifs, and within that, another treatment of design from any other textiles in the world. In looking at the detail in the Ajanta frescoes one is continually reminded of the friezes in Pompeian wall paintings, the patterns in Pisan and Sicilian silks, of high Renaissance detail in Florence or Mantua, of the silk fabrics of Safavid Persia, and so forth, all for the reason suggested, that interpretative and executive skill on the same instrument must run within the same gamut of effects.

But it is the transference of all these things into conditions of exotic heat that is the delight and wonder of Ajanta. The play of elephants is as facile to the painter's hand as the goldfinch and the wood-strawberry in the border of an illuminated manuscript, and the green parrot is as natural to him as in northern lands, the magpie or the red poppies in the corn. The exposition or statement of a mango on a ceiling at Ajanta is as assured as the ivy or Solomon's seal in the capitals at Southwell. They are an enlargement of the repertory while making use of the same method and devices, in the sense that Gaugain added motifs from the South Seas to the repertory of landscape painting. But their assurance in handling, not so much in the large figure compositions as in the compartment paintings of the borders, argues the existence of a whole school and not the workings of a solitary individual hand; of one or two great painters, it could be, in perhaps as many centuries, and suggests one of those golden ages among human beings as in fifteenth-century Florence when the hand of man could not go wrong. That they compare with the great cycles of frescoes in Italy is not in question, but we are seeing Ajanta too late. The officer sent by the East India Company to make copies of the frescoes, who spent many years on the task, but whose copies were destroyed by fire in 1861, gave a despairing report when his intermittent work of thirty years had perished. His words show how bad their condition was even in his day, and now it is so much worse that it is not easy to advise anyone but a dedicated enthusiast to go to the trouble of coming here, excepting always for the double bait that Aurangabad is only a few miles from the Kailasa of Ellora.

Nevertheless it is an unforgettable experience to go from cave to cave at Ajanta on the pathway built along the face of the rock, finding again and again the figures that have been familiar for more than half a lifetime. It is the equivalent of seeking out a person long admired, and discovering that he or she from old age has almost lost the power of communicating any message. Such are the ravages of time that it may even be difficult to believe it is the same person. Thus is it at Ajanta. The youth of the *Boddhisattva with the Blue Lotus* lasted for a thousand years, but it is now ended; we see little but the pose of his figure coming back out of the darkness and the curve of his eyebrows. Were we not informed, we could not know they are lotus and jasmine in his mitre of flowers. Chosroes II Parviz, or the god Kuvera, is still feasting, but in a sorry state; and the only certain thing is that his peaked cap is of Sasanid Persia, that the painter may have seen the

embassy of the Iranian King of Kings with his own eyes, and therefore touched or spoken to persons who knew of the Roman Caesars,
at least in their Byzantine incarnation. All that seems far away indeed
from this tropical langour of lotus and jasmine, where the flamboyant
and the jacaranda will grow when their time is come.

Pavilions of light and airy architecture abound in the paintings, as
in a fresco in Cave 17, near the end of the outside corridor where the
lightness of the columns which are like the pillars of a throne or four-
poster bed are a foil for the langorous farewells and love-making of
the figurants, a youthful prince who is breaking the news to his wife
that he has been exiled from his father's kingdom. The pavilion has
red columns—are these the 'pearl-red pillars' of Hsüan-tsang in his
account of the abbey of Nālandā?—and the exceptionally dark skin of
the prince is in contrast to the pallor of the princess. There is a
feeling of nervous tension in the painting as if some violent drama is
playing, this being achieved through their contrasting attitudes, his
resolution and her collapsed sadness. The group is completed by a
cup-bearer, another servant, and a dwarf at foot of the bed who looks
up at her mistress. The prince and princess appear again, only a few
inches below in the same fresco, as contrasting as before in the colour
of their skins, and with a graceful slave girl holding a parasol over
their heads. Dark of skin as is the prince, a palm-tree immediately
behind him is a coco-nut palm, and were there but a breath of wind
we would hear the rattle of the fronds. What one is at a loss to understand before this beautiful painting is why it should be here in a
Buddhist cave monastery with the monks living and sleeping but a
few feet away. Particularly with, in the words of the local guide, 'a
love scene from a dance fresco, where the royal pair is shown in a
mood of dalliance, enjoying full privacy,' which is the subject of
another fresco in the same cave. Yet another painting, there also, and
among the most beautiful of them all, is the standing figure of a
princess, mirror in hand, naked but for ropes of pearls and other
jewels, and depicted as though walking, or, at least, moving a step
forward, which gives to her figure a present immediacy that defeats
time.

The caves, if anything, are larger and more elaborate towards the
end of the curving, outside corridor along the valley. Cave 19 is one
of the biggest of the chaitya halls, with its forecourt, sculptured front,
and great mandorla-shaped window over the porch. Within are huge

columns that make the interior into a nave with aisles, a dagoba altar, and stone-ribbed ceiling. This cave is not far distant in spirit from the Roman catacombs. Another cave farther on (No. 26) is perhaps the largest of the chaityas, with pillars forming the aisles, and making a passage right round the dagoba at the back of the cave.

But if there is more sculpture in the caves towards the end of the valley, there is less painting; and this is the moment, at the last cave of all, to try and recall some of the incidents out of that lost world in the dark of the caves. They resolve themselves in the end into the tropical flowers and trees, the parrots and elephants and the parasols, and the graceful, long dead women of Ajanta; the young girl sitting on the ground in the first of the caves, with her back turned, dressed, unlike most of them, in a close fitting gown or tunic, leaning one hand on the ground, but the beauty of this figure is in the gesture with which she lifts her right hand to the wreath of jasmine flowers that binds her hair. There are the pairs of lovers in the same cave, painted to fit into the spandrels of an arch; the man in both instances owing to his darkness of skin being almost obliterated, but the young girls are paler of skin and lie out at full length in their lovers' arms; the more beautiful of them with her right arm marvellously drawn with the almost double jointing of her elbow, her shoulder hunched up against him, her right elbow and her right hand almost gone, but we can see even in the darkness her thin waist, her breasts, the huge pearls round her throat, and her almond eyes. And we see again the dark temptress who stands between two of the 'pearl-red' pillars, her left arm leaning on a column, but her wrist is in a long necklace or sling of pearls and her hand plays with her breast. She has stood between the pillars for fifteen hundred years, with left knee bent and the sole of her left foot resting against the pillar. She has bracelets and armlets of pearls, pearls round her leg between thigh and knee, and a girdle or belt of pearls. But it is round her hips, not her thin waist. Her black, black hair is sprinkled with pearls. She has long-lidded almond eyes. The tail of her hair comes over her shoulder. She has a coronet of pearls on her forehead, and an ornament like a huge white cockscomb across the crown of her head. Is it a head-dress of white frangipani petals? Were she to alter her pose but an inch or two, and move her head, we would smell the frangipani. But she does not move. She stands with one foot against the pillar as though to draw us after her into the cave.

Chapter Fifteen

◆◆◆◆◆◆◆◆◆◆◆◆ ◆ ◆◆◆◆◆◆◆◆

KAILASA OF ELLORA

IT IS A MUCH SIMPLER matter to get from Aurangabad to the Caves of Ellora for it is a journey of less than twenty miles. There are more than thirty caves in all, in different groups, Buddhist, Brahmanical and Jain, but, in retrospect, all fade from memory but the Kailasa which is a wonder of wonders and certainly one of the greatest works of art in India if, indeed, it is not among the wonders of the world.

As one approaches the long line of caves, among the groves below the cliff face there is to be seen the corncob summit of what is plainly a Hindu temple showing above the trees, and it is of advantage to go there first because it gives some sort of living link between the present and the tremendous past. We went to it, coming away from the Kailasa and still in the thrall of that mighty temple, but we should have gone there before entering on that huge experience. For this small building with mendicants and sadhus in waiting is an overture by an all but living hand to that work of the Ancients. It is the Jyotir Linga temple, in knowledge now of what a lingam means, built by 'a pious lady' no longer ago than the eighteenth century, and it is of minor interest that it is in southern Indian style, in mimic foretaste of the giant gopurams of Tiruvannamalai and Madurai. It has a little uneven court shaded by huge trees, and while a blind beggar accosted us the Brahman priest climbed the steps into the inner sanctuary, and we could hear what must be the blowing of conch-shell trumpets from within. The same mysteries were still playing that had inspired the hewing of the huge Kailasa out of the rock above. It is of little moment to be told this small temple is 'one of the twelve famous Jyotir Lingas.' All that matters is that there should be something alive near to the dead caves, some link in blood between them. The Caves of Ellora must not be as the dead fanes of ancient Egypt, the Kailasa being indeed of that canon of awe-giving solemnity. It is on the scale of the soon-submerging rock temple of Abu Simbel with the four seated colossi of Ramses II at its doorway that have looked for thirty centuries across the Nile waters into the sun. It is of the same labour, but not laboriousness, being indeed a very much greater work of art; the master work of the Indian sub-continent, and one of the great achievements, if more of sculpture than of architecture, of the world of human beings.

There are cave temples in both directions along the cliff face at Ellora, but we come to a halt in front of the Kailasa with a sort of flourish, and are left in an open court with a low screen of rock in front of us before there is time to realize quite what it portends. The enormous scale of it is not at once apparent. The sensation is that of standing at the walled entrance to a quarry. The Kailasa is not dug from outside into the rock, as with the temple of Abu Simbel and most if not all other rock temples, but it is dug down into the rock from the hilltop. Three great holes or trenches 100 feet deep were dug into the hill, and the temple buildings were then excavated from the blocks of stone left standing. In fact the Kailasa is not a building at all in the structural sense but a gigantic rock sculpture which has taken form as architecture. It is not, and never was a cave. Nor is it a building. Rather, it is one gigantic sculptured monolith, a rock heart carved out into a giant temple. There is no masonry in it at all, and the bridges of rock that lead from one interior part of the Kailasa to another are not true bridges but solid parts of the rock left *in situ*, standing free.

In fact the Kailasa was a stone mine, and as the stone was cut away they left standing in it enough bulk for a full size, double-storeyed temple. Round this they dug a series of chapels and monastic cells into the rock walls. The next step was to hollow out an interior in what was already excavated. When this incredible taking of pains was accomplished, the Kailasa was the absolute permanent replica of an erected temple, finished in every particular both within and without. It is not an interior hewn out of the rock, but the model of a complete, built temple, such as might have been erected on plain or hillside. The reason for this being that there was no exposed rock or cliff face at Ellora into which to dig. All the stone was below ground and must be mined.

It is difficult at first to realize this, and that the court of the temple as well as the passage leading all round it were hewn out of the hill from above. Indeed these open spaces represent as much, or even more labour than the temple itself. Fergusson, and other lovers of statistics, while giving the dimensions of the pit in which the temple stands—it is 100 feet high at the back, or, rather, let us say, 100 feet down to the rock floor from below the hilltop, and 270 feet long by 100 feet across, an area as big as that of the Parthenon and half again as high—have wasted much time in calculating that it does not in fact represent as many 'man-hours' in the quarrying out of the rock as would have been the case had all the stone been carried here to make the building. But 'man-hours' are of little value in dealing with so huge a sculptural conception, any more than it would be of interest were a collector of figures to tell us there are not as many notes in the *Meistersinger* overture as in the full scores of *Lilac Time* or Lehar's *Merry Widow*. What is certain is that a great mind, whether mass or group intelligence, or individual, was at work on the Kailasa. When they, or he, quarried down into the rock what was intended was known already. It was not haphazard. They had a plan that was to take a hundred years or more in the fulfilling.

It is now generally accepted that the Kailasa dates from the eighth century A.D. and was begun under Krishna I (757-783), of a dynasty who ruled over the Deccan. It is thus contemporary with Charlemagne but gives a more ancient impression. If for instance we try to relate it to what was in progress or had recently happened in other parts of the world it is difficult to think of the Kailasa as two and a half centuries later in date than Justinian's Santa Sophia, or the church of San Vitale at Ravenna built by the same Byzantine Emperor. The Kailasa comes to us out of the ancient world. It is of the epic or classical India; and in as much as it has affinity to anything outside India the relationship, if only of accident, is to ancient Egypt. Ellora, let us remember, is not far inland from the Arabian Sea. At that date when the Muslim were building the mosques of Cairo there must have been Hindus who had seen the Nile temples. Yet it is a similarity due more to a like solemnity of purpose than to deliberate design, and it is only that so giant a hand at work cannot but recall the Egyptian Pharaohs, with this one and important point of difference that the Indian King makes no appearance among the sculptures. The Kailasa is nothing else but a playground or theatre for the gods, and earthly kings have no part in it. The import of all this is more apparent when we are told what 'Kailasa' means; that it is the sacred Mount Kailasa of the Hindus in the Himalayas; that this mountain was the legendary home of Siva; and that the Kailasa of Ellora is therefore a temple of Siva. Further than that, the temple is even 'intended as an architectural replica of the sacred mountain', and the same authority goes so far as to say that 'the profile of the temple, with its central spires' rising above the porch and the rock screen at the entrance, 'seems to follow the actual contour of the real Mount Kailasa in the Himalayas,' in further argument of which we are told that many of the great shrines, like the Kailasa, were originally painted white in symbol of the sacred snow peaks of the Himalayas.[1] So may the Kailasa have been a thousand years ago, but it is time to walk under the rock-cut portico and set foot inside this most extraordinary of temples. But a step or two more, and the impression is quite overpowering.

We are in another, an ancient world which is so individual in form that it could be said to resemble a theatre-temple placed in a quarry. The theatre element in it is immediately apparent and the dramatis personae perpetually playing are the sculptured figures. But the very depth of the pit we are standing in precludes the light from striking down into it except when the sun is directly overhead, and so the shrines of the temple are placed high above in order to catch the light. They are as much as twenty or thirty feet above the rock floor, and we have to look up at them with something of the sensation of sitting too near the screen in the front row, side seats at a cinema. It is the same angle of vision and we have to crane our necks. But for easier entertainment there are the processions and battles of elephants in bas-relief below eye-level on the solid base of rock on which the temple stands. Were these problems of lighting foreseen and prepared for in the master plan; or did they present themselves during the century that the temple was being excavated while three generations of quarrymen dug down into the rock? They had, at least, time to ponder the problem and adapt their plans. But in discussing this we are losing the first impact of the Kailasa, with its simulated mountain peaks rising on all sides of us.

We have come through the porch on to the stone floor that most exactly could be the auditorium. In front of us stands the temple-theatre, a stage set back in depth to be looked at from all sides as we walk round it, with set scenes at different levels, the groups of sculpture being the players and we have to climb up, go in, and walk

[1] Benjamin Rowland, *op. cit.*, pp. 157, 174.

from stone cell to stone cell in order to follow the drama which is interior to those cells and invisible from outside. So much for the moment, until we go up into the body of the temple, but in the meantime standing here on the rock floor we are only a few feet away from a life-size stone figure of an elephant, and from a pair of columns, free-standing pillars that rise into the sunlight from the auditorium floor. But in fact this pair of columns fifty feet high stands at each side of the first and most forward standing of the temple shrines, which is the shrine or manger for Nandi, the bull of Siva. The lingam, his other symbol, was worshipped in the holy of holies which is the last and inmost shrine of all.

The shafts of rock from which this pair of columns is shaped had to be left intact from the start of the excavating, and no doubt this was pre-determined as a tour de force and part of the giant trick to which the mass of rock was to play unwilling partner. The columns were not dragged here and raised into position, but were hewn right down head first out of the hill. They are carved in flat relief; and it is probably on looking up at them, as their flat tops that are like the capitals of stylite-columns reach up into the sunlight from above, that the stupendous scheme and nature of the temple dawn upon one's mind. It is no building at all but a giant excavation worked down from above, going deeper still at the back, and all hewn out of the hill. The temple has three bodies or shrines, counting the porch as one, then the shrine of Nandi, and at the back of all the main body of the temple, all connected to each other by flying bridges.[1]

It is a matter of sculptured bridges. The first of them leads from the porch over the rock-screen to Nandi's shrine, and the second bridge leads straight on out of that shrine into the main temple. Both bridges are cut out of the rock. There would have been no span of air beneath them if it had not been cut away, and if the rock of the bridge itself had been demolished, the shrines and porches would have been left hanging, as it were, in air. These bridges are works of sculpture, and this knowledge makes the Kailasa more extraordinary still in purpose and accomplishment. The worked roofs of the temple just come up to the height of the quarry walls; it is as if some landslide or earthquake had ripped open the bowels of the earth and revealed these shrines standing inside, though, even so, the mind refuses to

---

[1] There are traces of another stone bridge between the upper storey of one of the caves on the south side of the court and the main temple, but this may have collapsed and fallen ten centuries ago.

accept the truth about the manner of their construction, and prefers to think of them as having stood within some great cavern from which the roof has fallen. So it seems to be another world thrown up out of the darkness into the light. Behind it all rise the broad planed surfaces of smooth dressed stone that are the walls of the quarry, and these give a continual reminder to the eyes of how this whole episode is taking place in a new medium—as much so, indeed, as if it were built out over the water.

And now, the notion of the flying bridges once grasped and in our minds, if we begin to look up at the sculptured bas-reliefs it is to note a curious feature about many of them. It is that the figures are in dance poses. This is something new to experience though it is found in some of the southern Indian temples. But it should be no matter for surprise in this temple dedicated to Siva, who in one of his embodiments was worshipped as Siva Nataraja, or 'Lord of the Dance'. The hundreds of apsaras on the bas-reliefs of Angkor are not of the same school; or they could even be said to have no school at all and to be quite untrained in the classical sense compared to the dancers of the Kailasa, which from its sculptures could almost be described as a dance temple, even if it lacks 'the pillared dance halls met with from end to end of India in temples and palaces, nostalgic witnesses to the need of dancing which was felt by kings and priests and people in the great days of India.'[1]

But the absorbing interest is that this is not the static dance of Cambodia and, supposedly, of India in which the dancers never move their feet. The dancers on the bas-reliefs of Angkor are as though weighed down by the heavy rings of metal round their ankles so that they cannot lift their feet from the ground. But neither do the dancers of the Kailasa in any sense or mood resemble the bayadères of Khajuraho, with whom the end in end is lascivious provocation. Nor, to judge from photographs of the sculptures, are the dancers of the Kailasa of the same school as those of 'the dancing ground of Siva, which centre is materially located in the great temple of Cidambaram, midway between Madras and Tanjore, one of whose entrance towers is an illustration in stone of the one hundred and eight poses of the dance described in the *Bharata Natya-Sastra*, the classic Hindu manual of dramatic procedure and dance technique'. It was at Cidambaram,

[1] e.g. 'the black marble pillared dance halls of the temples of Belur and Halebid in Mysore province'. *The Other Mind, a study of dance in South India*, by Beryl de Zoete, Victor Gollancz Ltd., 1953, p. 18. Further quotation in the next paragraph from p. 44.

according to legend, that Vira Chola Raja (927-977) saw Siva dancing on the sea-shore with his wife, Parvati, and built the 'golden shrine' in memory of the god. In short, and ignoring the beauty of the legend, Bharata Natya which was originally the dance of the devadasis or temple courtesans of Tanjore is not of the same school as the dance of the Kailasa. This one can tell, whether from the old sculptures, or in modern performance by troupes of Indian dancers.

But, rather, and even to the uninformed balletomane, what is portrayed in the sculptures of the Kailasa is the classical ballet in its grandest sense. High up on the exterior of the shrine of Nandi nothing other than a pas de deux is in performance; and if we come round to the left by the other of the 'stylite columns' and look up above the steps leading to the main shrine where the lingam was worshipped, there are more figures in recognized attitudes of the classical dance. Where a pair of figures is the subject, one of them is always partner and supports the other. Even when the figures are in repose and not shown dancing they are in the trained attitudes that could only be acquired in a school of dance. In standing figures, the pose in which the devadasi leans her head upon her partner's shoulder is even reminiscent of the supported arabesques of Princess Aurora in *The Sleeping Princess*; in the spell scene where she dances the 'Rose' *adagio* with her four suitors, taking a rose from the hand of each one of them in turn, and it is not carrying the analogy too far to remind ourselves that one of their number is a 'Hindu prince'. As we are admiring the bas-reliefs, in our imagination the grand airs of Tchaikovsky begin to echo through the Kailasa. And that this is only a slight magnification of the true facts will be even more apparent when we climb up into the temple and see groups of sculpture such as that of Ravana shaking Mount Kailasa which in posing and arrangement could be the final tableau in a ballet by some classical Indian forerunner of Petipa.

Continuing, meanwhile, our walk round the exterior of the temple, and all the while in this rock-cut corridor, leaving the left-hand of the pair of giant columns for the moment behind us, we are treading a sandy floor, the detritus of ages, through which a zigzag water channel runs some inches deep. It is witness to the age of the Kailasa; and playing with the centuries we may like to amuse ourselves with the thought that this was probably imperceptible for the first four hundred years. It may only have become visible ten centuries ago at a time when the Kailasa was already about as old as our Elizabethan buildings. Then the great age of the Kailasa comes upon us with a shock, and perhaps it is the last of the temples of the ancient world in a sense to which no church of the Christians, however early, can aspire. Other Hindu temples are mediaeval in their various phases, and evolve into a luxuriance as of Rococo. Only the Kailasa seems to hold the mysteries of the ancient world, and this with another flavour altogether from that of the frescoes of near-by Ajanta. Those speak of a golden age of painting with passages in their execution that cannot but recall other painters with known names. Perhaps the greatest works of art of all should rest in their anonymity and not be tied to persons, in which respect the Kailasa tallies with ancient Egypt and is more ancient in this finding than Greece or Rome where the names of sculptors and architects are on occasion known.

Perhaps the best point from which to view this strangest of temples is by retracing our steps a little so that we stand once more beside this left-hand of the stambhas, the correct name for what we have called the pair of 'stylite columns'. It is an experience that can be alternated by standing at the side of its sister column and seeing the enfilade of shrines, one behind the other, returning and coming back to us, when we have made the circuit. That is for the end of a visit to the Kailasa. This is but a beginning, even as our eyes catch again that little zigzag channel in the rock into which a keeper now sweeps the dust and debris of but another day.

From where we stand we see the slanting outside wall of the quarry rising higher at the back on our left hand, and are taken with a wish which unfortunately cannot be realized to look down upon it from above. It would be an experience indeed to see the tops of its shrines coming up out of the shadows below. That would be the place from which to grasp the stupendous nature of the quarrying even if, as one might suspect, the very compactness of the Kailasa, shrine after shrine, one behind the other, and all neatly contained and rooted in that same bowl, might alter from its hugeness and suggest at times a microscopic carving in a walnut shell. Looking back for a moment to the rock screen at the entrance, I remembered having read somewhere that the temple enclosure copied the traditional Vedic temple plan, and that its pattern was after the form of a primitive Aryan village— the whole essence of the Hindu caste system being pride in their

Aryan descent[1]—the mandapam or main shrine in the middle standing for the assembly hall, the chapels to each side mimicking the north and south cow-gates of the village, and the battlements of the rock screen copying those of a fortified town or village.

Coming forward again still nearer to the shrines we are in the shadow of the first of the flying bridges twenty-five feet above our heads. All three shrines are joined to each other by the two bridges. Who was to run along them? For whom were they made? It is a moment of excitement to think of that. This race with their choreographic tradition and genius must have intended some coup de théâtre for the Kailasa is the nearest they ever came to theatre according to our understanding of that. These opportunities which they had created could not be lost upon them. And now to the second of the bridges leading from the shrine of Nandi to the main shrine. It would be possible to run from end to end of both bridges, from the porch which was 'a double-storeyed gatehouse with ample accommodation for the temple guardians', through the shrine of Nandi to the lingam, with some dire message. For the desertion of the temple and the silence give a sinister purpose. What did the shell-trumpet portend that was blown in the temple down below? For the ancients had their mysteries as surely as the bell rings at the elevation of the host. It is only sinister because it is strange to us and coming from so far away that it is another world. We look up at the lingam shrine and back to the giant column, and see them both reaching up out of the dark shadow into the blaze of day.

There is time now to admire the procession of elephants and monsters carved on the solid plinth or keel on which the main body of the temple stands. For we are determined to walk right round it before we climb the stairs and go inside. Right at the back of it, and entirely in shadow, it is indeed as though one were making the circuit of some huge liner in a little rowing-boat and looking up at the sheer sides of it because the temple buildings, which are not buildings at all, only begin at about the height of where the lower deck should be. It is now we know we are in a cave, and the brow of it overhangs the

---

[1] As an example of which: 'in Southern India a Brahman considers himself contaminated by the approach of a Shanar (an unclean caste) within twenty-four paces', J. N. Bhattacharya, *op. cit.*, p. 255. Further (p. 107) 'a Tir who is a cultivator has to remain thirty-six steps off from a Brahman; a Malayaer hillman three or four steps farther. A member of the degraded Puliyar caste has to keep himself at a distance of ninety-six steps. If a Puliyar touch a Brahman, the latter must make expiation by immediate bathing, and change of his Brahmanical thread.' Social recognition, or ostracism, carried on as though by optical range-finder, are among the less pleasing practices of the Hindu mystique.

narrow passage where we walk. Not only this, but at the back here there are no more of the chapels excavated from the wall of rock. It is the deepest part of the quarry. The sunlight is 100 feet above our heads. In fact the direct light can only strike down to this depth for a few moments every day. And now directly under the bow of the temple, and making in this few steps from port to starboard, the whole Kailasa has, only momentarily, lost its scale. One cannot see its length and must come right round the end of it, and beside a projecting part of the main shrine, before it stands there long and enormous once again. Meantime the procession of elephants continues, and now the slope of the outer wall diminishes and runs slowly downward. We are out of the shadow. Light strengthens. We can see to the battlements over the rock screen. The other of the giant columns towers up into the air, and the Kailasa is entire and rises, mass behind mass, from off its quarry bed.

It is about here that another of the dance bas-reliefs stands out high on the shrine wall. The pose, or arranged attitude, are that of the choreographer in this shrine of Siva and temple of the dance. By now the cloister with its lesser shrines begins again opposite to where it left off at the other side, and there are chapels cut in the rock wall dedicated to the three river goddesses of Ganges, Jumna, and Saraswati. But although these lesser chapels are well worth entering for their sculptures one is now agog to climb up into the sanctuary, and we come round the front of the temple for this purpose and between the first of the giant columns and the Nandi shrine. The outside staircase is a little farther away and leads up into the main shrine, and here are more dance-panels high upon the wall, the local guide being as certain of this interpretation as we are ourselves for it remarks that 'the ancient as well as the modern dance art of India derives its inspiration from Siva Nataraja, that the master sculptors of the Kailasa have represented the god in different dance styles, and that in the bas-relief of the dancing Siva he is portrayed in an elegant dance pose,' the only name missing, we could almost say, being that of such a classical choreographer as Petipa, whose style is represented in all essentials in these bas-reliefs.

It is under such a panel carved high upon the wall that we climb the steps of rock that lead into the lingam sanctuary, and it must here be expressed that one anticipates a certain kind of feeling at this moment which is subtly differenced according to whether it is a

36 A 'stylite' Column at
Kailasa

37 R a v a n a s h a k i n g
Mount Kailasa

38   The Maharana's Palace at Udaipur

church, a mosque, or a pagan temple that one is entering. From the first instant of walking under the rock screen the Kailasa has proclaimed itself as being of the ancient world and of an antiquity that, we have said, it is difficult to believe is two hundred years later in date than Santa Sophia or San Vitale. This feeling grows stronger with almost every step of our circumambulation, and on setting foot into the dark sanctuary it becomes completely and utterly overwhelming. It is not just the bat-gloom of it as at the temples of Angkor, and the extraordinary sense of one despot of whom next to nothing is known having had the power in his hands to erect so huge a monument to his own egoism, but it is the sensation of being for so long as one is in his quarry-kingdom under other and ancient laws as though it is another and different classicism: an ancient and classical music in other tones, and a vocabulary, even a dictionary of poetic metaphors that are unknown. Here, the yellow cassia, the rose-apple tree, the scarlet kanaka are coinage or small change of poetry: to be sunburnt is to be blue of body by reason of the sun: blue lotus is the acme of ethereal beauty, and we could seek explanation of the curious 'pearl-red' pillars of Nālandā.

But, as well, it is as though one is entering into the Egyptian mysteries, and for as long as we are in the darkness the hocus-pocus holds. A priest in a mitre, which headgear is the one familiar thing come down to us, or taken over from that antiquity, and which relates us to the Egyptian Pharaohs, might be waiting in that inner gloom. But there is no one; not even another group of tourists. We were lucky to have the Kailasa to ourselves that morning except for a young Chinese-Californian in horn-rimmed glasses, on a world tour, who was eating his sandwiches at the entrance. There was nothing; not even a rustle of bat-wings. Had the columns but lotiform capitals it could be the interior of an Egyptian temple. One has the longing to penetrate right into its innermost shrine; but, as at Angkor Wat, the secret or that part of the mystery, at least, is gone and there is nothing. It is little different whether the image or the lingam is there, or not. The mystery is in the drama. Once that is explained, it is spoilt by standing in the wings to watch the play. There is not, and there never was more than the stone lingam symbol of Siva, in the inner shrine, and the mystery and the wonder are not in the palladium, but in the temple itself. This is most deeply and solemnly impressive, if more like a theatre for mysteries than a place for worship. The drama is in

o

the sculptures. But before looking at the one tremendous work of art among them in more detail it is irresistible to try the flying bridges, walk across the first of them into the shrine of Nandi, a pavilion of twenty feet square with nothing much inside it, and cross the farther of the flying bridges into the gatehouse. It has been said that no bridges of the sort occur in any masonry building so that it is an experience unique of its kind, and something as far removed from the ordinary as the Escalera Dorada of Burgos, 'a magnificent, though thoroughly secular double staircase'[1] of fifty-nine steps descending from the slope outside on to the floor of the north transept of the Cathedral, which comparison is brought in though it is hard to find a parallel, but the flying bridges of the Kailasa are by far the more impressive and spectacular of the two.

But leaving the purpose and the possibilities for those bridges until later, we come back across them in order to attend on the great sculptured group of Ravana shaking Mount Kailasa. This is a framed tableau, in even a kind of squared proscenium, set back from the spectator, and conceived much in the manner of a balletic finale or apothesis. But that is only as to the upper part of the composition. Beneath it the giant Ravana from the Rāmāyana is shown in his cave under Mount Kailasa, triple-headed, in a whirlwind of limbs, trying to shake the mountain. Most unlike the Atlas or the Titans of western classical sculpture who carry the burden of the world or of a mountain on their backs, and crouch under the weight of it, Ravana is fighting and struggling to shake and throw it off his shoulders and bring it toppling down. He has as many limbs as a spider, and is more wiry and sinuous than strong, as though the Indians of their own classical world had no notion of the muscles of a Farnese Hercules or a Laocoon.

Up above, on the conventionalized peak of Mount Kailasa, are the seated figures of Siva and his wife, Parvati. The restful curving of his left arm, stretched down as though he were reclining at ease on some lawn under the shade of a fruiting mango tree, is as a shield against which Parvati leans. She has not his self-confidence but clings to him in nervousness. He sits there, carelessly, not enthroned, with only one foot touching the mountain peak, and rides the Kailasa. He could be ambling along on it, as though mounted on an elephant, and with some reliable mahout to guide him. He needs to make no effort but is

---

[1] *Muirhead's Northern Spain*, edited by John H. Harvey, Ernest Benn Ltd., 1958, p. 204.

master of the mountain. It would be no surprise were he holding, Boddhisattva—like, a stem of blue lotus in his uplifted right hand. But now we see that graceful as is her pose she is clasping Siva's arm. She holds to him in terror while the mountain heaves and shakes. Out of the darkness behind her the smaller figure of a slave runs to her to find out what is happening. Other subsidiary figures in the background, or shown as upholding and forming part of the mass of Mount Kailasa, are more faintly indicated in the stone, whereas Siva and Parvati emerge from it, are more seated statue than they are bas-relief. It is interesting to think of the extraordinary circumstances of this sculpture for the stone proscenium had to be carved out before the sculptor could begin work and give life to his figures. Then, to the lifting of the curtain over months or years the final tableau or apotheosis began to take shape with Siva and Parvati not in hieratic position, but in a choreographic attitude and pose. It is this aspect of their grouping that has drawn at least one critic to invoke Bernini's *Ecstasy of Saint Teresa* when confronted with this sculptured group of Siva and Parvati.[1] But also the exceptional, or even transcendental conditions in which he was working may have inspired the sculptor to excel himself in this temple which itself is one huge sculpture, raised on a high plinth or podium to reach the light, and with its bodies of building joined high in air by flying bridges.

What exactly was their function? It is not enough to our imagination that they should be no more than connecting passages. Something other than that was surely born of the excitement of their setting. To think of them as mere corridors is to deny all opportunity to stone passages that are really and truly flying bridges. What is certain beyond contradiction is that the sculptors of many of the bas-reliefs at the Kailasa had much facility for watching dancing. It would appear that in the temples of southern India this truism becomes more obvious still. Large troupes of devadasis or bayadères were attached to temples where they performed in dance halls. In knowledge of which the flying bridges of the Kailasa are transformed in imagination into an equivalent of the hanamichi or 'flower-way' of the theatre in Japan, a raised passage which runs on the left-hand side of the auditorium from the back of the Kabuki theatre to the stage, and along which entries are made to a stir of excitement in the audience, at times even on horseback, processions pass, actors pause to disclose

[1] In the church of Santa Maria della Vittoria, at Rome. Benjamin Rowland, *op. cit.*, p. 176.

their identities, or even talk to those upon the stage. In one particular type of play which deals in extravagant fashion with acts of heroism and violence, and in which the actors even mouth meaningless words simply for their effect, the actors make their exit along the 'flower-way' in a series of leaps or hops. Let us consider, then, that it may have been here on the flying bridges of the Kailasa that the dancers learned not to be static but to tread the 'flowery-way'; here, in this rock-cut temple that is like a sacred theatre, stone scene always in place, stone dancers still in their attitudes, and with the stone bridges which were as gangplanks for the dancers to run along out of the bat-gloom into the glare of India.

Book Four

A VISIT TO CEYLON

Chapter Sixteen

+++++++++++++ ++++++++

TOUR IN CEYLON

WE ALL KNOW THE peculiar fascination in considering far off places one wants to go to, but will never get at, as though departure is imminent and every detail is arranged, the islands of the South Seas being perhaps that part of the world to which this especially applies because they cover so immense an area and it is difficult or even impossible to go from isle to isle. I particularly enjoyed for this reason talking to someone I met who had spent more than twenty years of his life in the Pacific Ocean. He could tell me of the different groups of islands; the Solomons, New Britain, New Caledonia, the new Hebrides, Santa Cruz, the Ellice Islands, Fiji, Samoa, Tonga, Tahiti, the Marquesas, Cook Islands, the Society Isles, and so forth, making due distinction between the fuzzy-haired negrito Melanesians and the taller Polynesians with their copper skins. Further to this, the National Geographic Society of America published in 1936 and 1943 two glorious maps of the Pacific giving the huge blue empyrean from end to end, from the Aleutians to New Zealand and across from Manila in the Philippines to Acapulco, with Pitcairn of the *Bounty* mutineers, the former convict purgatory of Norfolk Island, Easter Island of the giant monoliths, and the lizard-peopled Galapagos; and with more isles still, the Phoenix Islands, the Marshalls, Marianas, Carolinas, and insets of the more curious shaped among them, not so much islands like New Britain and New Caledonia which are two and even three hundred miles long, as the true atolls of the Pacific which have a freshwater lagoon in the middle.

In which way, unfolding those maps again on this snowy afternoon, we can embark in imagination for Clipperton in its coral reef; Rakahanga like a harp without strings and its lagoon where the strings should be; Christmas Island shaped like a lobster claw closing on its blue lagoon; Aitutaki, in the Cook Islands, obscene in shape like the bagpipe abhorred in alchemical lore, with a coral reef all round it; Jahuit, in the Marshalls, which looks to be a rampart of coral and nothing more; Nukufetau and Funafuti, in the Ellice Islands, coral walls and hardly land at all; Tarawa, in the Gilberts; Eniwetok and Wotje in the Marshalls; Manihiki in the Union group; Canton in the Phoenix Islands; most of them no more than three to five miles across, including their lagoons; with how many other coral atolls, Nukuono, Fakaofo, Aifutaki, Atafu, for the mere music of their names; and Wake Island, the only atoll in my own experience, where we touched down at four o'clock in the morning on the flight from Tokyo to Honolulu, and the only sensation was the damp on everything owing to isolation in so many hundreds of miles of salt ocean. With that pair of maps one could picture again in imagination the great war-canoes of Fiji; double canoes 100 feet long with 100 tattooed warriors on board, their carved and painted idols at prow and stern, as in paintings by William Hodges who sailed with Captain Cook to the South Seas; or, tiring in our minds of the Pacific Isles and the hibiscus, turn again to the lacquered Indies and search on the map for Sumba of the sandalwood, Komodo where the dragons live, Lombok, Flores, Timor and Celebes, 600 miles long, where there are still new genera of flowers to find, Amboyna of the conchologists, and slowly back to Borneo . . .

But one thing I have always remembered, that when I asked my friend where was the most beautiful place he had ever been to, he replied, 'Ceylon.' This island was in his opinion the most beautiful in the world. There was nothing to compare with Ceylon. It seemed therefore as if we should take the opportunity of being in India to make this little farther journey to the south in order to see it. But Ceylon is in no sense only an appendix or a supplement to India, and our survey of the atolls of the Pacific Ocean if it has served no other purpose will at least have effected a change of scene and driven the Indian names from mind. This is very necessary; or this other and different individuality would not have its chance.

So once more, but not for the last time, we took the long dull road from Bombay to the airport, where there was long delay and we found ourselves sitting out in the moonlight among the monster aeroplanes, with much light from flares and the slow crawling of the huge aeroplanes as they taxied in and let out their passengers, so many of them to so long and tapering a belly, while we watched the mechanical slow march of stair-turrets and other machines worthy of the Inferno of Hieronymus Bosch until, at last, near midnight all was ready and we boarded the huge, long aeroplane for Colombo, to be greeted by our Parsee stewardess with whom we had made friends during the hour in the air-line bus, and given iced champagne, a sign in itself that we were leaving India and going to Ceylon.

After so many delays it was towards three o'clock in the morning when we came down. There were further maddening obstructions by the Customs and a number of idiotic forms to fill in, and then we learned it was an hour or an hour and a half's drive from the airport into Colombo, which was exhausting in prospect, but an experience on no account to be missed. It was indeed something one will always remember, and the long after midnight passage through the forest of palm-trees tallies in my mind with that early morning boat trip on the klongs to the flower markets of Bangkok. This first breath of Ceylon, the Taprobane of the geographer Strabo, is certainly among the most marvellous of experiences to a traveller in the Orient, though it must be stressed that it is more Oceanic than Eastern. Ceylon is an island in the Indian Ocean, and it may be nearer in affinity to the Seychelles, to Mauritius, even to Zanzibar. It looked that night to be the mother isle of all the islands in the Indian Ocean, and yet another excuse for some preliminary mention of oceanic islands. It is quite apart from India. Persons living in Colombo will tell you they have been but once or twice in their lives to Bombay, and know nothing of Delhi. The hot plains seem far away from us now in all conscience. There are thousands of miles of ocean to the south, and the first landfall coming here out of Antarctica would be the southern point of Ceylon.

We are passing through a forest of palms of which the fronds seem like sleek feathers, and have an animal exuberance unlike the dusty palms of any oasis in Morocco or Algeria. Those are desert date-palms of the Arabs: these are palms of the tropics and of hills cooled by an ocean. One has seen nothing before to match their sleek exuberance. We go through villages where no one is awake, passing a large white church at one point which we learn later was built by Catholic fishermen, whose ancestors were converted by the ubiquitous Portuguese. But at last this paradisal journey that seems to have lasted for ever, and by the end of which one is no longer tired, is nearly over. We come into the suburbs of Colombo, which city is as bad as Bombay in point of the proportion of people sleeping in the streets, and after a preliminary stop at another and once famous hotel, being again by now almost too tired to speak, we reach the hotel where we are to stay and it is already half past five in the morning before we reach our rooms, to fall asleep in a dirty-looking dawn, and only be aware that the clean waves of the Indian Ocean break but the other side of the passage, when we ask for our rooms to be changed later in the morning.

We are on the Galle Face of Colombo, a term it is difficult to understand till we know it only means 'facing towards Galle', a town to the south which is in fact out of sight for it is seventy-five miles away. The ocean, we have said, breaks in large waves almost at the windows. The waiters in the hotel go barefoot, wear their hair in a chignon kept in place by a tortoiseshell comb in the Cingalese fashion, and have a short skirt-like apron which is the native dress. Tropical fruits are on the breakfast menu again, as at Bangkok, with the addition of king coco-nut water which tastes innocuous but is said to be good for rheumatism. The fresh lime juice is more than usually delicious. Alcoholic drinks are allowed again, and after a sojourn in India the inventor of Singapore Slings deserves commendation.

There is a kind of sloped glacis between the hotel and the town, grassed over, and except that we are at sea level and not at the top of a cliff, reminiscent of the Leas at Folkestone, with a club and bandstand to make suggestion doubly sure. The fort-like part of Colombo at the end of this has a clock-tower and the old government buildings. There are big stores with one or two English assistants still at work, and the rest of Colombo is less interesting for its buildings than its inhabitants. Compared to the Indians, there is a much greater percentage of persons with white hair. There are hawk-nosed Afghan traders, and the occasional Moor of a colony who have come here for centuries but may retire with their savings to the skyscrapers of the Hadramaut. There is no flower market, as such, which is a disappointment, and the Wolfendahl Church with a few monuments in its churchyard clearly cannot compare with the domed mausoleums in the Dutch cemetery at Surat,[1] or perhaps with those in the Dutch

[1] The old settlement of Surat is some two hundred miles north of Bombay. It has English tombs, as well, including that of the famous Oxinden brothers, with a pair of domes; and epitaphs, among others, to a president of the Honourable Company of English merchants who 'went unmarried to the heavenly nuptials in the year of Christ, 1649,' and to 'Mary Price . . . wife of the Governor of the Moghul's Castle and Fleet of Surat, who through the spotted veil of the smallpox, rendered a pure and unspotted soul to God, expecting, but not fearing death which ended her days, Anno Domini 1761. Aetatatis suae 23.'

church at Jaffna, on the northern point of Ceylon. Nothing else in
Colombo is interesting, except the shops of the jewellers who charge
extravagant prices for topazes and sapphires which are native stones
found on the island.

The interest and the beauty of Colombo are outside the town, and
it is only necessary to drive a mile or two to where the flowering trees
begin in the residential quarter of the town, past a hospital, a university and other buildings. What we see there may no longer be sensational to persons who have lived long in Indonesia, or in other parts
of the tropics, but it is a stimulant and a violent excitement if one has
not seen such things before. The real tropics are probably a disappointment in themselves in respect of flowering trees, as we are
warned again and again in Wallace's *Malay Archipelago* (1869), or in
other of the Victorian naturalists who saw these lands in their unspoilt, pristine conditions as, for instance, H. W. Bates, *The Naturalist
on the Amazons* (1863). Seldom is there a grouping or an 'effect' of
such things in nature, but they occur haphazard without, as it were,
making the best use of themselves. Also, now that jacaranda trees, for
example, have been brought from their native Brazil to flower
impartially all over the world where conditions are suitable to them
—including Lisbon, the only place in Europe where jacarandas can be
seen—the tropical flora although muddled, and it could even be said
shuffled by inexpert hands, has been given new opportunities and
new lands to conquer.

This was a first opportunity of seeing the yellow cassia trees in
flower. It is true that there are cassias in the tropical parklands of
Angkor, but their appearance is sporadic and ineffectual. Here, in the
suburbs of Colombo, they made one catch one's breath and are of a
classical antiquity—if Indian—to pair with the ilex glitter beloved of
Virgil. Their effect is to open new, but immensely old worlds of
metaphor and simile. There are some marvellous specimen cassias in
the gardens of Colombo. Many other wonderful trees, too, including
a banyan more venerable than any stone circle of the Ancients, the
mere thought of which recalls Milton's:

'The fig-tree; not that kind for fruit renown'd,
But such as at this day, to Indian known,
In Malabar or Decan spreads her arms
Branching so broad and long, that in the ground

The bended twigs take root, and daughters grow
About the mother tree, a pillar'd shade
High over-arched and echoing walks between:
There oft the Indian herdsman, shunning heat,
Shelters in cool, and tends his pasturing herds
At hoop-holes cut through thickest shade'

but we were told, incredibly, that this wonder of wonders was in imminent danger of demolition for a road-widening scheme.

Here, too, the frangipanis are in perfection, better even, I thought, than in the gardens of Bangkok. There would seem to be four sorts of frangipanis; the dark red, the pink, and a white frangipani with much staining of yellow along its petals, as well as the rarer and pure white, without a trace of any other colour, though it may be that this is but the exceptional form of the same white flower. They grow here in vigour with such extreme naturalness that one might well conclude the frangipani was native to Ceylon. It is in fact called 'the temple flower', both here and in Siam, because it grows so often near the Buddhist temples. Trays or bowls of frangipani petals are on every temple floor, the white kind being the variety most favoured for this purpose. So close is the association, and so appropriate the flower, that it is difficult to believe it may not have been growing in these lands even so little as a hundred years ago. It has a frangipani mystique of its own to which most persons who have seen it growing would readily accede. We read for instance that the Siamese word for frangipani rhymes with the word for 'anguish of heart' so that as a flower it has made quick conquest among the Thais. Indeed, one cannot visualize the temples of Siam or Ceylon (or, I am presuming, Burma) without the frangipani. It must be indigenous. But in fact it is nothing of the sort. The frangipani comes from Mexico and the West Indies, and it is an instance of quick adaptation, as much so as the fuchsia hedges of Connemara which can hardly have been growing outside the Irish cabins in the day of Daniel O'Connor. Now like the frangipani in Ceylon and Siam they are part of the national mythology. It is to be noted that the taxi-drivers from the hotels, such as our dark skinned and oddly named Mr P. M. Wilson—he had a lot of names of Catholic saints thrown in as well—were aware of the stranger's interest in the flowers and flowering trees and knew many more of their names than we did, ourselves. He was for ever halting at a particularly fine frangipani growing in someone's garden, and getting down to break off a flowering twig, or pick some un-broken flowers off the ground, hand them in at the window and drive on again.

Other attractions in Colombo are the two-wheeled carts drawn by a pair of oxen, but they are fast disappearing and will be gone altogether in a few years' time. They are covered in with a high barrel-shaped roof, and the sight of one of them must remind any lover of Japanese painting of the bullock-carts in pictures from the *Tale of Genji*. They occur in a famous pair of screens that are the masterpieces of Sôtatsu, where they are Court ox-carriages more than ox-carts, being therefore much more luxurious of finish, but the likeness is unmistakable and it is little strain on the imagination to think of a bevy of painted ladies behind their curtains. We were taken farther afield down a street of Hindu temples with fronts of over elaborate carving to a Buddhist temple which has a frescoed interior by a modern painter, the figures being perhaps too large and lifelike. Our companions, on this and other occasions, were a talented family, partly of Dutch 'burgher' origin. The daughter, who is still a child, shows remarkable promise as a painter, the son is a talented musician, and the uncle a distinguished painter and writer who studied in France in the great days of l'école de Paris. We went with the father and mother to Kelaniya, a famous Buddhist shrine said to date in its present form from the fourteenth century, though much restored. But Kelaniya has more than its share of that frangipane mystique and is one of those places that are physically beautiful in themselves with the white dome-shaped stupa near the temple rising directly out of the ground under the palms like a tethered moon, and the pottery stalls, however ugly the pottery, in the blazing, frangi-pani-scented morning.

It was on the afternoon of that same day that I remembered all I had been told of mangosteens, and inquired of our driver where they could be bought. His answer was at any fruit stall, and he came back with a handful of them and with some mangoes as well which made the mangosteens that much the cheaper. I had always heard they were the most delicious fruit in the world and now was the chance to prove it. We were lucky in that they had just come into season. If we had left Colombo a week or two earlier we would just have missed them. Mangosteens are a fruit of which the taste and the 'packaging', if it can be called that, far surpass all expectation. To those who have not had experience of them, I would say that they are enclosed in a medlar-like skin or casing of which you twist or screw off the top, where the stalk was, and the fruit rather resembling a lychee in texture but with a quite different and subtler taste, then shows, and can be bitten into. Or the whole rind can be broken off, and the naked mangosteen held in the hand.

The most sensational property of the fruit is its coolness. The taste of it, compound, as to some half of it, of fragole grape, nectarine and strawberry, and the other half all its own, I do not attempt to indicate further, but the fruit which is, also, about the size of a medlar, keeps ice-cool. We were given a large basket of mangosteens just before starting off on the trip I am about to describe, and this basket was put on the windowledge at the back of the car in full sun. When one felt thirsty, one had but to stretch out a hand and take a mangosteen. There they stayed for four days with sensibly dwindling contents as we helped ourselves. With their remarkable property of coolness, when lychees and mangoes and avocados now come regularly by air, it is the more curious that mangosteens are never sent to Europe. Their exquisite flavour degrades the rival pomelo, papaya, mango, good as those are, to the category of vegetable. The mention of them raised again one of the lesser mysteries of the Orient, concerning the 'celebrate eau de créole' which was made of mangosteens. I have been unable to discover where this scent was made, or when manufacture ceased, and it seems to pair off in mystery with the perfumed substance known as 'Goa stone', the invention of an Italian living in Goa early in the seventeenth century, and for which that town was famous for two hundred years, though the secret of it was lost long ago, and now at the time of writing, with Goa just fallen to the Indians, it is not likely to be heard of again.

But the time had now come for us to set off on a trip into the interior of the island, and it is a journey that after only a mile or two takes on the character of a nature lesson. It starts through a suburb with large churches attended, we were told, by Catholic fishermen; passes, which is indicative of its continuing character, the site of the old Cinnamon Gardens; crosses the river by the iron girder bridge; and we are in the coco-nut groves. Their feathery lushness is so beautiful that it was hard to agree with our Cingalese friends who on the day before had told us they longed for London fog and rain. The lovely heat of the tropics may pall after a time, but it was better to get the utmost enjoyment from this experience one may never know again.

It was not difficult. The coco-nut palms in this ideal environment which is their Garden of Eden have the identity to each other of carnations on the shelves of a greenhouse. They are in facsimile, and perfect, each in each. The highway is but a passage through the idyllic glades. They go on for mile after mile; and one does not know whether to admire most their straight stems or feathery crowns with the hard fruit clutched tight, as it were, in the armpit of the palm. Sometimes there would be a double or king coco-nut palm with yellow fruit. It was not much more than an hour before we drew up at a roadside stall to buy pineapples. But these were not the pine-apples that one buys in London. Still less were they the small green pineapples of Lisbon that come from the Azores. These were three or four a shilling, and as big as demijohns of wine or oil. One just cut big wedges from them and munched away.

Soon after this there was tea, coffee, and chocolate growing beside the road on their respective trees or bushes. Coffee plantations were formerly one of the main industries of the island till the plants were ravaged by a fungus nearly a hundred years ago, many of the planters were ruined, and the plantations were turned over to tea. Within the space of two years we had seen the low cushion-like, green tea bushes growing in Japan and, also, the coffee lanes of Guatemala, so it was not altogether an unfamiliar sight, though a sensation, to find both tea and coffee growing, side by side, with cocoa trees as well, and in addition, as though for sweetening, glades of sugar-cane. Huge pine-apples were still heaped every hundred yards or so at roadside stalls for a mile or two farther.

Now the character changed, and next thing we were buying bananas at another stall from a choice of ten or fifteen different kinds. That was what we were told, though it did not seem to me there were as many different sorts as that; but there were a pink kind and another sort called 'ladies fingers', and there were plantains and other kinds which had more yellow flesh, enough in any case to alter one's opinion on bananas. A little farther still and we halted at a delightful, leafy hut built of thatch and broad banana leaves, with a palisade per-haps of sugar-cane, where an attractive dusky maiden served hot, salted cashew-nuts wrapped in a piece of leaf. She was about fourteen or fifteen years old, in a somewhat skimpy skirt wrapped round her hips, her naked waist showing above that, and a handkerchief folded round her bosom, and was the perfect vahine of the South Sea Isles where Gaugvin lingered. So much so that we called at her stall for more cashew-nuts a few days later on the way home.

Thence, onward, the coco-nut palms continued endlessly, and there were wonderful vistas of deep hills and valleys with the feathery palms filling the distance with their fronds. Idyllic woods of palm-trees calling for a different and more tropical poetic imagery than Alexander Pope's 'Love whispering woods' and 'Lily-silvered vales'; musical not with the nightingale of our poetry but with paradise fly-catchers, rollers, minivets, orioles, painted thrushes, and for tympana the drumming of strange woodpeckers and the booming of the horn-bill. And even while trying to think for oneself of the noise a hornbill must make, whether a harsh chattering, or the sawing, grating of its huge beak, we got down to look at a cannon-ball tree.

There is one of these growing in the Botanic Gardens at Honolulu, but it was destitute of poetry at the time we saw it; a tree from Guiana, not in flower, and with but one or two of its negro-pated, wooden cannon-balls rolled on the turf beneath it. Here it was trans-formed, and flowering. But it flowers in a peculiar way. The flowers grow directly from the trunk of the tree without any stalk. The clearest way to describe their manner of growth would be to say that they grow like japonica apples, like the fruit of the old cydonia or Japanese quince, now, by authority, masquerading under a new name, chaenomeles. They have just the same spiky 'break-off', the same sensation of breaking though without the spike, but that is the way they come away from the tree. It is a system of growth belong-ing to another world than ours, and one I had previously associated in my mind with lychees and other fruits of China and Japan, as seen whenever there is a bowl of fruit in Japanese or Chinese paintings. But the cannon-ball tree is South American. The flowers, when in the hand, are of delicate nymphaea-like shape, and tropically scented, inferring that their scent is in the gamut of vetiver, ylang-ylang, or other smooth scents of the Far Orient, even of magnolia affinity, quite other than the peppery, more condiment than scent, patchouli which we were to encounter a day or two later in the Botanic Garden at Peradeniya. As for the 'cannon-balls', a few fragments of them were littering the ground as at an old battle-field of this other

39 The Lake at Kandy

40 Gate of Temple at Kelaniya

world where the cannon-balls were of wood, not stone; yet if one picked up a piece of an old shell it weighed like iron.

By now we were nearing one of the government rest-houses, and it was intriguing to read in a propaganda leaflet that 'the term is derived from the Dutch resthuys, a place of rest for the weary or benighted traveller' . . . and later that 'discernment, even genius, has been displayed in the choice of situation for their modern counterparts'. The road emerged from the glades of coco-nut palms into a small country town with piles of tropical fruits on sale, many varieties of them unnameable, and soon at a turn off the main road we reached the rest-house. But it was uninviting. Although it was long past midday the beds were unmade under torn mosquito-nets. Plumbing had completely broken down. A shadeless electric bulb was burning in a bathroom and would not turn off. Perhaps, too, they burned, inextinguishable, in the bedrooms for their Cingalese occupants of the night, as though cheated of sleep, dozed heavily, dark of countenance and disturbingly barefoot, in deck-chairs on the veranda. Two Americans ate curried wild-boar in the fly-blown dining-room while we enjoyed the mangosteens and sampled the different sorts of bananas under a tree in the garden.

After this halt there was an entire change in the landscape. The glades of coco-nut palms were left behind and it became wild country. The character of the vegetation had entirely altered, and there was the excitement of wondering what wild animals might cross the road in front of us, but this limited itself to two extremely large water lizards. Soon there are large stretches of water, shallow waters, but with the clouds reflected in them. They are the artificial lakes or tanks dug by the ancient Cingalese kings, some of them early as the fifth century A.D., and representing a feat of engineering, though it is an exaggeration to say that 'no similar constructions performed by any race, whether ancient or modern, excel in colossal magnitude the stupendous tanks of Ceylon', as it is, also, to write of the ancient capital, Anuradhapura, that 'ninety Cingalese kings had reigned there in continuous sequence, that it had once housed three million people, had a main street seven miles long, and has probably never been exceeded in size until our own era'.[1] None the less, some of the tanks are of remarkable extent, four of them covering, each, an

[1] *History of Ceylon*, by Sir Emerson Tennant, and *The Reefs of Taprobane*, by Arthur C. Clarke.

P

area of 6,000 acres. We were not able to get to Anuradhapura. Instead we were going to see the second capital, Polannaruwa, where more Buddhist remains are to be seen. At Anuradhapura there is from all accounts but little left, and some of that little has been too much restored. There are only the stumps of the granite pillars that upheld the 'Brazen Palace' or Royal monastery, a nine-storey wooden structure 'with precious fittings of jewels and ivory, and roofed with sheets of copper,' where, on a billeting system not practised elsewhere, 'the monks were accommodated hieratically on the different floors according to their level of enlightenment,' a building of the first century B.C. which may have rivalled the cloudscraper colleges of Nālandā.[1]

There was view after view of large areas of water as we neared Polannaruwa, the later capital from the eighth to the thirteenth century. For mile after mile we went on through this wilderness with scarcely a village, till at last, when least expected, the character changes once more and suddenly we are at the door of a modern looking, white rest-house built out over the waters of a not very large tank. We are at Polannaruwa and they are the waters of Lake Topawewa. This was, in parenthesis, a very different and much better rest-house, the tone of which was perhaps indicated by the exquisite swan-white frangipani floating in a bowl upon a wicker table in that wooden room with the lake in every window. After a rest, for it had been an exceedingly hot and cramped afternoon, we set out to see the ruins. This entails driving along the embankment of the lake. It is one of the smaller of the tanks, not more than three or four times the size of a lake in an English park, and very clearly artificial in origin. Sadly, at the time of our visit the huge red lotuses which grow in the lake were not in flower. They are supposed to be descendants of those grown ten centuries ago when Polannaruwa was a great city, and were worn as garlands in its palaces and given as offerings in its temples.

The embankment along the lakeside is an intimation that we are nearing the works of long dead human hands, and as soon as we come down from it we are among the ruins. They cover a large area which has entirely the character of a sacred park, and though the ruins are not nearly as impressive, this is as beautiful in another sense as the park surrounding many of the ruins at Angkor. The remains at

[1] Benjamin Rowland, *op. cit.*, p. 201.

Polannaruwa are entirely Buddhist for one thing. There is no trace of Hinduism; no multiple-limbed gods, or carved bas-reliefs from the Rāmāyana. The civilization which vanished from Ceylon as completely as it did from Cambodia, and at about the same time, seems to be an expression of religion in a purer and less cluttered form.

Having come down off the bund or embankment there are ruins in every direction. But, first, there is the strange, many times larger than life, figure of a king carved out of a rock which looks down upon the lake. He is bearded and, that apart, has the eyes and huge ears of a Chinese sage, holds a yoke in both hands—whether to infer the heavy load of kingship, or to show his subjects the yoke he is imposing upon them—and wears the Cingalese skirt through which, most substantially, his legs are seen. So sage-like is the mien of this forgotten king that in the park-like surroundings it would be easy to mistake his figure for a Chinese garden statue. Could it be, rather, that he is performing some agricultural ritual, a ceremonial ploughing, or other rite? High towers of brickwork now appear among the forest, some of them very tall indeed, but they are singularly free of ornament, and mere cores of masonry though 100 feet or more in height.

But there is a particular area of building which was clearly the centre of the ancient city. It is here that the red lotuses of the lake will have been on sale, and worn. One of the buildings, the Ata Dage or Temple of the Tooth, built of blocks of finely dressed stone, has panels of small, seated lions, looking like kylins, and doorways with classical mouldings. A few yards from this is the Wata Dage, a circular temple, with an inner and outer terrace and processional way, and four stairways leading to its inner shrine. The Wata Dage is much admired by the purists, but in its roofless state it is too much like a ceremonial gasometer to be a great work of architecture. Another, most curious building a little farther away, has little left but its stone columns, but these are shaped, or, rather, their stones are formed into lotus stems, and their capitals are the lotus buds. Fratel Pozzo, or whatever other virtuoso of the Baroque invented the Salomonic, or twisting corkscrew column, is surpassed in this, but it appears here, and here only, and is found nowhere else. Still more interesting may have been the paintings in another temple more than a mile away, but they have become almost obliterated in the eighty years since they were found. Anyone who has seen the paintings at Sigiriya will want to know what these vanished frescoes at Polannaruwa may have been.

It is a ruined city more beautiful in the aggregate than in detail. To the extent that we would not have lost very much had we missed the buildings just described, but it is another matter altogether with what we were to see next. After some mile and a half of ruins we came into a part of the park where there are whole monkey-families leaping in the rocks—and they were another race of monkeys, at that, from those of the temples in India and Nepal—with more white in their coats and on their heads, and a rather silkier fur. A little farther on we walk down a grassy slope to where strata of rock come up out of the earth. This is called the Gal Vihara; there is a rock-cut figure of Buddha coming out of a panel in the rock, and a colossal statue of Buddha's disciple, Ananda. They are figures twenty, or twenty-five feet high.

Very near to them is the reclining statue of Buddha in Nirvana, not asleep, still less, dead, as some old accounts describe him, but having attained Nirvana, the state of oblivion which is beyond death, yet, not being dead, is substantive. It is a portrayal of Buddha frequently met with, and one which more often than not carries no message. Here, at Polannaruwa, in this holy place, it is quite otherwise. The most lovely of white frangipanis grows only a few feet away from him, and a little higher on a grassy mound there grows a marvellous yellow flowering tree. There are more of the trees with their yellow flowers in the sacred park at Polannaruwa, and it can only have been by accident that we saw them nowhere else. Neither were we able to discover the name of this yellow flowering tree. The broken frangipane petals were littering the ground. Only now and then was there an unpillaged, an unspoilt frangipani. As for the yellow flowers, they grow with few leaves up near the sky, like yellow cups spread wide, holding, yet spilling down the glorious sun-wine and ichor of the light. There were whole unbroken flowers of them among the frangipani, the two sorts lying together. We have to go stooping in the shade of the tree to find a perfect flower with all its flanges, lifting some, rejecting others, till we had one, whole and entire, no petal missing, like a huge yellow lily-cup, though no lily at all, and now had the yellow grail in our hands and held it to our faces, looking up at its brother-flowers against the sky, in the ecstasy of scent out of the grail-cup—like the promise, and almost the spoken word! Unworthy I, who believe in nothing. And yet! And yet! Angkor Wat and Angkor Thom may be among the dead wonders of the world, but, to myself, Polannaruwa was a holy place.

The road, thence, to Sigiriya is in part a return along the same track, but it diverges again and, eventually, late in the evening, the rock of Sigiriya loomed up, inexplicably, against the sky. It is not the only rock of its kind in Ceylon. There are more of the huge boulders starting up alone out of the plain, and we had caught sight of one or two of them far away above the coco-nut glades. The rock of Sigiriya may not even be the most sensational of them but the sight of it gives a strange excitement to arriving at the rest-house under the semi-tropical trees. There it is, standing over them for no reason at all, or for some fixed purpose, and there it was still in the moonlight looming up like a rock island in the milky sea. The rest-house is comfortable with verandas to sit out on, even though the table-cloth was dominated by a praying mantis with its triangular visor-head and saw-toothed forearms clenched up, waiting to strike. A Buddhist funeral with chanting and lit torches went down the road in the moonlight under the feathery boughs and flowering trees.

In the morning there was the mystery of Sigiriya, and it is mysterious indeed, beginning at the rock foot. Its history is that Kasyapa, a sixth-century king of Ceylon who reigned from A.D. 511-529, built a fortress and a palace at the flat top of it after adventures worthy of the House of the Atridae. Kasyapa was a parricide. He had a brother, and a sister who was married to the commander-in-chief. When the sister complained to her father that her husband ill-treated her, the old king caused her mother-in-law, that is to say the mother of the commander-in-chief, to be burned alive. He, then, used Kasyapa, his brother-in-law, as a tool against the old king and Kasyapa had his father buried alive. He seized the throne, and his brother fled to India. It may have been in dread of his brother's return to avenge himself that Kasyapa took refuge on the rock of Sigiriya, to be defeated by his brother years later below the rock, and commit suicide on the field of battle.

Steep flights of stairs begin at the foot of the hill, and climb the slope to where the rock rises sheer from the ground. There the more serious steps begin, contained by brick walls, between a pair of lion's paws which come threateningly out of the foot of the hill. They are of alarming appearance, with the nails of their claws some three feet long. Not much else is left of this colossal lion figure, but his giant paws are frightening and seem to hold up the rock. There is flight after flight of steps up the rock till they can go no farther, and then a long gallery along the face of it, some half-way up the rock, and a spiral stair at the end of that with perforated treads. It is quite nervous work to climb this stair, looking up the face of the rock to the frescoes rather than down to the dizzying drop below. The paintings are visible from the foot of the rock, but it is only now that the extraordinary nature of them which is the mystery of Sigiriya becomes apparent.

For they are painted on wet plaster, it would seem directly on the cliff face. We are now on the narrow platform or passage which stops or caves in at the end, and the paintings are but a foot or two above our heads. The containing wall of polished plaster on which we put our hands, and which looks quite new as though it had been built at the same time as the spiral stair, is covered, we notice, with graffiti that are scratched into the plaster. The paintings are half-length figures of women, twenty-two of them in all, of a very marked physical type. All have big, globe-like breasts, thin waists not much thicker than their necks, aquiline noses, particularly if painted in profile, and high flower-decked head-dresses. All are markedly yellow-skinned, but it is only their waists that are naked, their apparent nudity is covered by thin gauze-like materials. The start of their striped Cingalese skirts can be seen below their naked waists, and all the figures end on what are clearly painted clouds. What are the women doing; and how, and why are they painted on the cliff face? It cannot be that they were always meant to be seen from this crow's-nest gallery just beneath them. How in fact did the painter, for all but one of the figures seem to be by the same hand, contrive to work on the sheer cliff face? But, as we shall see, it is an even deeper mystery than that.

It is ridiculous to think, as has been suggested, that they are the idle doodlings of one of the palace guards. And were they so, it only makes more inexplicable his descent of the rock in order to paint, which would have needed a house painter's cradle. They are by a professional hand beyond question; and various theories would explain the figures as heavenly dancers or apsaras, or, more romantically, that the fairer of them are 'lightning princesses', and the dark ones 'cloud damsels'. Looking at them in detail, all have big, hoop-like ear-rings, many strings of necklaces, and most hold flowers in their hands. In one part of the paintings, a second female who must be a goddess of divinity offers a bowl of flowers, and appears to lean forward out of another element in order to do so. She must be one of the 'cloud damsels' offering lotuses to a fair-skinned 'princess of the lightning', who is certainly one of the 'golden-coloured ones'. Else-where there is, also, a second female in the background holding a tray of flowers, who is perhaps a servant. One of the ladies with many bangles on her wrists holds a huge blue lotus. All the head-dresses are of extreme elaboration, and made obviously of the same materials as the masks of Cingalese dancers.

But the ultimate mystery of Sigiriya is that the polished surface of the wall which looks so new, and the graffiti which could have been scratched there no longer ago than the year before last, are themselves a thousand years old. There are nearly 700 of the inscriptions, and until very recently no one has been able to decipher them. But, lately, an almost incredible labour of detection and translation has been devoted to them, and a Cingalese scholar, Dr Paranavitarne, the Commissioner of Archaeology, has published a two-volume work upon them. It emerges from this that the inscriptions, dating from the ninth to the eleventh century, are all expressions of admiration, or jokes or riddles about the painted ladies who are referred to through-out as 'the golden-coloured ones' and their blue eyes, or what passed for blue, are fervently admired. In fact the persons who made the graffiti were even more astonished by the paintings than we are our-selves. Some of the poems addressed to the 'golden-coloured ones' are beautiful to read, and the work of poets; and it is to be inferred that the writers were in a state of innocence and had never before come across profane paintings of female figures. They seem to have undertaken the journey to Sigiriya specially to see the paintings which in their time were mysterious works of art four or five hundred years old. It is salutary to remember that there could be few graffiti of this date in Britain for none but monks and scribes had learned to write. One of the poets mentions 500 'golden-coloured ones', a palpable exaggeration, but it is clear he must have seen more than the twenty-two of them that are extant. So others must have fallen from the cliff face; or there were more painted galleries or cells. And now it is borne in upon one that there must have been other galleries along the cliff; but it is difficult indeed to form an idea of their purpose, or of how they stood. The paintings, though of the same date as the frescoes in the Caves of Ajanta, are very different in style and in the physical types portrayed, and must be regarded as typically Cingalese. The mystery as to how this isolated pocket of frescoes was left, and where the other apartments or galleries were which have fallen, is never likely to be solved. Was the wall with the graffiti only put there for the poets and literati who came to see the paintings? It is all a mystery. Now, ten centuries later, we can read the poems addressed to the 'golden-coloured ones', the 'cloud damsels' and 'princesses of the lightning', by poets no less mystified than we are ourselves.

The rock of Sigiriya stayed long in sight as the road led into the jungle once more on the way to Kandy. Moreover, improbably, it rained and thundered, and there were clouds of mist, giving just those effects that are admired in Japan as 'masculine' weather so that it was no surprise, when we got there, to find Kandy looking like a pocket edition of Nikko without its temples. It is like Nikko with the temples taken away and a lake added. The lake, it is true, is a small one, built by one of the kings two centuries ago, and not much larger than a glorified duck pond. There are clipped trees at the edges of it, to add to the Japanese effect. But, also, the hills round Kandy and the miniature scale of everything, remind one of Japan.

From the garden of the private house up the hill where we stayed it looked as though it would be easy to jump or fall into the lake far below. The world famous Malegawa or Temple of the Tooth on the lakeside has nothing interesting in it, and is yet impressive and even beautiful in memory. The heat, and the press of frangipani petals in the holy of holies where the sacred relic lies on a golden lotus flower under seven bell-shaped shrines, must be the reason for this. But, also, the perpetual beating of drums reminds one of the Kandyan dancers, and of the festival of the Perahera which is held here in August. Probably Kandy without the dancers or the Perahera is an even greater disappointment than Seville without the Semana Santa or the Feria. But for an account of the fire-fly nights, when more elephants process along than in a month of circuses, howdahs on their backs, their trunks gold-sheathed like the golden fingernails of the temple dancers, to continual and fevered drumming; the fire-flies dropping like sparks or meteorites among the heavy leaves, and on the lit night air the smell of frangipani, the reader must look elsewhere.[1]

Though we missed the Perahera and the Kandyan dancers we saw the Botanic Garden, outside the town, at Peradeniya. There can be nothing to equal this garden of tropical plants and trees, unless it be the Botanic Garden at Buitenzorg in Java. The gardens at Peradeniya were laid out rather more than a hundred years ago on 150 acres of ground with a loop of the river running nearly round them on both sides. They are one of the masterpieces of Victorian landscape gardening, nicely preluded by the tropical gardens along the road that leads to them. The drive round the gardens goes along several avenues; one of heavy leaved rubber trees, and another of silver-stemmed cabbage palms with straight stems of prodigious height, too easily compared to the pillars of a cathedral. There is a notable banyan worthy again of the passage in Milton's *Paradise Regained*. There are cannon-ball trees in their curious flowering, as incongruous as if some kind of a nymphala grew out of the bark of an oak tree; and all sorts of other tropical trees.

The orchid houses are all that owners of nineteenth-century stove houses could long for, full of the orchids for which collectors risked their lives in Borneo and Sumatra, in the forests of the Amazon and in the jungles of Central America; and in any case the region of Kandy is famous for orchids. But one of the sensations of Peradeniya is the bamboo groves. Down by the river they grow thirty or forty feet high; dozens of varieties of them, differing in their leaves and in the jointing of their stems. There is one sort with almost black stems. Bamboo glades in all their feathery and rustling beauty, the sight and, also, the noise of them, are a revelation, and one can comprehend how there was a school of bamboo-painters in China who were poets and literati. The spice grove is not less of a fascination; and it adds up to a tropical experience in little to be shown the different peppers, know the sources of so many condiments, and breathe in the heavy patchouli that cloyed the curtained alcoves and clung about the crinolines of Cora Pearl and other courtesans of the Second Empire. There are camphor trees and bread fruit, and cacao trees and coffee-bushes; and at the gate a glorious *Amherstia nobilis*, no less spectacular than its namesake the Amherstian pheasant, but where that painted paragon of metallic green and white has a tiara of little feathers this

---

[1] The Perahera is described in *Dance and Magic Drama in Ceylon*, by Beryl de Zoete, Faber and Faber Ltd., 1957.

has a flower that is almost like a cockscomb, hundreds of cockscombs of coral and yellow on the leafless air.

It only remains now to return to Colombo, down the deep ravines and once more into the groves of coco-nut palms. But before we reach the paddy fields where coolie-like peasants in wide-brimmed hats are working ankle-deep in mud, and the water-buffaloes are but grey shadows, and a little time before we halt on the road to have a giant white flower pointed out and be told it is the talipot, we reach a place where elephants are bathing in the river. There were several elephants lying, wallowing in the water at the hot midday, and one in particular who the driver told us was the biggest elephant he had ever seen, even taller than the 'casket' elephant who takes the chief place in the Perahera. How sad to have missed those processions in which eighty, or on occasion more than a hundred elephants, tread slowly along with jewelled hoods over their ears and embroidered housings! But it is not always so solemn. Sometimes an elephant is in *mast* and the whole procession gets wind of him and runs amok. We had to be content with watching the elephants lying on their sides in the river, six or seven of them, and later, feeding off boughs of the kitool palm which is their provender.

It was but an hour or two more to Colombo; and then, next day, to Bombay and back to Delhi. From there I came home where, indeed, with all those scenes so near in mind, I dreamed of the Perahera, and the ghostly processions of Angkor were joined in memory to other wonders across the stone bridges of the Kailasa.

INDEX